CU00724942

TIDELINE BOOKS
RHYL, N. Wales
Tel:
RHYL
54919

All about Your Dog's Health

All about
Your Dog's Health

GEOFFREY WEST M.R.C.V.S.

PELHAM BOOKS

First published in Great Britain by
Pelham Books Ltd
44 Bedford Square
London WC1B 3DP
1979
Revised edition first published 1985
Reprinted 1986

© 1979, 1985 by Geoffrey P. West

All Rights Reserved. No part of this publication
may be reproduced, stored in a retrieval system,
or transmitted, in any form or by any means,
electronic, mechanical, photocopying, recording
or otherwise, without the prior permission of the
Copyright owner.

West, Geoffrey P.
   All about your dog's health. — Rev. ed.
   1. Dogs
   I. Title
   636.7'083   SF427

ISBN 0-7207-1627-6

Filmset and printed in Great Britain by
BAS Printers Limited, Over Wallop, Hampshire
and bound by Dorstel Press, Harlow

Contents

TEXT ACKNOWLEDGEMENT

The author and publishers thank Dr Eleanor Frankling and the Hutchinson Publishing Group for permission to quote the paragraph on page 156 concerning 'token resistance' rather than aggressiveness which appears in *Practical Dog Breeding and Genetics*.

List of Illustrations

Photographs

Figures

ILLUSTRATION ACKNOWLEDGEMENTS

The author and publishers would like to thank the following for permission to use copyright material:

Photographs

Agricultural Research Council (16)
Animal Virus Research Institute, Pirbright (42)
R. D. Barrett-Lennard (8)
Commissioner of the Police of the Metropolis (5)
Fox Photos (2)
Marc Henrie and Pedigree Petfoods (23–5)
Milk Marketing Board (27)
Ministry of Defence (4, 17)
Novosti Press Agency (9)
Royal Veterinary College (15, 19, 26)
Swiss National Tourist Office (6, 7)
University of Cambridge Department of Veterinary Clinical Studies (22, 28, 29)
Wellcome Foundation (20)
World Health Organisation (43, 44)

Figures

A. & C. Black (5, 16–17, 19)
British Veterinary Association (15)
Hamlyn Group (23)
Longman Group (12)
Pedigree Petfoods (24)
Pergamon Press and B.S.A.V.A. (25)
Universities Federation for Animal Welfare (1, 28)
Wellcome Foundation (13–14, 29–30)

Photographic credits

Photographs (copyright by the photographer) were taken by:
Angela Cavill (11, 32–41)
Dave Parfitt (14)
Sally Anne Thompson (1, 12–13)

Figures 2–4, 6–9, 13–14, 20–21 and 26–7 are by Terri Lawlor and Paul Buckle

Acknowledgements

I should like to acknowledge my indebtedness to all those veterinary surgeons whose names are given in the references and in the text. My thanks are also due to the Editor of the *Veterinary Record* for permission to make abstracts from letters or papers. I am grateful to Mr Gordon Knight F.R.C.V.S., a former Reader of the University of London and in charge of the Beaumont Animals' Hospital, Royal Veterinary College, for reading with a critical eye a large part of the typescript and making helpful suggestions; and to Gilbertson & Page Ltd, and Mr Edward Askwith, Editor of *Countryside Monthly* from the pages of which I have included or enlarged upon in this book several notes on canine health which I have contributed over the years. Not least, I should like to thank Mr R. N. Fiennes M.A., M.R.C.V.S., for his valued contribution of chapter 28; and others who have helped with illustrations or in other ways, not forgetting the Librarian and her staff at the Royal College of Veterinary Surgeons.

Preface

This is not just another dog book. It is different. There are several which offer good advice on first-aid; and some which mention briefly a few, a very few, illnesses. It seemed to the author that dog owners might prefer something in greater depth, which would offer explanations, dilate a little on cause and effect, and be a source of information on canine ills not available in any hitherto published book with this readership in mind.

Not *all* of the conditions described are very common (indeed some are rare), but it is felt that an owner encountering a less familiar one will be glad of information about it. Busy veterinary surgeons, with a waiting-room full of clients and patients, do not always have as much time as they would like for explanations. Moreover, they sometimes use technical terms, many of which may be meaningless to the dog's owner. Accordingly, a glossary has been provided.

A unique feature of this book is the use of case histories, both to amplify and enliven the text. Some are based on the author's own experience in practice; others have been abstracted (and shorn of technical jargon) from the veterinary literature of several countries.

An index will help the reader; but so, it is hoped, will the grouping of topics under appropriate chapter headings; e.g. 'Accidents and Other Emergencies', 'The Itchy Dog', 'The Dog's Face', etc.

Causes, symptoms, first-aid or prevention are given, as appropriate; with emphasis on avoidance of trouble, so far as this is possible. There is a whole chapter devoted to rabies, a subject also referred to in a special chapter for overseas readers, 'In the Tropics'.

The special hazards of dogs on farms is another unique topic of the book, which also deals with risks facing the owners of boarding kennels. To put the whole into perspective, there is the opening chapter, 'The Dog in Society', which not only pays tribute to dogs in the service of man, but tells how one solved a murder mystery, and deals with that important topic — aggressiveness.

PREFACE to second impression

The need to reprint this book has provided the opportunity to expand the text, and to include additional case histories and new topics. Some of the latter will be found in the Appendix at the back of the book, some on previous pages, but all in the index.

1 The Dog in Society

Before discussing canine health, illness, and first-aid, with which this book is mainly concerned, a brief look at the dog's place in society seems highly relevant. Social attitudes towards dogs, ever since their domestication, must have always affected their health and well-being. Equally, the way dogs are managed today, or mis-managed, has a greater effect on canine health than most dog-owners probably realise. In turn, failings or shortcomings in the management of dogs influence public opinion, and all too readily encourage demands that further restrictions should be placed on dogs.

The ancestry of dogs, and how man may first have come to admit them to his primitive social groups, in the common quest for food, is discussed in chapter 28 of this book, 'The Origins of the Dog', contributed by Mr R. N. Fiennes.

By the dawn of history, it seems, man was employing dogs for three main purposes: hunting, guarding, and making war; and by 'between four and five thousands years ago,' to quote Charles Darwin, there already existed 'various breeds, e.g. pariah dogs, greyhounds, normal hounds, mastiffs, house dogs, lap dogs, and turnspits.' As this list implies, the dog has had not one niche in society but many, and has been pampered or exploited, well-cared-for or ill-treated, according to its role in a particular human society, as well as to cultural beliefs or prejudices.

To the urgent, and sometimes desperate, quest of game for food were gradually added the pleasures and skills of the chase, and if hunting introduced an element of sport, so sport introduced an element of privilege. This had an effect on the status of the dog, which became the esteemed companion of kings. In Arabia, royal Salukis were at one time each accorded a slave, carried on litters, and adorned with gold ornaments. In the literature of Iran there is a reference in a national epic to 'seven-hundred hounds collared with gold'. The king of one African territory maintained a guard of two hundred dogs, and in his domain two slaves were exchangeable for one dog; even twenty slaves if it were a superb dog from Europe! In the old Hebrew (as the Moslem) culture, the dog was a generally despised creature, not admitted into the ordinary dwelling house, yet very much at home in the palace.

There remained for centuries this great gulf between, at one end of the scale, the scavenging dog or its often hungry and ill-used working counterpart, and, at the other, hounds which literally dwelt in marble halls.

Somewhere between these two extremes was the dog, valued for hunting or as a herd dog or watch-dog, even if despised on religious grounds, which found a place in a commoner's yard or household.

In the present century the dog has maintained most of its historical roles, though thankfully not that of executioner. One can be glad, too, that the turnspit dog has long been emancipated. In war, dogs have continued to be highly valued as scouts to warn of an enemy ambush, as messengers, as pack-animals, and also for tracking. In peace, the cattle-herding role of dogs has declined, but the economic importance of sheepdogs has considerably increased as flocks have become larger. The inestimable value of guide dogs for the blind (not altogether a new role, but one enhanced by careful selection and skilful training) is widely appreciated. Guard dogs are as necessary as ever, and people who enjoy country pursuits continue to gain pleasure and companionship from many categories of sporting dogs.

Companion Dogs

Most of the five million or so dogs in Britain are companion animals. According to a survey carried out on a small scale by the Consumer Association, with the findings published in a 1977 edition of *Which?*, dogs' popularity rating is above that of horses, ponies, cats, and budgerigars. It would be safe to say that dogs are more versatile, and can enter into family

Below: Sheepdogs. The increasing interest in Trials perhaps disguises their continued economic importance

Right: Achievement. An English Springer Spaniel bitch during a pigeon shoot

life – both in the home and out-of-doors – to a greater extent than any other animal.

A housewife, alone most of the day, may well be glad of a dog's company; the animal – if a reasonably good watchdog – can give a sense of security, the more so after dark.

For those whose occupation is largely a sedentary one, taking the dog for a walk is an incentive to obtain a breath of fresh air and exercise. Of course, Fred Basset, Graham's engaging cartoon character, would be the first to point out that sometimes a husband's eager offer to take the dog for a 'walk' is a pretext for a visit to a pub, but be that as it may, there is no denying that dogs as companion animals fulfil a need in modern society.

For some people living in large towns or cities, but whose parents or grandparents were country dwellers, a dog – like a garden or an allotment – may satisfy an instinctive need for contact with the flora and fauna which they would otherwise miss. Dr Kenneth M. G. Keddies has recently emphasised in the *British Journal of Psychiatry* that for an elderly person living alone, a companionable dog can make the difference between a tolerable life and intolerable misery.

Some examples of Companion Dogs Saving Lives. Many untrained, companion dogs have given timely warning of fire, so that lives as well as property have been saved. To give but one example, an 11-year-old boy was woken by his Corgi, and found that his mother was lying unconscious beside her blazing bed. Though badly burned, she made a good recovery; but for the dog, she would certainly have died, and probably her son. Dogs have alerted families to escaping gas too.

In the Tyrol an Alsatian gave warning of a landslide. Normally quiet, this animal kept running about the sitting-room, and when let out rushed to a small apple tree and barked furiously. His owner then noticed that the tree was moving in the direction of her house and a neighbouring one. She barely had time to warn nine adults and eleven children before the first home was engulfed.

A sheepdog carried to the farmhouse a scribbled message, tucked into his collar, after his master had fallen and broken a leg. Another farm dog saved the life of her master by going for help after he was involved in a tractor accident.

In January 1977 a Labrador, though injured in a car crash, struggled to the side of the road and waited, in due course attracting the attention of a milkman, who obtained medical help for the dog's owner, who – badly injured – had to be cut free from the wrecked car, which was lying concealed from the road.

Companion animals have saved many people from drowning. A water spaniel saved the life of a boy seized with cramp while swimming in the Seine. A Keeshond jumped over the side of a Dutch barge and rescued a child which had fallen overboard, and swam ashore with him before anyone had discovered the accident. A crossbred dog went a mile and a half to obtain help for a boy half buried in mud near Weymouth.

Anti-crime Use of Dogs

Three of the greatest threats to modern society in Europe and America are an alarmingly high crime rate and (as facets of this) addiction to dangerous drugs, and terrorism. In helping to counter all three, specially trained dogs are rendering valuable service, and are now regarded as indispensable.

Imagine the dilemma of H.M. Customs, warned in advance that a parcel from India, due to arrive in a named ship, would contain cannabis; and faced, on that ship's arrival, with about five-hundred sacks containing several hundred parcels each! To open, examine, and re-pack the hundreds of thousands of parcels would have been a mammoth task — impracticable in terms of both time and man-power. Trained dogs overcame the difficulty quickly and effortlessly. They were led along the sacks, which had been laid out in 10 rows about fifty yards long, and showed keen interest in one sack. This was opened, and its parcels spread out on the floor. A particular parcel was quickly indicated to the Customs officers and found to contain cannabis concealed in a table-lamp.[1]

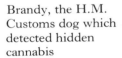

Brandy, the H.M. Customs dog which detected hidden cannabis

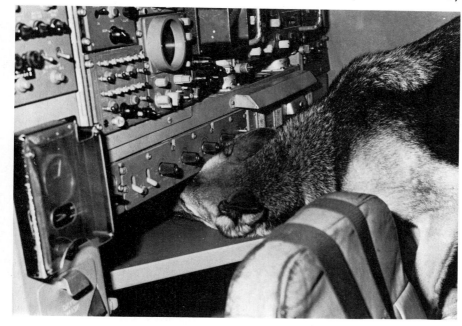

Rhona, an R.A.F. Police dog, searches for explosives in a VC10

In 1977, the barking of Brandy, a Labrador used by H.M. Customs at Gatwick airport, alerted them to a crate containing oil paintings. When the frames of these were opened, £100,000 worth of cannabis was found. The man who had smuggled the drug into Britain from Kenya was arrested and convicted – thanks to the dog.

The report for 1976 of the Commissioner of Metropolitan Police mentioned that Labradors, specially trained in the detection of narcotics, were successful in 421 out of the 749 calls which they attended; this resulted in the arrest of 1,068 people for misuse of drugs. As one understands that a proportion of young people who start with cannabis go on to 'hard' drugs such as heroin, ruining their own lives, bringing misery to their parents, and becoming a burden on society, the work of such dogs is clearly important in the extreme.

In searches for explosives, other trained Metropolitan Police dogs were called on 772 times during 1976; and, of course, similarly trained dogs have rendered splendid service in detecting bombs for the Army in Northern Ireland.

When it comes to locating mines or caches of arms and ammunition, one is made aware that the dog must have a very remarkable 'extra' sense. The dog can achieve what the electronic mine-detector cannot. Pieces of metal on the surface interfere with the performance of that instrument, which is also useless when it comes to locating mines made of plastic. The trained Army mine-detecting dog, on the other hand, ignores surface metal, and will indicate the position of a plastic mine as readily as a metal one. I have watched them doing this. A trained Army dog has also indicated the presence of buried arms and ammunition, the topmost of which was $4\frac{1}{2}$ feet below ground, covered with concrete slabs.

POLICE DOGS

At the end of 1976 the Dog Section of the Metropolitan Police had 365 dogs on strength: 292 operational, 64 under training, and 9 breeding bitches. Officers of the Section were responsible for 8,334 arrests and 2,844 summonses; 27 missing persons were found; 292 items of property recovered. The operational unit organised 41 large-scale searches during that year, and provided security patrols at prisons and courts.

Police dogs can sometimes achieve results very quickly where other methods of detection would either fail or be impracticable. For example, a cigarette-machine was once found broken open. There was blood on the machine, and also on the pavement around it. A police dog, brought to the spot, led his handler five-hundred yards to a house where both gained admittance. The dog then led the way upstairs to a bedroom where a man, with one hand bandaged, was in bed. Nearby was a quantity of cash – and cigarettes. The man admitted breaking open the machine. This is an example of a dog both identifying the criminal and finding the evidence.

When thieves take to a car a dog is often thwarted, but not always. Police were on the lookout for a stolen car reported heading in their direction. The car duly appeared but when its driver saw the police van, he turned off into a side road, and the car was soon found abandoned. Two police dogs were set to search the neighbourhood, and within a quarter of an hour one of them indicated the presence of two men in a garden, and kept them there until the arrival of his handler. Put to search the garden, the dog soon began digging. At the spot indicated, the handler unearthed the keys of the stolen car, together with housebreaking instruments which had been hastily buried by the arrested men. Both admitted stealing the car, and also thirty housebreaking offences. Subsequently £2,000 worth of stolen property was recovered.

In another incident an automatic burglar alarm led to the arrival of police at a house, and the arrest of a suspect seen in the garden. A window of the drawing-room had been smashed. This room, the doors of which were locked, had already been searched when a police dog was brought to the scene, and put to make a second search. Within minutes the dog gave tongue and began to scratch at a part of the wall of the room. His handler pressed the part indicated, and a door opened leading into a small, secret room where two men were found hiding under a table, and were arrested.

Dogs have solved murder mysteries. Here is one example, for which I am indebted to the Australian Police.

One of the three hundred or so operational dogs of the Metropolitan Police

A small girl in a town 30 miles from Sydney was reported missing. Her anxious parents obtained the help of several people to make a search, but no trace of the girl was found. Suspicion fell on an elderly gardener. Questioned, he admitted speaking to the girl but said that she had left him, and that he had not seen her since. Police searched a hut in the grounds of a house where he was employed, but found nothing suspicious. Then Scottish-born Sergeant (later Inspector) Adam Denholm and his Alsatian, Tess, were sent for. Tess was offered one of the child's diminutive dresses to scent, and taken to the place where the child had last been seen. There she circled round and then, despite all the comings and goings, she was able to pick up the scent and led the way into the drive of the big house where the gardener was employed. The ground outside the hut seemed to interest her. Then she went inside. After a sniff around, she jumped on to the bed and pawed at the bedclothes. Then she jumped down and went outside, lying down as though that were the end of the matter.

Sgt Denholm told his colleages that he believed that her behaviour indicated that the girl had been on the bed, but had not left it alive. They, however, were not impressed, and felt that they were no nearer to finding the child or incriminating the gardener.

However, Tess's handler had more faith in her than the local police, and offered her one of the gardener's tattered old shirts. Her reaction was immediate. She led the way to a secluded fernery – a spot which had been overlooked in the previous search – and showed great interest in it. She then went to a gate, across a street, and into a churchyard. Increasing speed, she crossed a paddock and came to a water-course. Here she swam, and indicated an object in mid-stream.

Still, the local police were not impressed, for they had already looked in this area and found nothing. Sgt Denholm was not to be put off, however, and the object Tess had indicated was recovered. It proved to be an old paint-stained sack – containing the body of the dead girl.

Her father had, on the previous night, accompanied home a friend who had been helping in the search. During their walk, very late, they had suddenly come upon the gardener who had exclaimed: 'Caught at last!'

This fact helped in a reconstruction of the crime. What had apparently happened was that the child had been murdered on the bed, her body hidden in the fernery until late at night, then taken and dumped in the water, the murderer probably expecting the sack containing it to be carried away by the current.

The paint on the sack matched that on a fence which the gardener had recently repainted, and was a useful piece of evidence. But without Tess would he ever have been convicted?

Dogs' Versatility

During the air raids on London in the 1939–45 war, a trained Civil Defence dog was able to indicate the location of a body buried 20 feet below ground. She and a half-sister, between them, found no fewer than 233 people, of whom 21 were rescued alive.

In current times, several skiing enthusiasts and mountaineers have cause to be grateful to avalanche rescue dogs, shown in the pictures on a training exercise.

Trained dogs have carried out most varied tasks. They have been employed to detect gas leaks; in Canada, I understand, they have been trained as mineral prospectors, searching for copper, lead, zinc, etc., all of which occur in nature as sulphides, and give off minute traces of sulphur dioxide. In preliminary trials, Labradors were reported to have discovered mineral-bearing rocks missed by human prospectors. It has been suggested, too, that trained dogs could help in the *early* diagnosis of certain illnesses in which a faint but characteristic body odour is produced.

Pet-facilitated psychotherapy (P.F.P.) is a newish development in human medicine in America. It was a subject discussed by an Ohio psychiatrist, Professor S. A. Corson, at a symposium organised in London by the British Small Animals Veterinary Association. 'Dogs; no drugs' was the motto for the treatment of schizophrenics, the Professor said. Touch, personal affectionate contact, and a feeling of trust had all been regarded by therapists as important factors aiding recovery, and a dog could provide

Avalanche rescue dogs
on a training exercise
in Switzerland

these. P.F.P., Professor Corson maintained, might help patients not reached at all by currently available methods of therapy.

It is an interesting idea, though one must have some reservations concerning what the patient might do to the dog – either physically or mentally. A dog needs confidence in, and a consistent attitude from, its owner. My impression from veterinary practice is that some neurotic dogs with a tendency to viciousness may have been so because their owners were, or seemed to be, under mental stress themselves – but that, of course, is only an unsupported personal impression.

An untrained dog solved a problem for the Electricity Generating Board. Attempts to pass a cable along a 150-ft tunnel below the Severn Estuary had failed. Then one of the engineers brought along his terrier, a keen rabbiter, and fitted the animal with a light harness to which a light cord was attached. At the other end of the tunnel two other terriers (encouraged to bark) were stationed, along with a dead rabbit or two. Hearing the barking, the terrier raced along the tunnel, no doubt encouraged also by the scent of rabbit. According to *The Daily Telegraph*, which reported this incident, a great deal of money and time were saved.

In an earlier century, Barbichon was a dog that went shopping, taught, by a cook employed in a French château, to take and bring back various objects. There were three or four people who could be named, and Barbichon would go to them, taking in his mouth a basket with money and a note inside stating what was required. He usually fetched coffee, sugar, cheese, cod or tobacco, but one day the cook wanted eels. The dog started home with these, but on the way they managed to wriggle their heads free of the cloth at the top of the basket and escaped. (As this was the first time that Barbichon had been sent to fetch live creatures, a boy had been sent to

This dog (in Switzerland) takes two churns of milk to the dairy each morning, and then carries the handler back with the empties

Huskies are familiar working dogs, here about to haul a sledge for a Soviet frontier guard

keep a discreet watch.) The dog did the only thing possible; he killed each eel, and replaced it in the basket, arriving in good time for the cook to prepare them for a meal.

A strange skill, self-taught, was acquired by a dog called Caesar, after which Lake Caesar in New Zealand is named. A crossbred which accompanied for eleven years the explorer-naturalist, Andreas Reischek, Caesar learnt to catch butterflies, alive, in his mouth and bring them back to Reischek.

Many dogs have learnt to catch fish, both in coastal and inland waters, and – as they never ate what they caught – presumably did so as a pastime. The tenth Earl of Home wrote in a letter, which I am able to quote through the courtesy of the Hon. Caroline Douglas-Home: 'My uncle . . had a Newfoundland dog which was celebrated for catching salmon . . . The then Lord Tankerville instituted a process against the dog . . . The case was brought before the Court of Sessions, and the process was entitled "The Earl of Tankerville v. a Dog". Judgement was given in favour of the dog.'

Awareness of the seasons of the year would seem implicit in the observations by Professor Archie Carr of the University of Florida. While in Costa Rica he found that each May and June dogs from towns along the railway line far inland made their way to the Caribbean shore, where they located, dug up, and ate turtle's eggs.

Knowledge of the day of the week is suggested in several stories about dogs. One in Australia was reported to sit out on high ground every Friday evening, watching for the country bus which brought his master back for the weekend after work in a distant town.

Mr R. H. Smythe M.R.C.V.S. has kindly allowed me to quote from his book *The Mind of a Dog* (Country Life) his experience with a Retriever named Ben, which he had bought from a gamekeeper on an estate seven miles away. 'At that time I was in the habit of shooting on a Monday and a Thursday. It was on these days that Ben used to meet me in the mornings with my old cartridge case. Then Ben started to disappear from home on Tuesdays and Saturdays, but was always at home on other days of the week. The mystery was solved when a bus conductor stopped me in the street and asked who was responsible for Ben's fare (seven miles out into the country to his old home and back) for it appears that he regularly travelled alone by bus. Those days, Tuesdays and Saturdays, also happened to be the regular shooting days on the estate where my gamekeeper friend was employed!'

Problem Dogs

So far, this chapter has been concerned with the loyal service of dogs to their owners, with the sagacity of dogs, and their ability to learn. All this is not irrelevant in the context of the dog's health, because I believe that an occupied, as opposed to a bored, dog – a dog which can do something useful for his owner and be aware of the fact – is less likely to become neurotic and aggressive. Undoubtedly, there are clever dogs and stupid dogs, and many of indifferent potential; but I think that the generalisation holds good within those limitations. If more owners would encourage their dogs to perform useful tasks, I think that there would be fewer problem dogs in our society.

NOISE

Incessant barking, whining, or howling can be very aggravating to neighbours. A few dogs are noisy at the best of times, but many – especially puppies and young adults – become so if left alone for hours on end while their owners are out. Some dogs are descendants of those used for centuries to give warning of the approach of strangers to isolated mountain farms. It is not the dogs' fault if what was expected of them in the Pyrenees is 'wrong' for them to do in night-time Peckham.

I was once asked for advice by a friend of a couple who were engaged to be married, but had one problem to solve first. This problem was a dog belonging to the fiancée, who was very fond of it. Her spouse-to-be, however, was not enamoured of the animal, which he regarded as excessively noisy. Would it help, I was asked, if she had it 'doctored'? I replied that, in my opinion, it would be most unwise to pin any hopes of noise abatement on castration.

Nor did I advise the operation of 'muting' – an operation performed during the 1939–45 war on some Army dogs, which might otherwise betray by their barking troop movements to the enemy. This operation involves excision of the vocal cords, and has occasionally been carried out in peace-time where the apparent choice lay between putting the dog down or stopping the barking.

It seemed to me that the dog in question should not be subjected to either operation. One alternative, which the fiancée had already considered, was having the dog put down, but I later heard that a new home had been found for it: a traumatic enough experience in itself, but one which *might* turn out well.

I recall another marriage where the new husband was never able to get on 'speaking terms' with his wife's dog, a Pekingese, which haughtily ignored him at all times.

AGGRESSIVE DOGS

A very real problem about which veterinary surgeons are often consulted is aggressiveness in a dog. This can obviously lead to embarrassment of the owner, to difficulties with neighbours, postmen, and other dog-owners; and it can also involve the dog's owner being sued for damages. It may even reach the stage where the *owner* is repeatedly bitten!

Of course, aggressiveness may be transient, as in a nursing bitch fearful for her puppies. Persistent aggressiveness can be occasioned by jealousy, when the birth of a baby means a decline in status for the dog. Ill-treatment; attacks by some local pugnacious dog; being kept for long periods tied up in a yard, or shut in an empty house – any of these causes may change a previously good-natured dog into an ill-tempered one. I have already suggested the possibility that the sheer stress of boredom or frustration may do the same for an unemployed working dog, removed from country to town, where the only exercise may be twice-daily walks to the park, tied to the handle of the pram.

Then there is the gene lottery; that is to say, heredity. A tendency to aggressiveness may be there from puppyhood (though one can never be certain to what extent aggressiveness is due to heredity, or environment, or both). I knew one long-suffering couple who were inexplicably devoted to a crossbred bitch which had always been wild in her behaviour. Near meal-times, she gave her owners no peace, leaping over furniture, barking till human nerves were frayed, and snarling if reproved. Husband, wife and daughter were all bitten by this animal, but there was never any idea in their minds of getting rid of it. In my experience, continued ownership of such a dog is by no means as rare as might be expected – unfortunately.

A change of temperament may occur as the result of a brain tumour, or of brain damage following a virus infection (e.g. distemper, rabies) or, rarely, a bacterial infection. In such cases aggressiveness may result.

An extreme example of aggressiveness was related by Dr Phyllis Croft PH.D., F.R.C.V.S., in the *Veterinary Annual*, and concerned a miniature Poodle given as a wedding present to a couple who both went out to work. Delightful as a puppy, it began, as it grew up, to guard objects excessively, and to bark at – and occasionally bite – visitors it had seen many times before. When it was two years old, both husband and wife had to enter and leave the flat with their hands held above their heads; otherwise the dog bit them so severely that they needed medical treatment! The owners hoped for a 'cure' but, sensibly, the dog was put down on veterinary advice.

Responsible Dog Ownership

This brings us to responsible dog ownership which, in my view, precludes the keeping of a dog such as that Poodle once it had shown persistent viciousness (perhaps engendered by being left alone all day). It also entails giving much thought to the pros and cons before acquiring a dog in the first place, or replacing one that has died. Can enough time be spared for exercising the animal? An elderly semi-invalid may have the time but not the stamina to cope with an exuberant young dog, but could manage an older one obtained, say, from the Battersea Dogs' Home. A busy housewife, who goes out to part-time work as well, is not likely to be able to

'Many no-longer-wanted dogs are turned away', and may, like this phlegmatic mongrel, be rescued by The Dogs' Home, Battersea

offer the necessary attention to a dog. Some people take their dogs with them when they go out to work; this is often a good solution, better, at any rate, than leaving the animal shut up on its own at home.

Often, dog ownership starts when a child sees an attractive-looking young puppy in a pet-shop window, and the parents yield to a plea to buy the animal. Later they may grow disillusioned, when the puppy has turned into a large dog, with an appetite to match, or when the dog licence becomes due. As a consequence, many no-longer-wanted dogs are turned away and become strays, or are taken to an animal welfare clinic to be 'put to sleep'.

One even hears of dogs being bought, as the result of a whim or fancy, to match a particular colour scheme at home; one suspects that many large or rarer breeds are bought as a boost to the ego or to impress friends and neighbours, rather than because of the breed's innate qualities.

SIZE AND TYPE

Size and type of dog are important considerations. Mr D. R. Highet M.R.C.V.S., in a paper given at the 1977 annual congress of the British Veterinary Association, commented: 'We have a theory in our practice that the size of the dog (bought) is often in inverse ratio to the income of the owner and the size of his house. A little persuasion that Bloodhounds and Irish Wolfhounds are not suitable for a family in a small modern house will do much to reduce the problems that arise in this type of dog from inadequate management, and which cause physical and psychological problems in both dog and owner.'

Mr Highet also referred to the findings of Pedigree Petfoods Education Department (which runs a Selectadog scheme to advise owners on what sort of dog, if any, would be suitable to their circumstances) that there were 'nearly four hundred known cases in 1975 of Pyrenean Mountain Dogs having to be rehoused, even up to five or six times, because their owners were unable to cope.'

COSTS

Nowadays the cost of feeding a dog, especially a large one, has to be borne in mind, since it will form a by no means negligible item in any household budget. Allowance has to be made, too, for the incidental expenses of dog-keeping, for veterinary fees, and perhaps for a stay in boarding kennels. Kennels will insist on a certificate of inoculation against distemper.

GENERAL POINTS

Responsible dog ownership requires kindly (but not *over*-indulgent) treatment of the animal; provision of good food in adequate quantity at regular times; regular exercise, grooming, and worming; preventive inoculation against the major canine infectious diseases; and veterinary care, when the dog is ill, injured, or, for example, suffering from a contagious or irritating skin disease. (It is prudent to register your dog as a potential patient and yourself as a client with your veterinary surgeon, and not leave this until some emergency arises.)

As regards hygiene, keep separate bowls and dishes for the dog and wash them up separately – do not let a dog feed off plates used by people. Hygiene entails not letting the dog sleep on your bed or go into food shops. It also, along with the regular worming mentioned above, means preventing fouling of pavements and the grass of children's playgrounds.

Elementary obedience training is essential, and the dog should be kept under control so that it does not cause a traffic accident or worry farm animals. 'We hear', said Mr J. Swift at an annual general meeting of the National Farmers' Union, 'a great deal of criticism from some quarters about fox hunting. Is it realised that for every fox killed by hounds, over one hundred sheep are torn to pieces alive by dogs?'

Buying a dog licence and providing a collar with the dog-owner's name and address on it are statutory requirements. (See Insurance.)

REFERENCE
1 Mahir, Tom C.B.E., G.M. *Police Dogs at Work* (J. M. Dent & Sons)

When a dog cannot be regularly exercised, a running chain can make for health and freedom from stress. This is especially valuable with farm and guard dogs

chain running on a wire

2 Health and Food

Your dog's health will depend over the years upon many different factors which will interact with each other, and change. First, there is what people loosely call the dog's 'constitution': here heredity is clearly of prime importance. Dog-breeding, like breeding racehorses or pedigree cattle, is an art, but even the most skilful breeders have to contend with the fact that heredity is something of a 'gene lottery'; there may be – from the health aspect – significant differences between puppies of the same litter.

After heredity comes environment. In its widest sense this means not only whether the dog sleeps indoors or in a kennel outside, but also the food the dog eats, the infections it is exposed to, and the chemical substances (many harmless, a few causing allergies in susceptible individuals, some causing poisoning) with which it comes in contact. All environments have their hazards. The farm dog may be less likely to be hit by a car than a town dog, although the latter may have a better traffic sense. Farm chemicals represent a hazard for sheepdogs. While distemper tends to remain

The points of a dog

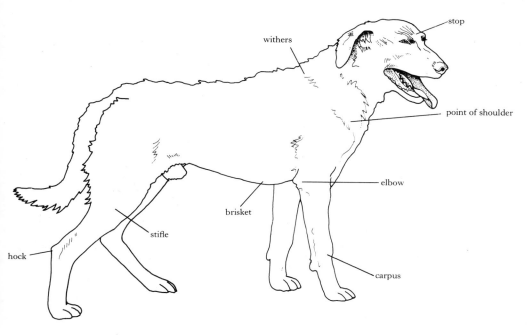

endemic in towns and cities, sudden epidemics may prove disastrous in the country, where preventive inoculation is as necessary a part of responsible dog ownership as in towns.

Infection and Disease

Exposure of a dog to infection may or may not be followed by illness, depending upon whether the dog has a useful degree of immunity against that particular infective agent; whether the animal is well nourished (and that includes its not lacking essential vitamins, minerals and trace elements in the diet); is not under stress; and has not any other existing major infection, disease or defect which might reduce its ability to resist the new infection. Stress can result from repeated dog fights, from being left alone for long periods, from a change of ownership, ill-treatment, etc.

Sometimes the normal immune response of the body's natural defence mechanisms may be suppressed. Some viruses can do this, e.g. the canine distemper virus (particularly some strains). This explains why there are apt to be so many complications in cases of distemper. Bacteria such as *Bordetella* are enabled to multiply and cause bronchitis, or other organisms may multiply in the intestines, with resultant digestive upsets which often accompany distemper. Treatment with cortisone may likewise bring about immunosuppression, as it is called.

The virulence or otherwise of the infective agent, and the quantity of it which enters the animal's body, will also have a bearing upon whether illness will follow. For example, a dog may be bitten by a rabid animal but not itself become rabid because the quantity of rabies virus entering the wound, from the biter's saliva, was too small and the bodily defences were able to cope, which they would not have been able to do had the dose of virus been larger. (I am referring here to an unvaccinated dog.)

One must appreciate, too, that the average dog may be host to several different parasites at one and the same time. Viruses, bacteria, fungi, worms, insects, and mites – several of these may be present without the dog's owner being aware of the fact.

Dog breeders sometimes attach scant importance to lice in puppies, overlooking the fact that a heavy infestation can cause anaemia, which may be exacerbated by worms in the intestine.

Some parasites may be too few to be causing active disease. Some, owing to the host's powers of resistance – the immune response – may be on the decline. Others may have a sudden opportunity for increased activity as the host's resistance becomes lowered by an additional infection, or by stress, or as the result of a severe chill.

A dog may recover from an illness, e.g. leptospirosis, but remain a carrier, when the *Leptospirae* (corkscrew-shaped bacteria) persist in the kidneys but in smaller numbers, able however to cause a flare-up of the disease under conditions adverse to the host, and able to infect other dogs. *Leptospira canicola* infection can be spread under these circumstances – a 'tree or lamp-post' infection transmitted by the male's urine.

Food and its Effect on Health

Your dog's food is obviously important to health. Most dog-owners wisely feed their animals on a mixed diet, arranged to offer some variety and at the same time provide the essential nutrients – proteins, carbohydrates, fat, minerals and trace elements, and vitamins.

Variety is important both for the sake of palatability and in order to obtain a balanced diet. A monotonous diet leads to animals 'going off their food'. On the other hand, a sudden complete change of diet can lead to diarrhoea and other digestive upsets. When taking home a new puppy, for instance, it is best to ascertain what it has been fed on, and to offer similar food; make changes gradually.

It is important to remember that in the wild state the carnivore eats not only a little greenstuff and other vegetable matter, but also *virtually the whole of its prey*. In the context of the domestic dog's diet, 'meat' should therefore not be taken to mean only red meat or muscle; yet some dog-owners have the idea that red (muscle) meat is a complete food for dogs. It is not. For one reason, it fails to provide enough calcium.

At the 1976 congress of the British Veterinary Association, Dr R. S. Anderson stated that a diet of unsupplemented raw meat was found at two university veterinary hospitals to be the main factor responsible for bone disease in young dogs, particularly of the large and giant breeds. (Canine juvenile osteodystrophy is referred to in chapter 17.) Commenting on the calcium and phosphorus content of muscle meat in relation to dietary requirements, Dr Anderson remarked: 'thus a 22-lb puppy would require 1 cwt of muscle meat per day to supply its recommended calcium requirements.'

On the same subject, Dr D. W. Holme commented:

'Muscle meat is an excellent source of good-quality protein, and usually contains appreciable quantities of fat. Most meat, other than liver, is deficient in vitamin A, and all meats are particularly deficient in calcium. This is of great importance, because although meats do not have a high phosphorus content, it is high enough to give a very adverse calcium: phosphorus ratio.

'Meat is a good source of most other minerals and of the B vitamins. However, it does not have any miraculous properties which confer benefits on dogs. We have compared dogs maintained for over a year on biscuit plus raw meat, supplemented with minerals and vitamins, and dogs maintained on other foods, and could not detect differences in health and appearance, blood chemistry, or health of the teeth.'

Should the meat be cooked or raw? Some dog-owners favour raw meat and seldom or never give their dogs cooked meat. Logic could be said to be on their side, for wild, as opposed to domestic, dogs obviously never eat cooked meat. However, raw meat is not always safe, since it may contain parasitic worm cysts or harmful bacteria, both of which would be killed by cooking. On the whole, it is wiser to feed cooked meat, which the dog may prefer and which is safer and less likely to cause digestive upsets.

An all-muscle meat diet is one to be avoided because, as already mentioned, the correct calcium:phosphorus ratio for the diet as a whole will not be achieved, and disease may result. Secondly, such a diet will be monotonous. Thirdly, as readers know, the proteins which an animal eats are broken down into their constituent amino-acids – the 'building blocks' with which the various special proteins required for the body tissues can be created. Certain amino-acids are essential for health, and the more varied the diet, the less risk there will be of a deficiency of a particular amino-acid arising.

It is a good idea to offer liver once a fortnight, since this is a useful source of protein, fats, and vitamins, and is liked by nearly all dogs. Eggs, cheese, and milk are all excellent items for the dog's diet. Cooked fish may be given for a change but should have the bones removed first. Canned fish may be used occasionally.

Canned dog foods from reputable manufacturers are usually both palatable and nutritious, and formulated so as to constitute balanced rations. However, they should be fed not alone, but with biscuit or meal, household scraps, vegetables, etc. In an American survey, the known vitamin requirements of dogs were compared with the average levels of vitamins in canned dog foods. All those canned dog foods examined needed supplementing with vitamins A, D, and E. With a mixed diet, comprising canned food plus the various recommended fresh foods, there should be no need for special vitamin supplementation by the owner for adult dogs.

While a deficiency of vitamin D may lead to rickets in the growing dog, over-dosage with vitamin D may do actual harm. Cod-liver oil and yeast are best not given continuously over long periods, especially at high dosage. This is not to say that cod-liver oil is not an excellent source of vitamin D, and a useful additive for a puppy's food, but, generally speaking, it is best to leave vitamin supplementation to your veterinary surgeon.

How Much, How Often, and What?

Dogs, like people, vary in their food requirements, so that it is not possible to state precisely what any individual will need per day, to the nearest ounce. Moreover, a dog will need more food in very cold weather than when it is warm. The amount of exercise a dog is having will obviously have a bearing, too, upon the quantity of food needed.

However, as a rough guide most authorities suggest that a dog weighing

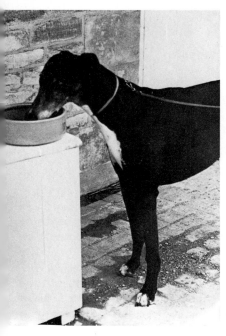

between 20 and 25 lb should have 4 to 6 oz meat a day, about 1 oz of vegetables, and 8 oz of biscuit. A dog (e.g. a Labrador) weighing between 60 and 80 lb may need $1\frac{1}{2}$ to 2 lb of meat a day.

Dishes used for dogs should be kept clean; likewise drinking bowls. Do not allow dogs to eat off plates used for human food.

For adult dogs, the best plan is obviously to give two meals a day. The dog should have time to rest for a while after the main meal, and not be subjected to violent exercise immediately afterwards.

Fresh drinking water should always be available.

Food, other than dry biscuits, should not be left down for more than a quarter of an hour or so. If it has not been eaten within that time, it should be removed.

Some dogs, if they are allowed to, will develop fads. 'He will eat only so-and-so.' It is a mistake to pander to dogs in this way, for not only can such fads prove highly inconvenient and expensive to the owner, but they may result in the dog becoming too fat, or frankly unwell.

A case history of a fad. To take an example from my own practice, there was a brown crossbred dog, 8 years old, which answered to the name of Toby. This animal could barely waddle into the surgery the first time I saw him.

'What do you feed him on?' I asked my client, when Toby, ungainly and panting, stood on the examination table.

'Ginger biscuits', she replied with a deprecating smile.

'Yes, but what else?'

'Nothing. Just ginger biscuits. He won't eat anything else.'

My subsequent advice must have been followed, for three weeks later – aided, I like to think, by the hormone treatment prescribed – Toby was able to walk without distress; and he was no longer gross.

Above left: Although for most breeds, the bowl can be placed on the ground, it is often easier for larger breeds to eat from a raised platform

Above right: 'When called upon for that extra exertion . . .' A healthy, well-fed Border Collie

Another bad diet. A 1953 survey showed that a high proportion of Scottish sheepdogs had to subsist on a daily diet comprising ½ lb oatmeal, ½ lb maize, and ½ pint milk ('when available'), the first two ingredients being made into a mash by pouring on boiling water. Occasionally a rabbit, or a little boiled mutton from a sheep found dead, and – at lambing time, the afterbirths – supplemented this inadequate diet.

Such additions may have enabled the sheepdogs to survive, but were too infrequent to prevent the onset of black tongue, the result of a nicotinic acid deficiency, in 11 per cent of the dogs in the survey. (Nicotinic acid is a component of the vitamin B_2 complex which includes also riboflavin, pantothenic acid, choline, and biotin.)

When called upon for extra exertion, the sheepdogs on that cereal diet can have had little but will-power in reserve. The authors of the survey suggested that some horse or cow meat, fine bone flour (sterilised), and a little salt should also be given.

STORAGE OF DOG FOODS

Conditions under which dog foods for use in kennels are stored are important. For example, in a later chapter reference is made to stored biscuit meal contaminated by rats' urine containing warfarin, which had been eaten by them in poisoned bait. Unfortunately, Greyhounds eating the contaminated biscuit meal died as a result. For rare cases of poisoning by biscuit meal contaminated with dieldrin and aflatoxin respectively, see chapter 23.

SAFE BONES . . . AND DANGEROUS BONES

Sometimes one hears a person say: 'I have had no trouble from giving my dog bones of any and every sort over the last twenty years.' Such an owner has had more luck than he or she deserved, and it is not an example to follow; for there is no doubt that the wrong sort of bone *can* kill – unless surgery is resorted to in time.

Cooked bones are better not given as they are less digestible than raw bones. Chop, cutlet, and poultry bones should never be given; nor the backbones from fish or rabbit. A chop bone is liable to become wedged across the roof of the mouth, making the dog frantic. If part of a chop or cutlet bone is swallowed, it may pass some way down the oesophagus (gullet) and then become lodged there, causing an obstruction to the passage of food.

Consider what happened to an 8-month-old Scottish Terrier, to take but one example from many. When operated upon at the Royal Veterinary College's animal hospital, the bone had been there eight days, completely obstructing the passage of all solid food to the stomach. By then, of course, the animal had lost much weight and was in a sorry state.

Trouble occasionally arises from sharp splinters or fragments of bone,

The right kind of bone to give a dog – marrow available at the sawn end, and large enough to ensure that there is no danger of choking

and these may abrade the mucous membrane which lines the digestive tract. Sometimes – particularly in the elderly dog – a hard mass of bone particles obstructs the rectum, causing the animal to strain in its unsuccessful attempts to defaecate. A few drops of blood may be passed. In view of this risk, it is better not to give bones to elderly dogs.

For other dogs, a marrow bone, from the sawn end of which the dog can lick out some of the contents, is much enjoyed, and is good for the teeth and jaw muscles.

MEAT NOT FROM BUTCHERS

Previous references in this chapter to 'meat' were about butcher's meat (i.e. that intended for human consumption) or canned dog food, and these are the only sorts which many owners ever buy for their dogs. However, meat sold in slab or other form at pet stores may consist wholly or partly of knacker's meat.

There have been instances where such meat originated from a horse, cow, sheep, or goat which had been humanely 'put down' by means of barbiturates or chloral hydrate. Cases of dogs being poisoned as a result of residues of these drugs in the meat have been recorded; and though far from common, they are worth mentioning.

One dog was found by its owner lying on its side, and making paddling movements with its legs. Taken to a veterinary surgeon and examined, it was treated for barbiturate poisoning, and was normal again in 48 hours. In another incident, a Fox Terrier was found dead 24 hours after eating horse meat. Barbiturates were detected in the stomach contents.

Other poisons might be involved, too, and there was in fact the case a decade or two ago of a pony being found dead by the roadside. The dead animal was removed to a knacker's yard, from where the meat reached – through the usual trade channels – the owners of dogs and cats, of which about 100 died as a result of poisoning by a fluorine compound – from which the pony itself had died. However, that was a rare and isolated case, and it would be alarmist to imply otherwise; but there is another, far greater risk associated with meat not from a butcher: that of infection.

Many a farmer's dog has accompanied his master to a knacker's yard and been allowed inside – to be tossed, or himself to drag off, a piece of offal or red meat. A misguided treat, indeed! For there is still the T.B. risk (admittedly smaller now that our dairy herds are virtually 100 per cent free, but tuberculosis in pigs must not be forgotten). There is also a very real likelihood of the dog becoming infested with tapeworms, and certain kinds of tapeworm in the dog can lead to cysts in the brain of human beings. The dog in the knacker's yard may acquire other infections, because the knacker slaughters not only otherwise healthy animals which have broken a leg, but also animals *in extremis* from an infectious disease; and he collects, too, the carcases of farm animals which have been found dead on the farm.

In the U.K. the Meat (Sterilisation) Regulations 1969 require all knacker's meat to be sterilised before being supplied to trade outlets for pet-animal owners, Hunt and other kennels, etc. These regulations may sometimes, like all regulations, be broken or evaded and equivalent regulations do not apply to all countries. However, the idea is to protect both the animals being fed on knacker's meat and also the housewife; for even if cooked by the animal-owner before use, *unsterilised* knacker's meat can contaminate kitchen working surfaces, the cook's hands, and utensils. Outbreaks of food-poisoning can arise in this way, salmonella and *E. coli* organisms being most frequently involved.

Not infrequently a dead calf or sheep is offered in good faith by the farmer to local Hunt kennels for feeding to hounds. The following diseases have been recorded in foxhounds after eating such meat: anthrax, botulism, and Aujeszky's disease. It should be added that brucellosis, salmonellosis and *E. coli* infections could similarly be transmitted, and probably have been on many occasions.

Hormones in meat. Another type of food to be avoided is poultry waste containing the head and neck of birds which have been chemically caponised. Such material – with the unabsorbed remainder of the caponising pellet still present and active – has been fed to mink with unfortunate results, and could prove harmful in kennels if added to normal dog food. Ears from beef cattle which had been receiving sex hormone implants have been fed in breeding kennels with disastrous consequences. Ears are hardly rich in desirable protein, being mostly skin and cartilage; and as in this instance they contained the hormone pellets, the purchaser paid dearly for those ears, whatever the price.

Cases of accidental poisoning are discussed in chapter 10.

3 Skin, Hair, Claws and Feet

Skin and Hair

The skin is, of course, a protective covering for the body, and consists of two main layers. The outer of these (the *epidermis*) has a hard, dry, surface part, with flat plate-like cells which flake off to form dandruff, and a deeper, soft, moist part with cells multiplying and being gradually pushed upwards, away from blood vessels in the deeper, second, part (the *corium* or *dermis*) until they too flatten, die, and flake off.

The corium consists of a network of fibrous tissue, including elastic fibres, well supplied with blood vessels, and containing the hair follicles, sebaceous glands, lymph vessels and nerves. The topmost layer of the corium is dove-tailed, so to speak, into the epidermis by ridges and nipple-like projections.

Each hair has a shaft – the visible part – and a root embedded in the hair follicle. Tactile hairs have follicles which are abundantly supplied with sensory nerve endings. Ordinary hairs are pigmented, giving to the coat its characteristic colour. Special muscles enable the hairs to be erected when the dog is afraid, angry, or very cold.

As well as protecting the body, skin and hair assist in the heat regulation processes which are aimed at maintaining a constant body temperature. Dogs can be regarded as non-sweating animals. It is true that sweat glands can be found in the skin, but only from the pads of the feet is cooling achieved in this way for all practical purposes. The dog depends upon panting, and to some extent upon salivation, for getting rid of excess heat.

The dog's natural coat, and especially the air trapped between the hairs, provides insulation against cold. In very low temperatures the hairs can be raised and heat generated by shivering.

A heat-regulation centre in the brain is able to influence the rate of metabolism, constrict or dilate surface blood vessels, initiate panting or shivering, and bring about the effects mentioned. However, in extremes of cold, or under an anaesthetic, shivering may cease and **hypothermia** ensue. If this is not recognised, the animal will die as its body temperature falls. In extremes of heat, the heat-regulation centre may likewise be unable to cope, as seen in the dog shut in a parked car on a warm sunny day or in a non-indigenous dog in the tropics, with resultant **hyperthermia**.

Being on the outside, the skin is naturally exposed to damage by violence, parasites, chemical irritants, the temperature changes already

A picture of good health: an excellent glossy coat

mentioned, and to damage from what Professor I. A. Silver M.A., M.R.C.V.S., University of Bristol Medical School, has described as 'misdirection of normal protective responses, e.g. allergic reactions'. Like muscles, the skin can atrophy, or over-develop (hypertrophy), and can show abnormalities in its formation. Like all organs and tissues, the skin can be affected by benign or malignant tumours.

As we all appreciate, a glossy coat in a smooth-coated breed is one of the signs of good health, whereas a lustreless appearance suggests that all is not well. This latter may be due to the dog not receiving enought fat in its diet, which can easily be corrected. Vitamin deficiencies, and the presence of worms in the intestine or of external parasites are other factors which may affect the appearance of the coat.

Parting the hairs, one can see whether the coat is scurfy or clean, dry or oily, and whether the skin is of normal colour and appearance. In cases of **seborrhoea** there may be an abnormal amount of dandruff, and sometimes a greasy skin. An abnormal and unpleasant odour is present in some skin diseases and some illnesses; e.g. mange and uraemia.

MOULTING

The hairs of the dog's coat are constantly being shed and replaced by others, though the extent to which this occurs and becomes noticeable may be greater in the spring and autumn. At such seasons dog hairs become inconveniently conspicuous on carpets and furniture; more frequent grooming will obviate this to a large extent. There is no cause for alarm at the quantity of hair shed, provided that the skin remains covered; i.e. there are no bald patches.

FELTING

Regular grooming is all the more necessary with long-haired breeds.

Unfortunately it is not always carried out. Of many dog breeds neglected in this respect, one particularly recalls Old English Sheepdogs, on which the formation of large lumps of a felt-like consistency may occur. These lumps have to be *cut* away – a painstaking task – as combing is by then impossible.

One recalls also dogs which had hair around the anus so matted and soiled after a bout of diarrhoea that they were in great distress, being unable to defaecate after the diarrhoea itself had cleared up. A very unhygienic and malodorous situation!

Grooming is also, of course, an essential part of parasite control.

BATHING

It would be rash to make a firm recommendation as to how often a dog should be bathed. Twelve times a year? Six times? Or only when the dog has returned in a filthy or smelly condition, or is continually scratching and obviously in need of an insecticide shampoo? Much will depend upon the breed or type of dog, and the owner's inclinations.

Use warm water and either a hard human toilet soap, or a dog shampoo of a reputable make. Avoid the use of soft soap and household washing-up liquids. Rinse the dog thoroughly afterwards, and rub him dry with an old towel. Ensure that the dog is in warm surroundings after a bath, or the less hardy types may suffer a 'chill'.

Some dogs apparently dislike the smell of their coats after a bath and – if given the opportunity – will go out and find a deposit of excrement to roll on; returning home more in need of a bath than ever! So guard against this.

It seems sensible to make a bath a dual-purpose occasion; for both cleansing and parasiticide. Accordingly a shampoo containing derris, BHC, Dichlorvos, or other insecticide safe for dogs may be used; follow the instructions as regards strength of mix: with BHC, for example, fits can result from too strong a concentration.

ALOPECIA

This is only a rather grand word for baldness, and in dogs it tends to be reserved for bare patches which occur when there is a hormone imbalance; i.e. a deficiency of a particular hormone or an excess of another.

There are several of these disorders, not all of which are fully understood; but the best known is undoubtedly that resulting from a deficiency of the thyroid hormone thyroxine. Bald patches, which are usually symmetrical, are seen first on the flanks, and the loss of hair may extend to the limbs. the skin may become thickened, pigmented, and in a few cases affected with seborrhoea. A lack of energy and obesity may accompany the alopecia, which usually responds well to hormone treatment.

Another form of alopecia is seen in the male dog only, at an age of five years and upwards. Often there is ultimately very little hair left. Such an animal may be seen to be attractive to other male dogs. Hormone therapy may fail, then castration succeed. This latter may seem a rather drastic measure, you may feel, but a normal coat regrows as a rule within three months of the operation.

A Sertoli-cell tumour in the testicle gives rise to similar symptoms, i.e. hair loss and feminisation. (See also chapter 22).

Symmetrical bald patches and lethargy are seen in the canine equivalent of the human Cushing's disease, but additional symptoms are present, such as thirst, the passing of more urine than normal, sometimes wasting of the temporal muscles, and a 'pot belly'. The appetite is often ravenous. Cushing's disease, or syndrome, is associated with over-activity of the adrenal glands.

A case history of the Cushing syndrome. At the University of Cambridge School of Veterinary Medicine a 9-year-old bitch, showing symptoms similar to the above, was brought for treatment. Should surgery be attempted, or would euthanasia be preferable? That was the question. Removal of both adrenal glands is, of course, a major operation and invariably fatal unless steps are taken to provide, by means of implants, a suitable dose of the vital adrenal hormone.

The operation was carried out with all the 'supportive therapy' which would have been given in an intensive-care unit for human patients, and the bitch made a successful recovery, becoming energetic and alert again, with regrowth of hair.

Loss of hair is occasionally seen in puppies, and in a recently whelped bitch; rarely it is the result of poisoning, e.g. by selenium.

Hair loss associated with eczema and parasitic diseases of the skin is referred to in chapter 4.

A blackish pigmentation of the skin, which becomes thickened and wrinkled, occurs in a disease called **acanthosis nigrans**, occasionally seen in Dachshunds and other breeds. Parts of the body involved are chiefly the axilla ('armpit') and neck. This is a chronic condition, slowly progressive, not painful or itchy, but very unsightly if present on the neck.

Urticaria ('nettlerash') is characterised by the sudden appearance of raised blisters or weals on some part of the body. The eyelids may become swollen. Urticaria is regarded as an allergic condition, and an anti-histamine is used in treatment. However, many cases of this non-painful skin disease disappear spontaneously, within a matter of a day or so.

It may be of interest to mention a rare and unimportant abnormality in which the skin appears too large for the dog. The skin of one Dachshund stretched, when pulled, to form (momentarily) a living cartoon of a dog. Unfortunately, the skin was so fragile that a rose thorn could produce a tear several inches long.

Claws and Feet

A dog's nails are derived from the same layer of cells in the developing embryo as the skin and hair; and as with the skin, the hard outer part of the nail is composed of modified epidermis, and the soft inner part – the quick – of corium.

Just as a hair grows from its follicle, so the nail grows from its matrix, which is supplied by blood vessels and nerves. Extending into the matrix is a projection of the third phalanx bone.

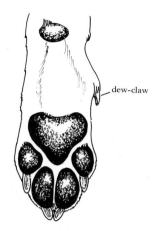

The normal dog's foot, showing a dew-claw

DEW-CLAWS

All normal dogs have four functional toes on each foot. In most dogs each front leg also carries a rudimentary fifth toe, known as a dew-claw, which does not touch the ground. On the hind legs, dew-claws may be present or absent. If present, they may be double.

The nails of the dew-claws grow like any other nails, but do not become worn down through friction. This fact, and their curve, may result in ingrowing nails which eventually pierce the skin. Before this happens the dog is often noticed licking the claw.

Because dew-claws are troublesome both on account of the ingrowing nail risk and also – especially if they are loose – because they are liable to be caught in tangled vegetation, etc, and wrenched off or otherwise injured, they are commonly removed when a puppy is three or four days old. At that age, anaesthesia is unnecessary, and trauma is minimal. In the older dog dew-claw removal is a surgical operation which must be carried out under anaesthesia.

NAIL CARE

Some dogs, especially those of large breeds, do not need their nails (other than dew-claw nails) cutting, as they wear them down sufficiently during exercise. However most dogs do need to have their nails cut regularly.

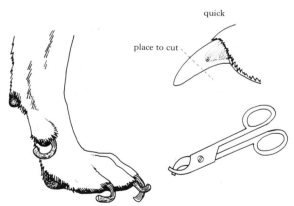

quick

place to cut

How the dew-claw grows if left untended; how the nails grow; what to do about it

If this chore is neglected, the nails become too long and cause the toe to be raised in front, so that muscles and tendons will then be functioning at an abnormal angle, which virtually constitutes a deformity and will distress the dog. If further neglected, overgrown nails may curve round and penetrate the pad, causing pain and sometimes an abscess.

With unpigmented nails, the quick can be seen as a pink core, and this is a guide as to how far it is safe to cut. Always allow a short space of solid nail between the sensitive quick and where you cut, otherwise you will hurt the dog.

With pigmented nails, the quick may be hard to see, or completely invisible; in this case one needs to proceed cautiously, cutting too little rather than too much.

Injuries to Nails

Sometimes a nail becomes torn or broken. If only the tip is injured, any ragged part should be cut off; otherwise there is no need to interfere, and new growth of horn will repair the damage. If the nail is broken higher up, involving the sensitive quick, the nail may slough off, a new nail eventually replacing the lost one.

Infection sometimes follows an injury, with pus visible or oozing – when pressed gently – at the junction of nail and skin. As a *first-aid* measure put the whole foot into a big jam jar containing warm saline, or warm diluted TCP, for example. (It needs one person to hold the jar firmly, while another copes with the dog, and holds the paw in the water.) If veterinary services are not available, or do not seem urgently necessary, repeat the fomentation in three or four hours' time. Pain and swelling can both be relieved by this means.

Injuries to the Pads

Thorns sometimes penetrate the pads, causing pain and lameness. Broken glass may inflict a deep cut. The latter may require sutures to draw the edges of the wound together; otherwise healing may be protracted.

If, for first-aid purposes, you wish to bandage the foot, always put a thick pad of cotton-wool underneath the full extent of the bandage; in other words, the bandage should not be touching the skin at all. This will prevent interference with the local circulation. (Tight bandaging, with no such cushion of cotton-wool, will cause the foot to swell and, unless the pressure is very soon relieved, could result in gangrene.)

Children sometimes put elastic bands on to the legs or feet of dogs, and the consequences can be similar to those of tight bandaging; except that a narrow rubber band will gradually cut through the skin, as well as interfering with the blood supply to the part below the constriction. Necrosis (death of cells) in the part deprived of its blood supply follows, and if infection supervenes there will be gangrene.

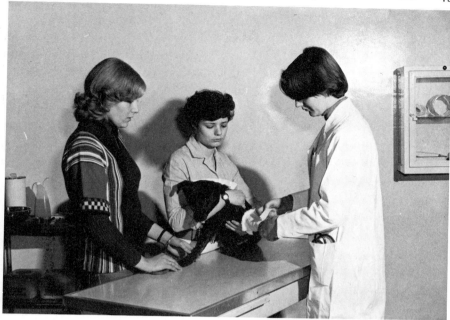

Bandaging an injured
foot: notice the
cotton-wool padding

BETWEEN THE TOES

The dog may lick between his toes if there is an inter-digital cyst or abscess caused by a foreign body such as a grass seed or piece of road grit. This condition seems to be far more common in some breeds than others, and an individual dog may have a succession of cysts, with two or three present at the same time in bad cases.

Fomentations, using a large jam jar as described earlier, may afford relief, if only temporarily. If there is a true cyst, or an abscess with a foreign body present, surgical treatment will be needed. Even this often fails, cysts recurring time and again. Cryosurgery (for example, use of a metal rod cooled in liquid nitrogen to a temperature of $-196°C$) has been used with success in treating these cysts, where other methods had failed to obtain a lasting cure.

Intense irritation between the toes, causing the dog to lick frantically, may be due to one of several causes: atopic disease (the canine version of hay-fever), when other symptoms will be shown too; an irritant liquid such as petrol, in which the dog has walked; hookworm larvae or harvest mites (and, in the tropics, the guinea worm), to give some examples.

4 The Itchy Dog

Anal Gland Disorders

When a dog is seen to drag itself along the ground in a sitting position, apparently attempting to rub an itchy part, people often remark: 'He's got worms.' This is seldom the case, for the dog does not have a thread worm such as causes anal irritation in the horse, and although the segments of a certain tapeworm can move and may cause irritation, the usual cause is a disorder of the anal glands.

There are two of these, situated slightly below and to each side of the anus, and they produce a fluid which probably acts as a lubricant to aid defaecation, but is also comparable with musk. It is the odour of the gland's secretion which other dogs take such an interest in.

Each gland has a tiny duct opening just inside the anus. These ducts may become blocked by a grass seed or other foreign body, so that their secretions cannot escape and the glands swell; but more commonly there is infection, and the normal secretion is replaced by brownish, foul-smelling pus. Irritation or pain may then result.

As a first-aid measure take a piece of cotton-wool about three or four inches square, place it over the anus, and apply pressure to the glands (which, when enlarged, can easily be felt), with finger and thumb on either side of the anus. An evil-smelling fluid may then spurt out into the pad of cotton-wool, which serves to protect one's hands, clothes, furniture, etc. Sometimes it is easy to empty both glands simultaneously. Sometimes the gland contents are waxy in consistency and difficult to expel. Professional help may then be required, as it will be if the dog shows signs of pain when the glands are squeezed.

Tail-chasing, and yelping on sitting down, are regarded as other symptoms of this disorder, which some veterinary surgeons call anal sacculitis.[1]

PERIANAL FISTULAS

An entirely different disorder is a perianal fistula, perhaps most common in Alsatians. The fistula is a short passage, opening on the surface of the skin near the anus, and connecting internally with the rectum. It is a cause of discomfort, and the dog may lick the part frequently. Some blood or pus may be seen, and difficulty in defaecation may be observed. First-aid measures are not effective here, and professional treatment is necessary.

External Parasites

HOOKWORM LARVAE

Especially in Foxhounds, racing Greyhounds, and other sporting dogs confined in kennels and runs, redness of the skin of the abdomen and accompanying irritation may be due to hookworm larvae, which can penetrate the unbroken skin. The pads of the dog's feet may become itchy as a result of these worm larvae.

FLEAS

If a dog is scratching or biting himself, the most likely cause is fleas, since these are the most common external parasites. Fast-moving, they are dark brown in colour and have very narrow bodies (tall and thin). These insects have mouth parts adapted for piercing the skin and sucking blood, and if numerous can cause anaemia in young or debilitated dogs.

Moreover, dogs may become sensitised to a substance which fleas secrete when biting, and then even a single flea can cause a severe allergic reaction – one type of eczema.

Many women dog-owners seem to find it shaming to be told that their dog has fleas, though why this should be so is a little puzzling. Any but the most unsociable dog is virtually bound to acquire fleas at some time in its life; it is only if they are knowingly allowed to remain that the dog-owner need feel self-critical.

The dog may be infested with fleas of several different species; and in a survey of flea-infested dogs in Dublin it was found that of 128 dogs 86 had dog fleas only; 24 dogs were infested entirely by the human flea; 12 by both dog and human fleas; 4 by cat fleas; and 2 by dog and cat fleas.[2]

All these species of fleas may bite people, another reason for not tolerating fleas on your dog. Then again fleas transmit the larvae of the common tapeworm of the dog which becomes host to the adult tapeworm after swallowing an infected flea. (Children may become infested, too, through tapeworm larvae contaminating their fingers when playing with dogs, and not washing their hands afterwards.)

A dog heavily infested with fleas will have a dirty skin. If the hair is parted, blackish dots of flea excrement may be seen, and fleas will not be hard to find. Eggs are laid on the dog's bedding or on the floor of a room. They hatch into small, active, maggot-like larvae after 2–12 days in summer, or after perhaps several weeks in winter. When full grown they spin a cocoon, from which in due course a flea will emerge.

Getting rid of a dog's fleas involves two separate courses of action: (1) applying a wet shampoo containing a suitable parasiticide such as rotenone or BHC to the dog; (2) destruction of existing bedding used by the dog, and attention to places where flea eggs may hatch (e.g. cracks between floorboards, skirting boards, cracks in woodwork or concrete of kennels);

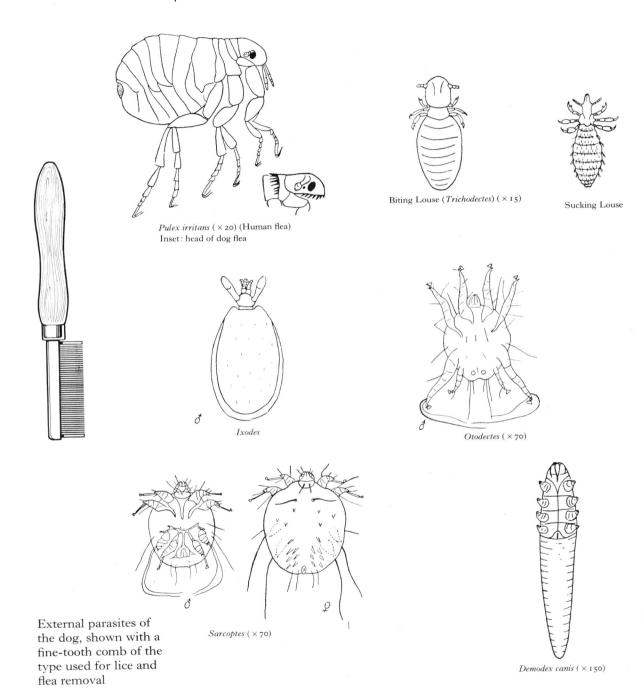

Pulex irritans (× 20) (Human flea)
Inset: head of dog flea

Biting Louse (*Trichodectes*) (× 15)

Sucking Louse

Ixodes

Otodectes (× 70)

External parasites of
the dog, shown with a
fine-tooth comb of the
type used for lice and
flea removal

Sarcoptes (× 70)

Demodex canis (× 150)

repeated washing of such places with a rotenone preparation, or use of a flame-gun on concrete work in kennels is essential, as otherwise re-infestation will occur. In the modern living-room, a vacuum cleaner will gather up at least some of the flea eggs and larvae.

Mention should be made here of the 'stick-tight' or chicken flea, likely to infest dogs only where poultry are kept, though wild birds and their nests are another source. The female attaches its mouth parts to the skin, sometimes of the dog's ear, and remains there tightly secured.

LICE

Without a good light and a magnifying glass, lice are hard to see. Whereas a flea, with its dark brown colour and its quick movement, attracts the eye, the greyish louse merges into its background. The eggs or 'nits' are laid on the host, are white, and each is attached to a hair.

Lice are of two types: biting and blood-sucking. The former can cause intense irritation to the dog; the latter, in obtaining their meal of blood, cause anaemia in young, old, and debilitated dogs – and even death.

Unlike the flea, the louse's whole life-cycle is spent on the host's body, and may be completed in one month. Such a short period increases the risk of a dog carrying a very large number of lice.

People buying a puppy should beware of accepting one with lice.

Lice often congregate on the ear-flaps of dogs. Like fleas, they can transmit the larvae of a tapeworm.

While lice are readily killed by means of a rotenone (the active ingredient of derris), derris, or BHC shampoo, this will not affect the hatchability of their eggs. It is consequently essential to repeat the wet shampoo in a fortnight's time, or to give three treatments at ten-day intervals. Clipping of heavily infested long-haired dogs may be necessary.

TICKS

In Britain ticks which are found on dogs include the common sheep tick, *Ixodes ricinus*, often acquired by dogs on country walks; *Ixodes hexagonus*,

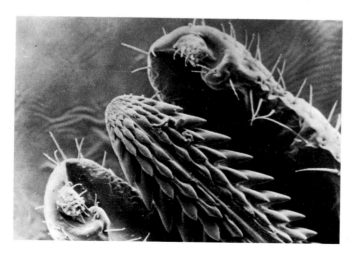

The mouth parts of a tick (× 2,000 approx.)

not uncommon on suburban dogs; *Ixodes canisuga*, the 'British dog tick': and *Dermacentor reticulatus*, also found on cattle and horses.

The brown tick, or kennel tick, *Rhipicephalus sanguineus*, is distributed throughout the world, and has been brought to Europe on dogs coming from the tropics, with a resultant problem for the owners of quarantine kennels, where it establishes itself in buildings and may spread to nearby houses with central heating. *I. canisuga* may likewise establish itself in buildings.

The ticks mentioned above are all three-host ticks; that is to say, the larva, nymph, and adult each feeds on different animals, dropping off the host after doing so. Tick larvae climb up blades of grass, etc., and attach themselves to a passing animal.

A single tick may be found on a dog's head, for example, or two or three, or sometimes a large number of larval ticks around the lips. To anyone unfamiliar with ticks, an engorged female may look more like a small tumour than a parasite, since legs and mouth-parts will be hidden underneath the body. Once recognised, a tick must be removed. This may be facilitated by applying a drop of ether, surgical spirit, or lighter-fuel to the tick, and waiting a little; the parasite may relax its grip and back away. It can then be removed with forceps or tweezers. If it is merely pulled, the mouth-parts may break off and be left in the dog, which will result in an abscess.

Ticks cause local inflammation, some secrete a toxin, and all suck blood and worry the host. (In parts of the U.S.A. and in the tropics, a single tick on the neck of a dog can cause tick paralysis, involving all four legs.)

While ticks can be removed by hand, or killed by means of a wet shampoo containing BHC (unless they are already resistant to this), there is no effective tick-deterrent which can be applied to a dog's coat. However, it may be of interest to mention that Dr I. C. Horak,[3] writing in the *Journal of the South African Veterinary Association*, found that a plastic collar impregnated with Sandran (propoxur) effectively controlled the adult brown dog tick for seven weeks, and immature ticks for a period of at least ten weeks. (This was in a trial involving four dogs.) The same type of collar also killed all the ticks, fleas, and lice on a severely infested dog within 48 hours, he stated. In Britain, too, owners have found such collars effective in killing ticks of all sizes.

Such plastic collars are on sale in many shops in Britain and elsewhere, and are impregnated with different parasiticides by different manufacturers. Dichlorvos, used in resin strips which are attached to the dog's ordinary collar, are claimed to be effective for up to three months against fleas, but probably 10 weeks is a safe maximum to allow.

As ineffective collars of this type sometimes come on to the market, dog-owners are advised to buy from a reliable source, and to judge for themselves how effective a particular make is. Any signs of skin inflammation should be watched for, as a few dogs are allergic to one or two of the chemicals used.

PARASITIC MITES

If your dog is frantically licking between his toes, or nibbling there, try to examine the area under a good light. If you see an orange or reddish speck, it is likely to be the larva of a harvest mite or 'chigger'. This is an occasional cause of intense irritation in a localised part of the body.

The larvae occasionally cause itching in man, and are found on many domestic and wild animals, so that it is not easy to prevent infestation of the dog. Benzyl benzoate kills the larvae; but as a home remedy you could try applying a few drops of water in which a little washing-soda has been dissolved to allay the itching. To kill the mites, use a little of one of the shampoos already mentioned in connection with fleas and lice.

Cheyletiella mites are also reddish in colour and a cause of itching. They infest rabbits, hares, birds, and cats – as well as dogs and sometimes man. A wet shampoo containing one of the insecticides mentioned earlier can be used, and should be applied along the dog's neck and back especially. Repeat in a week's time.

EAR MANGE

This is the most common cause of a dog shaking his head or scratching his ears, and is caused by the mite *Otodectes*. The names ear mange or parasitic otitis are preferable to the word 'canker', which is used indiscriminately to describe a variety of differing ear troubles.

If a pledget (small wad) of cotton-wool be inserted into the ear and wiped around, it will, in a case of ear mange, be found to bring with it a waxy-powdery deposit, brown or blackish. If this is examined under a powerful magnifying glass, mites may be seen moving.

Again, you can use a little of one of the insecticide shampoos to kill the mites. If there is much wax present, a little warm water containing a pinch of washing soda to an eggcupful may be used as a preliminary cleaning agent.

Be sure to avoid poking around inside the ears with an orange-stick or any other sharp object, and avoid also any 'canker powders' bought over a shop counter, as some tend to clog the ears without doing any good.

If there is a painful condition of the ear, any sign of pus or blood, or a foul-smelling discharge, seek veterinary advice.

SARCOPTIC MANGE

This is what might be called the common, or ordinary, type of mange. It is a highly contagious skin disease, caused by mites (too small to be seen with the naked eye) which spread rapidly from dog to dog – and occasionally from dog to man! (In people, the itchy skin disease is known as scabies.)

The mites burrow their way into the thickness of the skin, a fact which makes treatment less easy than when dealing with surface parasites such as fleas. Intense irritation is caused, the hair drops out, and on the bare patches the skin begins to take on an abnormal appearance; becoming spotted, thickened and folded. Mange often begins on the dog's face and spreads backwards.

If sarcoptic mange is not checked, the bare patches may become very extensive, and the dog may suffer exhaustion and become ill. As a first-aid measure, use one of the shampoos recommended above; do not listen to any neighbours recommending lavender oil, turpentine, tar, carbolic acid or creosote, or you may kill your dog.

The dog should be kept away from others, and bedded on newspaper which should be burnt after use. Old blanket or other bedding previously used should be boiled if practicable before re-use, or else destroyed.

It really is advisable to obtain veterinary treatment for mange, as even repeated shampooing with wet BHC and similar preparations cannot be relied on for other than first-aid; other means of treatment will be necessary. A diagnosis is important, too, and this means a microscopical examination of skin scrapings to find the mites.

FOLLICULAR MANGE

This is also known as demodectic mange, since it is caused by a roughly cigar-shaped mite with stumpy legs called *Demodex folliculorum* (or *D. canis*). These mites live in the hair follicles and sebaceous glands, and may be present without any symptoms being shown.

In contrast to sarcoptic mange, follicular mange is not very itchy and it is slow to develop. When it does so, it results in a loss of hair and a thickening of the skin.

Two types are recognised: (1) the *squamous* type, in which the skin becomes scaly, wrinkled, and often resembles ringworm – for which it may be mistaken. This type is seen mostly in young dogs, and usually begins on the face or forelegs. It may be followed by (2) the *pustular* type, in which secondary bacterial infection occurs. This is always very serious, and constitutes an illness as well as a skin disease, since the dog often suffers from toxaemia.

Professional treatment and advice are highly desirable, likewise a diagnosis first. Dressings will be needed to kill the mites, and antibiotics to control or prevent secondary infection. If extensive areas of skin are involved, it may be necessary to treat only half at a time, owing to risk of poisoning. The outlook is always serious with advanced cases of follicular mange, and sometimes euthanasia is the only course.

A difficulty in treating follicular mange is that the mites are difficult to reach at the depth where they are living. One way of overcoming this difficulty is to use the technique of iontophoresis, but unfortunately it is a very time-consuming method and not widely available. It is an electrical treatment involving an electrolyte – such as methylene blue in this instance – in which pads are soaked and attached to electrodes connected to a battery. The methylene blue reaches the mites and kills them. It is a painless method, and has been used with success experimentally in severe follicular mange at the Hannah Research Institute, Scotland.

A case history of follicular mange. A client bought a dog from a very reputable-sounding source and requested a health check. The animal was a golden Labrador, under one year old, handsome, fit, and free from the usual detectable congenital defects, *but* a small yellowish patch of bare skin, about ¼-inch across, caught the professional eye. Under a magnifying glass it looked as though this small area had been dressed with a sulphur preparation. Suspicion aroused, a skin scraping was taken. This was later examined under the microscope, and the client informed that the dog had follicular mange. She was advised to return the dog – which she did – at the seller's expense. (It *might* have been one of those non-progressive cases of follicular mange which would yield to treatment; but why should she take the risk?)

Ringworm

This is a contagious disease caused by the growth of certain fungi, especially – in the dog – species of *Microsporum* and *Trichophyton*. Ringworm is not very common in the dog, but by no means rare. It is likely to become noticeable to the dog-owner at the stage where hair has fallen out of a small patch of skin (usually but not always circular). The skin there becomes reddened, with raised edges and tiny 'blisters' (vesicles). Later it becomes thickened and covered with a crust which is greyish or yellowish white. Ringworm may be itchy, so the dog tends to rub or bite the part; (in some cases there appears to be little irritation).

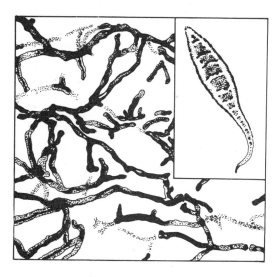

Ringworm: the branching filaments of the fungus (× 100 approx.), and a spore (inset × 1,000)

Circular patches of ringworm may coalesce to form larger areas of irregular shape. The face, head and neck are common ringworm sites, and less often the spaces between the toes – occasionally in or around the nails.

Ringworm should be treated early, before it has time to spread. As a first-aid measure, tincture of iodine may be applied around the edges of the lesion (the fungus is growing from the centre outwards); but if the dog is being taken almost immediately to a veterinary surgeon, do not dress the place first. Diagnosis depends upon an examination of the dog under ultra-violet light, or the taking of skin scrapings and the demonstration of the fungus and its spores on or in the hairs.

Except in dogs in poor condition, or where ringworm is neglected and left untreated, it is not a long-lasting or serious disease in dogs. Treatment involves either the use of local dressings, or the internal administration of an antibiotic called griseofulvin, which can be given in the food. This antibiotic is expensive, and should not be used in a pregnant bitch; otherwise it is an excellent method which is suitable for treating a kennel outbreak of ringworm, obviating the hand-dressing which can so easily lead to kennel staff themselves becoming infected.

Dogs become infected by other dogs, cats, rats, mice, rabbits, hares, etc.; and a farm dog could be infected by calves, in which ringworm is a common disease during the winter months.

A dog with ringworm is best bedded on newspaper, which should be burnt after use. Care must be taken by anyone handling a dog with ringworm, as the infection sometimes spreads to human beings.

Eczema

This is an inflammatory condition of the skin, which takes various forms, but which is often characterised by a bright red, moist appearance ('wet eczema'), or by a scaly, dry appearance ('dry eczema'). Itchiness is associated with many forms of eczema, for which sarcoptic mange is sometimes mistaken. The acute moist type, which may appear overnight, is especially distressing to the dog. Calamine lotion can be recommended as a soothing application for first-aid purposes.

Some cases of eczema are examples of allergic dermatitis. Substances present in carpets, rubber, household cleaners may give rise to an allergy. Dogs are protected to some extent by their natural coats, and for this reason the inflammation may affect the muzzle, abdomen, or inside of the ear flaps. Redness, itching, and often biting or scratching at the affected part, are symptoms of allergic dermatitis – one of the commonest causes of which is sensitisation to flea-bites. Sensitisation may take months to develop, but once established the reaction will follow every contact, although there is often a delay of one to five days before symptoms appear.

Individual dogs may become sensitised to a particular food which is harmless and beneficial to the majority. Certain kinds of fish, cow's milk, certain canned foods, oatmeal, pork, chicken, egg, beef and mutton, have all been cited; of course this does not mean that dog-owners should ban all these valuable items of diet. After all, there would not be much else left to offer a dog!

It is easier to relieve the symptoms, in many cases, than to identify the substance producing the skin inflammation. Treatment may include the use of an anti-histamine, to neutralise the excess of histamine liberated from the tissues.

Not all cases of eczema, however, are due to allergies. A vitamin deficiency may be one cause, and it is always advisable to vary and improve the diet – especially if there has been a long succession of meals consisting of fish, or if the dog has had little to eat but dog biscuits.

Eczema may be associated with disease of the kidneys, sometimes with diabetes, possibly with obesity.

An itchy area of inflamed skin on the front of the foreleg or side of the hock may become the site of what is sometimes called a 'lick granuloma'. This is an area of chronic skin ulceration, with a reddish, raw-looking appearance. Licking it becomes an obsession with the dog, and interferes with healing. Veterinary treatment is necessary – and sometimes the use of an Elizabethan collar to prevent the licking.

Viral Infections

Finally, brief mention should be made of Aujeszky's disease, although it is likely to be encountered mainly in farm dogs or hounds, and even in these it is not common. An important, but not invariable, symptom of this disease is intense irritation which is so severe that the dog will scratch and bite itself to an extent amounting to self-mutilation. A dog with this disease has been known to bite off its own tail. Another name for this infection is pseudo-rabies.

Rabid dogs may mutilate themselves in similar fashion. A burning or tingling sensation, rather than itching, is – to judge from what human patients have said before their death – common at the site of the bite wound made by a rabid animal. Possibly the sensation of burning or tingling is that felt in Aujeszky's disease, too, and not mere itching.

REFERENCES
1 Halnan, C. R E. *J. Small Anim. Pract.* 17 (1976), 527
2 Baker, K. P. & Hatch, C. *Vet. Record* 91 (1972), 151
3 Horak, I. G. *J. Sth. Afr. Vet. Assoc.* 47, (1976), 17

5 The Dog's Face

The first time that a client brings a dog to the surgery, or that a veterinary surgeon makes a call to the house, the animal is – from the behaviour point of view – an unknown quantity. The late Professor William C. Miller commented: 'The animal which gazes up into a person's face with an expression of interest and frankness will generally allow itself to be handled without any trouble, but the sly-looking creature which watches every movement of one's hands out of the corner of its eyes should be treated with respect.' Such a dog, one might add, will often make slight anticipatory movements of its lips – a sign that it has half a mind to bite.

At the house a dog may stand with ears pricked, keenly alert, giving the visitor the benefit of the doubt; or back may go those ears flat against the head, hackles may rise, lips be drawn back. 'His countenance likes me not', the visitor might quote to himself.

Eyes, ears, lips and teeth all enter into the dog's expression, both in good health and bad. Anyone can tell from a dog's dejected or anxious expression that something is wrong; and a veterinarian may be able to detect that a dog is unwell 24 hours before the owner, merely by noting that the eyes have lost some of their lustre.

A vacant stare is another important guide to illness in the dog, as

Expression. *Near right*: intelligent, alert (an R.A.F. Police dog); *far right*: somewhat apprehensive (at a veterinary surgery)

mentioned in the chapter on 'Fits and Hysteria'. Involuntary alteration of the expression may occur in tetanus, although fortunately very few owners indeed will ever see the sardonic grin (the *risus sardonicus* referred to by the classical authors). In the rare muscle disease, eosinophilic myositis, the affected dog's face may assume a foxy appearance. Wasting of the temporal muscles is one sign of Cushing's disease, among others. The face may develop a lop-sided look if there is an abscess or tumour present. Paralysis of the facial nerve may also alter the appearance of a dog's face.

The appearance of the third eyelids, like curtains partly drawn across a window, may be due to absorption of fat during the course of an illness, (i.e. a sign of general ill-health), or to a local eye condition.

Abscesses

An abscess may follow penetration of the skin by a cat's claw, a grass seed or awn, a splinter, or other foreign body, and may give rise to what the owner thinks of as a small wound which fails to heal.

Facial abscess. Case history 1 : The owner of an 8-year-old Poodle had been assiduously bathing away the discharge from a small swelling on the face, but the discharge continued and there was evidently some irritation there as the dog sometimes scratched or rubbed the place. Two or three times they thought that healing had occurred, only to find that there was a scab over the surface. Examination at the surgery revealed a small abscess. This was opened and a grass seed found. After its removal, permanent healing quickly occurred.

Another cause of facial abscess is illustrated by *case history 2 :* A small crossbred dog was brought to the surgery with what his owners described as 'a hole in the face'. They added: 'It won't heal. We've tried everything. The man in the dog-food shop in the High Street said that it was a rat-bite and told us to bathe it with antiseptic and it would get all right, but it hasn't – not after weeks and weeks.'

Examination very soon showed that the 'hole' was the exit of a *fistula* – the channel taken by pus in a break-out to the skin surface from an area of suppuration. At the other end of this fistula was the root of the carnassial tooth. It was explained that there would never be healing until the infected tooth had been extracted. This was later carried out, and the 'hole' soon disappeared.

In the tropics a small swelling on the face with a non-discharging hole indicates the presence of a larva of the tumbu fly, or other tropical warble fly. Swelling of the head and neck may occur in some cases of anthrax.

Tear-staining

The face of a light-coloured dog may show reddish-brown tear stains if there is any obstruction to the free flow of excess tears into the nose. The discolouration is due to a pigment in the tears (or lacrimal fluid) which takes on this colour when exposed to the light. Tear-staining occurs also in atopic disease (canine hay-fever). Allergic dermatitis often appears first around the eyes, and many parasitic skin infestations begin on the face, e.g. ringworm, sarcoptic and follicular mange.

The Nose

A cold, moist nose is accepted by most dog-owners as a sort of barometer of health, and quite a good one, since a dry nose may indicate a fever, and should certainly prompt the taking of a dog's temperature.

In **canine distemper** there is often a nasal discharge; indeed, the nostrils may become caked with greenish-yellowish mucus, but in the 'hard pad' type of distemper infection this discharge is usually absent and the nose may become dry and cracked and horny.

Acute rhinitis (inflammation of the nostrils) may be associated with infection by several viruses other than the distemper virus, and also by bacteria such as *Bordetella bronchiseptica* and *Klebsiella*.

Violent sneezing or snorting, and a mucopurulent discharge from only one nostril, suggests the presence of a foreign body, such as a grass seed or awn.

Chronic rhinitis and **sinusitis** may result from the continuing presence of a foreign body, or from a fungal infection, especially aspergillosis, described in chapter 20. The fungus, *Aspergillus*, tends to spread in the nose and nasal sinuses, giving rise to symptoms of a muco-purulent discharge from one nostril at first, sometimes from both nostrils later, and some bleeding. If there is destruction of bone by the fungus, there is liable to be slight deformity of the face and tenderness over the bridge of the nose.

Case history. A 10-year-old working Collie, alert but rather thin, had been suffering from intermittent nasal catarrh, which antibiotics had failed to control. At the University of Glasgow's veterinary hospital this dog was examined under general anaesthesia – and not allowed to regain consciousness, for unfortunately the findings were cancer of the turbinate bones and a severe fungal infection.[1]

Fungal infection often follows a chronic inflammation, or trauma, or the presence of a tumour. It can be treated surgically, where there is not already too much destruction of bone, but when a malignant growth is associated, euthanasia is the only course. If the growth is non-malignant, surgery often gives reasonably good results.

Swelling and tenderness of the bridge of the nose may indicate a fracture involving one of the nasal bones.

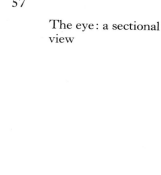

The eye: a sectional
view

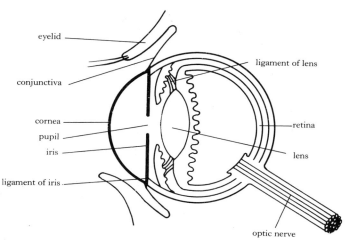

eyelid

conjunctiva

cornea

pupil

iris

ligament of iris

ligament of lens

retina

lens

optic nerve

The Eyes

A healthy eye is lustrous; naturally and adequately moistened by the tears.
The white of the eye should show no tinge of yellow, nor redness due to the
presence of blood vessels not normally seen there. The pupil should be
sensitive to light.

A discharge from the eyes indicates an inflammation of the conjunctiva,
the membrane lining the eyelids and, in modified form, covering the
visible part of the eye. **Conjunctivitis**, as we all know from personal
experience, leads to 'watering' of the eyes, often to redness and swelling of
the eyelids or their edges; sometimes to a sticky, thicker discharge, with
tenderness or pain, and a reluctance to keep the eyes open in a bright light.

Among common causes of conjunctivitis are local infections with
viruses, mycoplasmas, bacteria, fungi; exposure to draughts (looking out
of a moving car window, for example); exposure to dust, lime or smoke. In
some dogs a hyper-sensitivity to inhaled pollen or to other particles of
foreign protein gives rise to **atopic disease** ('hay fever') with conjunctivitis. The latter can also be a symptom of some generalised illness
such as canine distemper, and of canine herpes virus infection.

Inturning eyelashes or eyelids cause inflammation and 'watering' of the
eyes. These conditions are referred to below.

In the tropics and sub-tropics, and the U.S.A., *Thelazia* worms are not
uncommon parasites of the dog's eye, living behind the third eyelid or in
the lacrimal gland or its duct. Transmitted by flies, these worms affect
cattle in Britain, and could easily be transferred to the dog's eye.

Severe inflammation and '**watering**' of *one* eye may occur if there is a
blocked tear duct, or a grass seed or piece of grit present. Pain and irritation
may cause the dog to paw the face or rub it along the ground.

Sometimes it is possible to flush out the piece of grit, and for this purpose a piece of cotton wool can be soaked in warm saline and held close to the eye so that a few drops fall on to its surface. An eye-dropper intended for human use could serve the same purpose but there is the danger that if the dog jerks his head, the end of the dropper may come into violent contact with the eye. If the grit has been moved by the liquid and become visible, it can often be removed with a piece of moistened cotton wool.

A grass seed or awn is more difficult to remove. Flushing may move it so that what looks like a hair becomes visible, but this is difficult to grasp. (Household tweezers, which usually have sharp ends, should *never* be used anywhere near the eye.) Usually a local anaesthetic is indicated and then removal by a veterinary surgeon. As a first-aid measure, apply a drop of castor or olive oil to reduce friction and discomfort.

Keratitis means inflammation of the cornea – the eye's window, so to speak, which admits light through the pupil to the retina. Keratitis often follows conjunctivitis, especially if there is a severe infection present; or it may be due to inturning eyelashes or eyelids; or to violence such as a whip lash or a cat's claw causing injury; or to a thorn, a minute piece of glass, or some irritant chemical. It may also be a sequel to canine viral hepatitis.

Symptoms of keratitis include the profuse watering seen with conjunctivitis and a tendency to keep the eye closed, but then there follows an opacity which at first may be only pin-head in size but, if treatment is not forthcoming, may spread to the whole of the cornea, when the dog becomes blind in that eye. People often refer to 'a film over the eye' but in reality the opacity involves the substance of the cornea.

It is a pin-head size opacity which may be a clue to the presence of a thorn embedded in the eye. The thorn itself is seldom noticed, being too small and inconspicuous – what attracts attention is the tiny circle of white around the thorn. It must be removed by a veterinary surgeon under anaesthesia.

Pannus is a complication of keratitis, and the term implies the appearance of very small blood vessels which grow out from the margins of the cornea, stopping at the edges of an ulcer – if one is present.

Ulceration is another common sequel to keratitis and is always potentially dangerous, since penetration may occur, leading sometimes to a hernia of the iris, sometimes to infection of the anterior chamber and permanent blindness.

It will be appreciated therefore that eye conditions such as these should receive professional attention without delay. If treated in time, most cases of keratitis will clear satisfactorily, leaving a virtually undamaged cornea and no impairment of vision except, perhaps, for the tiny opaque spot where the thorn had been or where other injury had occurred. In a few cases part of the cornea becomes pigmented after keratitis, but usually does not render the dog blind in that eye, though sight will be imperfect.

It seems that anything which causes drying of the surface of the cornea, such as an insufficiency of lacrimal gland secretion (i.e. tears) may result in conjunctivitis and keratitis of one or both eyes. 'Dry-eye' may follow infection or injury of the gland or its nerve. 'Blue-eye' is referred to on page 77. Sometimes the edge of the third eyelid becomes thickened and causes friction, leading to keratitis.

The appearance of a red, raw-looking 'lump' at the corner of the eye is due to an enlarged and displaced Harderian gland. This will need surgical attention, which will remove both the discomfort and the unsightly appearance associated with it.

Turning in of the eyelashes, technically known as **trichiasis,** and turning in of the eyelids – **entropion** – are sometimes the result of a chronic inflammation but far more often are inherited defects which appear during puppyhood. The eyelashes irritate the cornea and, if left untreated, keratitis with opacity will follow. A minor surgical operation, involving removal of an elliptical piece of skin of the eyelid, and suturing the two cut edges together, corrects the defect and prevents further trouble.

Ectropion means a turning outwards of the eyelids – a condition virtually normal in Bloodhounds and St Bernards, but which usually needs correcting in other breeds by means of a minor operation.

The eyelids are sometimes the site of sebaceous cysts, warts, or – in the older dog – malignant growths.

ACCIDENTS

A major accident sometimes befalls Pekingese and other breeds of dog with prominent eyes – as a result of violence of some kind the eyeball becomes partially displaced from the orbit. Sometimes the eyeball can be re-positioned, but if long delay has occurred or if the eyeball is damaged, it may have to be removed.

Case history. A Pekingese was chased by another dog and lost sight of by the owner and, judging from the sound of a car braking suddenly, may have been struck by the latter. Whether the eye protrusion was caused by car or dog fight was uncertain, but at the surgery next day there was evidence of exacerbation of the condition by road grit. It was not found possible to ease the eye back into the orbit and the eye was removed. It was explained to the owner that as an empty eye socket is very unsightly, and an eye patch not practicable for dogs, the eyelids would be operated on so that they could be sutured to close the gap. This was done, and the dog looked afterwards as though he had always had only the one eye. After a period of convalescence he became as lively as ever.

Gunshot wounds. Occasionally dogs have the misfortune to be shot in the face. Apart from sometimes multiple wounds of skin and underlying muscle, there may also be penetration of the eyeball. As can readily be imagined, damage may be severe and permanent impairment of vision often follows.

Case history 1. An 11-month-old Labrador, shot with a 12-bore, suffered injury to the iris, which became partly adherent to the lens (a condition technically known as posterior **synechia**). However, six weeks after the accident the iris was mobile with the pupil able to respond to light. Where the cornea had been penetrated, an opaque pigmented spot remained.[2]

Case history 2. An 8-year-old Springer Spaniel had to have amputation of part of the iris protruding through a gunshot wound in the cornea. Sutures had to be inserted in the latter; being removed after 10 days. One lead shot had lodged in the lens and gave rise to a cataract.[3]

CATARACTS

A cataract, or a cloudy appearance of the lens, may also form in the elderly or diabetic dog, impairing vision. Cataracts are often bilateral. An inherited predisposition to cataract is said to exist within some breeds. There is no effective treatment for cataract other than surgical removal of the lens, which is occasionally performed in canine surgery.

OTHER CONDITIONS

Dislocation of the lens is seen mainly in wire-haired Fox Terriers, Sealyhams, or terriers with similar ancestry, and there is a hereditary predisposition to this condition. If the lens becomes displaced in a mainly downwards direction, it does not seem to cause much discomfort to the dog. Usually, however, the lens is displaced forwards as well as downwards, when there is likely to be interference with the drainage of the eye so that pressure builds up. Within a matter of weeks or even days, the sight then becomes poor and the dog miserable.

Swelling or bulging of the eyeball becomes noticeable; but first the pupil is larger than normal, and the white of the eye shows some redness. Observed carefully, the lens may be seen to wobble, if it is still attached to some of its supporting fibres and not yet completely dislocated. A crescent of bright green irridescence between the edge of the pupil and the edge of the lens later affords an indication of the degree of displacement. Both eyes are nearly always involved eventually. An operation for the removal of the dislocated lens can be carried out by veterinary surgeons who specialise in ophthalmic work.

Glaucoma is the swelling of the eyeball due to intra-ocular pressure. It may follow the lens dislocation mentioned above and also atrophy of the retina. Some of the causes of glaucoma are not yet understood.

Progressive retinal atrophy (P.R.A.) is an inherited condition which develops in certain breeds. The dog suffers from 'night blindness', being unable to see properly in conditions of poor light. The pupil dilates widely, even in daylight, and the dog appears to stare. No treatment can halt the progressive degeneration of the retina, and the dog gradually becomes blind. Neither a dog nor a bitch with P.R.A. should be bred from.

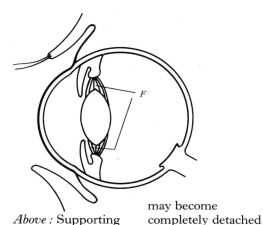

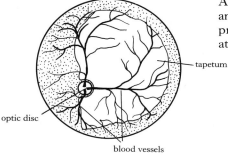

A normal eye (*above*) and one affected with progressive retinal atrophy (*below*)

tapetum

optic disc

blood vessels

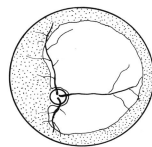

Above : Supporting fibres of the lens are indicated by *F* in this diagram of the eye. If the lens becomes partly detached it can, at a veterinary examination, be seen to wobble. Later, it may become completely detached from its supporting fibres – dislocated. If it falls forward into the front part of the eye, it interferes with drainage of the fluid there, and causes the dog great discomfort

Detachment of the retina is another eye disorder with a hereditary basis, being one feature of the so-called 'collie eye anomaly'. Mr D. G. Lewis F.R.C.V.S. gave a paper on this subject at the B.V.A. congress not long ago. Much of the research had been carried out in Australia and the U.S.A. on this condition in the Rough Collie. Bleeding within the eyeball and/or detachment of the retina may occur. If the latter is extensive the dog is likely to be partially or totally blind. The bleeding is usually seen in the young puppy.

Mr Lewis's paper was concerned mainly with the Shetland Sheepdog, and he stated that of 206 examined during 1972–73 after appearing in the show-ring, only 19 per cent could be regarded as completely normal. But 'the incidence of normality in the merles alone was 63 per cent. This fact rather confounds suggestions that have been made among breeders that the merle coat colour combination is directly related to the hereditary pattern and occurrence of "collie eye anomaly".' Isolated cases of this have been reported in Old English Sheepdogs, Smooth Collies, Beagles, and Poodles.

There are many other abnormal eye conditions, some due to hereditary factors; some to diet (e.g. a lack of vitamin A); some to infections such as distemper (involving the retina and optic nerve), toxoplasmosis, tuberculosis, and various fungal infections.

Filarial worms may infest the interior of the eye, and rarely they can be seen moving in the anterior chamber. They have been removed surgically. *Angiostrongylus* and *Dirofilaria* species are among those found in this situation (mainly overseas).

Blindness has been mentioned as either a symptom or a sequel to other conditions. A tumour or brain disease of some kind may cause blindness; while some poisons, such as metaldehyde, carbon monoxide, and quinine (to which the dog is very susceptible) cause temporary blindness. In old age vision is apt to become impaired, and a few old dogs do go blind.

The Ears

The shape and carriage of the ears varies greatly between the different breeds of dog – not content with which some breed societies insist on the barbaric practice of ear-cropping, without which done a dog cannot compete in shows; owners acquiesce. Fortunately, ear-cropping has been banned in the U.K. and Canada. The modern dog, unlike the medieval felon punished by ear-cropping, has the benefit of an anaesthetic, but that hardly justifies an operation performed purely for reasons of fashion. An example of re-shaping of an ear for veterinary reasons is given in the chapter on 'Accidents and Other Emergencies' (page 91).

Inflammation of the ear, **otitis**, is very common in the dog and leads to scratching and shaking of the head. Sometimes a small blood vessel becomes damaged during the course of these activities, and blood clot collects beneath the skin of the ear-flap (pinna), forming a large swelling – a **haematoma**. This is not as painful as an abscess but may cause some discomfort to the dog, and worries the owner because it is unsightly. If left untreated it causes crinkling of the ear, but this can be prevented by minor surgery.

Otitis is frequently caused by **ear-mange mites** described in chapter 4, 'The Itchy Dog', where symptoms and treatment are given. An uncomplicated case of ear-mange can easily be overcome, but if allowed to persist infection often supervenes; and inflammation, pus formation, and ulceration can result in a painful and very unpleasant condition. Parasites other than ear-mange mites (*Otodectes*) may also infest the ear (including the larvae of flies, in the U.S.A. and elsewhere). Along the borders of the ear flaps, lice and fleas often congregate, sometimes ticks.

Wax and Foreign Bodies

Infection may also follow an excessive secretion of wax, and give rise to an offensive odour. Spaniels are very prone to ear trouble of this sort, and the large flap hanging down is probably a disadvantage. A first-aid measure consists in fixing, by means of adhesive plaster, the ear-flaps inside-out above the head. This allows air to circulate, and the mere ventilation by itself is sometimes sufficient to clear up this objectionable disorder. In long-standing cases of purulent otitis, a surgical operation called aural resection may be the only satisfactory method of treatment.

A foreign body such as a grass seed may become lodged in the ear and worry the dog.

A little olive oil dropped into the ear and worked around may help to ease irritation from a foreign body or soften wax, and can be used as a first-aid measure where there is no pus. A pledglet of cotton wool can afterwards be used for cleaning, but should not be wrapped around an orange-stick or other pointed object. Ear-drops specially formulated for the condition present in your dog's ears can be obtained from your veterinary surgeon. Ingredients include wax softeners, antibiotics, local anaesthetic, or parasiticides – according to need. Avoid the use of so-called 'canker powders' sold over shop counters, as some of these preparations may be ineffective, merely clogging the ears. (See also the Appendix.)

DEAFNESS

Deafness can be a congenital defect associated with a white coat (e.g. in the white Bull Terrier), and this should be borne in mind when buying a puppy. Injury to the ear-drum is another cause of deafness and underlines the danger of poking about in the ear. Nerve damage, blockage of the Eustachian tubes (which lead from the throat to the middle ear), and a brain injury are other causes of deafness. Carbon monoxide poisoning may, in a few cases, cause deafness. In the human subject the antibiotic streptomycin is a well-recognised cause of deafness. Aspirin has this effect, too, in a very small proportion of people. Such findings may be relevant.

THE INTERNAL EAR

Inflammation and infection of the internal ear gives rise to loss of balance and to circling movements. It requires veterinary treatment, or infection may spread to the brain.

The Jaws

The average young-to-middle-aged dog will derive benefit as well as pleasure from being given, periodically, a knuckle bone to chew. This is good for the jaw muscles which – in the domestic, as opposed to the wild, dog – seldom receive much exercise. With soft food, quickly gulped, and without the normal carnivore's prey, jaws and teeth have little of the biting and tearing and grinding movements which occur in natural conditions. Dog biscuits help, but to maintain the health of jaws and teeth, a large marrow bone is ideal.

Jaw injuries include fractures and dislocations, but these are uncommon apart from in car accidents, falls, blows, etc. A temporary paralysis or **paresis** of the jaws is seen occasionally in dogs which carry too-large pieces of wood in their mouths. A slightly dropped lower jaw, with inability to close the mouth, is one symptom of rabies.

So-called '**rubber jaw**' is associated with some cases of chronic inflammation of the kidneys. The bone becomes so soft that, at autopsy, it can be cut with a knife.

A hardening of the jaw muscles occurs in an uncommon disease seen mostly in Alsatians – **eosinophilic myositis**. The effect is to give the dog's face a foxy appearance, and the nictitating membranes may be much in evidence. Diagnosis is made or confirmed by examining a blood smear. The outlook is not hopeful.

Atrophy of the jaw muscles is a feature of **atrophic myositis**. The causes of this are not fully understood, but possibly one of them is over-extension of the tempero-mandibular joint when the mouth is opened too wide, with resultant nerve damage. Symptoms include a inability to eat solid food or to lap. There is very little voluntary movement of the jaws, and the dog resists when any attempt is made to open them. Recovery usually takes place within three to six months.

The Teeth

The average adult dog has 42 teeth; the upper jaw contains 6 incisors, 2 canines, 8 premolars, and 4 molars; the lower jaw has 6 incisors, 2 canines, 8 premolars, and 6 molars. There is some breed and individual variation in the number of permanent teeth; the average Pekingese, Boxer, or Bulldog (i.e. breeds with a short skull) has slightly fewer teeth.

From the dog-owner's point of view – once the purchase of an animal with an undershot or overshot jaw has been avoided – the main concern should be the maintenance of healthy teeth and gums.

Sometimes, persistent temporary teeth need removing in order to make way for the permanent teeth and avoid these being badly positioned. Supernumerary teeth or those which do not meet so as to give a correct bite may also need professional attention.

The brown discolouration, or mottling, of teeth, which occurs after some cases (usually mild ones) of distemper, cannot be rectified by ordinary cleaning, and remains as a permanent blemish. The only way of overcoming this is a sophisticated (and expensive) dental technique carried out by some veterinary surgeons; it involves cleaning with a dental drill, etching of the enamel around the defects, and sealing the enamel with a composite filling material comprising two resins – one to form a mechanical bond with the etched enamel, the other to form a chemical bond. There are other stages, including shaping, in this technique,[3] also used where it is desired to restore teeth damaged by stone or wire chewing.

Tartar, or dental plaque, represents the greatest threat to the health of teeth and gums. Bacteria normally present in the dog's mouth may act on

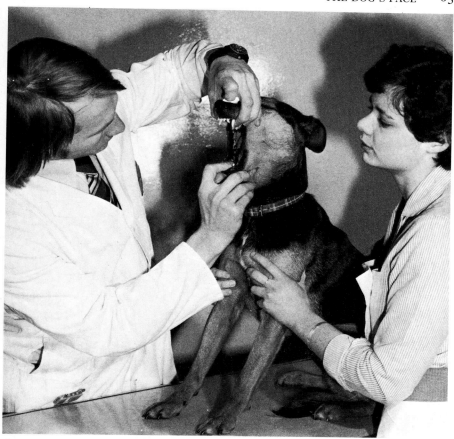

Examination of the dog's mouth is not painful to it, but requires a little expertise. The dog's lips are held between its teeth and the fingers, to ensure that even a frightened dog cannot bite

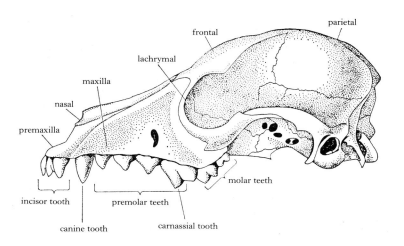

The dog's skull and teeth. Note the carnassial tooth

soft, sweet foods. Gradually, a soft deposit, at first composed of food particles and dead bacteria, becomes impregnated with calcium and other mineral salts contained in the saliva, and eventually attains a considerable hardness. Not only that, for the tartar attains also a considerable bulk in neglected cases, forming hard masses over several teeth which are completely covered and masked.

Where the tartar reaches to the gums and encroaches on them, inflammation is caused (**gingivitis**). This is followed by an increasing degree of infection, and a foul odour from the mouth. If still not relieved by professional treatment, the condition progresses to one of **periodontal disease**, with shrinkage of gums, and later of the underlying bone. As the gums recede from the teeth, fresh sites are formed for food particles to lodge, for bacteria, and for more tartar. Loosening of the teeth occurs, and the general health of the dog suffers.

There is absolutely no need for this deterioration. If the dog is taken to a veterinary surgeon for regular health checks once a year, the teeth can be scaled and tartar removed. In any event, seek professional help whenever the gums seem tender, inflamed, ulcerated or bleeding, or when there is marked halitosis.

Loose teeth cause pain, reluctance to masticate, and sometimes loss of weight. Signs of toothache including pawing at the mouth, rubbing the face along the ground, and whimpering. In addition, dogs with tooth trouble may dribble.

People often ask whether anything can be done to prevent tartar formation and tooth decay, such as a mouth wash or brushing the teeth. In the U.S.A. dog tooth pastes (appropriately flavoured!) are on the market; if the dog-owner is prepared to add teeth-cleaning to grooming chores, and if the dog does not protest too vigorously, I would suggest that there is no point in going to the expense of a canine dentifrice – use a little common salt in water. Far more important is the annual scaling of the teeth, which as a rule no regular cleaning can supersede or render unnecessary.

An abscess at the root of a tooth has already been referred to at the beginning of this chapter; such will soon dissipate after the tooth has been extracted.

REFERENCES
1 Bedford, P. G. C. & Heaton, M. G. *Vet. Record* 101 (1977), 327
2, 3 Schmidt, G. M. *et al. J. Small Anim. Pract.* 16 (1976), 33

6 Parasitic Worm Control

'My dog never has worms' is as empty a boast as the statement 'my dog never has fleas'. True, the dog-owner may not see the worms, but that does not refute their presence. It is virtually impossible for any dog outside a laboratory to escape worm infestation perpetually. Roundworms and tapeworms would not have continued to exist were they not successful parasites, able to ensure survival of the species through successive generations.

Even the most hygiene-conscious and fastidious person cannot prevent a dog becoming infested; but by periodic dosing with an effective anthelmintic (anti-worm drug), he or she can control such infestations. It is highly desirable that this is accepted as a part of responsible dog ownership, and carried out regularly, in the interests of both canine and human health. This is especially necessary in farm dogs.

The word 'control' is used advisedly, because it would be misleading to imply that one dose of an anthelmintic will dispose of every worm in the dog's body. The larval stages of some worms are not affected by drugs which kill the adult worms; and so a second dose will be necessary to remove them. Again, not all anthelmintics are equally effective against all types of worm; choosing an appropriate one is important – your veterinary surgeon can advise on this.

Great progress has been made in recent years in the development of new anthelmintics which have both a wider margin of safety and effectiveness against a wider range of worms. The days when a nauseating dose of areca nut – given after fasting – was necessary to expel tapeworms are happily long past. Now tasteless preparations are available, and fasting is unnecessary. Similarly, progress has been made in formulating drugs which can safely be used in puppies only a few weeks old to control roundworm infestations.

ROUNDWORMS

All roundworms in the digestive 'tunnel' steal nourishment which should be going to the dog. Some worms cause additional harm through the secretion of toxins. Damage to the mucous membrane lining the gut is caused by worms, which facilitates the entry of bacteria. A massive infestation can lead to actual blockage of the intestine. On the other hand, many light infestations give rise to no observable symptoms.

If you are intending to breed from a bitch, the time to begin worm control in her prospective puppies is before they are conceived; in other words, ensure that she is wormed before she is in oestrus prior to mating.

Congenital infestation with roundworms is common in puppies. Larvae of the ascarid worm *Toxocara canis* can cross the placenta and enter the pups before they are born. It is sound policy therefore to try to ensure that a pregnant bitch is free of these worms. The risk to human health associated with Toxocara worms are discussed in chapter 25; but this worm is important also from the canine health point of view, since it can cause failure to put on weight, abdominal pain, vomiting, and sometimes convulsions. Over two thousand of these worms have been found in a single dog. Rarely they penetrate the gut wall, causing a fatal peritonitis. Puppies should be wormed when between three and four weeks old, according to current recommendations; and again at fortnightly intervals up to the age of 12 weeks; then at longer intervals.

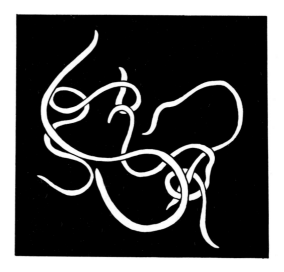

Toxocara canis, an ascarid roundworm. This drawing shows adults ($\times \frac{1}{2}$ approx.)

The body's defence mechanism forms antibodies against parasitic worms just as it does against bacteria and viruses, and before long it may be possible to produce an effective vaccine against *Toxocara*. As it is, the number of these worms found in adult dogs is only a fraction of those found in the puppy, and may even be nil.

Another ascarid worm, *Toxascaris leonina*, is – compared with *Toxocara* – relative harmless, and not often found in puppies under three months old.

Larvae of the roundworm *Trichinella spiralis* give rise to cysts in the muscles of dogs. Trichinosis is a serious problem in sledge-dogs in the

Arctic after eating walrus, bear, seal or fox meat, but is rarely diagnosed in dogs in Britain.

Hookworm (*Uncinaria*) larvae have been found in bitch's milk, and can gain entry into her puppies by this means. The larvae can also penetrate the unbroken skin, and in doing so cause great irritation between the toes and on the skin of the abdomen of adult dogs. Hookworms feed not on gut contents but on blood. They do this by abrading the intestinal wall until blood flows, and then they secrete a substance which inhibits the normal clotting process. As would be expected, a dog with severe hookworm infestation is likely to be anaemic, weak and thin.

Hookworm eggs hatch in water or moist soil: some are swallowed, others penetrate the skin. The advantages of concrete over grass runs are discussed in chapter 23 as a means of control.

Of 63 soil samples taken from public parks in Milan, 57 contained hookworm eggs. Ascarid eggs were present in 17 samples, and whipworms in 35. In the U.K., soil sampling in parks and playing fields has shown that on average 7 per cent of samples contain viable Toxocara eggs.

Whipworms (*Trichuris*) live in the large intestine and can cause diarrhoea, loss of condition, and a harsh coat.

Faecal samples from 1,000 well cared for pet dogs in a suburban area of north-west London were obtained in a survey carried out by Mr T. Turner B.VET.MED., M.R.C.V.S., and showed an infestation of Toxocara in 7.2 per cent, Toxascaris in 2.7 per cent, whipworms in 1.3 per cent and hookworms in 1.3 per cent. The age of the dogs, of both sexes, ranged from three weeks to 18 years. An interesting feature of the survey was that very few dogs showed symptoms.[1]

Roundworms found in other organs are listed in the table below.

TAPEWORMS

A tapeworm has a head bearing suckers or sucking grooves (and, in some species, a number of sharp hooks as well, to enable the worm to cling to the wall of the intestine), and behind the head and neck are a number of segments which increase in number as the worm grows in length. These segments are, respectively, immature, mature, and (furthest away from the head) gravid (i.e. containing fertilised eggs). These older, gravid segments become detached from the rest of the worm and pass out with the faeces.

The presence of adult tapeworms in the dog may give rise to few, if any, symptoms or, on the other hand, to indigestion, a capricious (sometimes ravenous) appetite, and anaemia. Occasionally convulsions or a complete blockage of the intestine (when an unusually large number are present) may occur.

The life-cycle of tapeworms requires two different hosts, sometimes three. (The broad tapeworm *Diphyllobothrium* is an example of one with three hosts. It may attain a length of 60 feet in man – less in the dog – and

TABLE OF PARASITIC ROUNDWORMS AND THEIR CHARACTERISTICS

ORGAN(S) AFFECTED	NAME OF WORM	WHERE FOUND	MAIN SYMPTOM(S)	INTERMEDIATE HOST(S)
Oesophagus/ stomach/ arteries	*Spirocerca*	S. Europe/ tropics	vomiting haemorrhage	cockroaches/ various beetles
Trachea	*Oslerus*	U.K. and world-wide	coughing/ retching	
Heart/ arteries	*Dirofilaria Angiostrongylus*	tropics Europe	panting anaemia/ stiffness/ swellings	mosquito slugs/ snails
Kidney	*Eustrongylus*	Europe/ America/ Asia		fish
Bladder	*Capillaria*	Europe/ world-wide	those of cystitis	
Skin	*Dracunculus* (Guinea worm)	Africa	skin/ paw damage	crustacean
	Uncinaria Ancylostoma (hookworms)	Europe/ U.S.A./ tropics	ditto	
Muscles	*Trichinella*	U.K./ Europe world-wide	cysts in muscles seldom diagnosed	pigs, rats are main hosts
Small intestine	*Toxocara*	world-wide	see page 68	
	Toxascaris	world-wide	diarrhoea	
Large intestine	*Trichuris*	world-wide	diarrhoea	

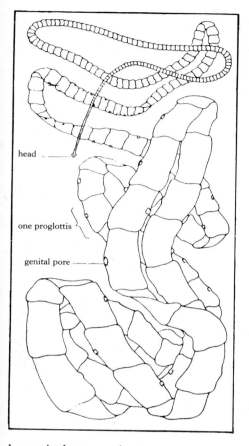

A typical tapeworm.
Each segment is called
a proglottis

head

one proglottis

genital pore

has as its hosts a minute crustacean and a fish. Species of this tapeworm are distributed through most parts of the world but are rare in the U.K. Infestation occurs through eating raw fish.)

The tapeworm *Echinococcus granulosus*, of which the dog and fox are the usual hosts, is the cause of human hydatid disease (see chapter 25). Eggs passed in faeces are later swallowed by grazing cattle, sheep, and horses, and these animals may also become infested through drinking water contaminated by wind-blown eggs. The eggs hatch in the intestine, and larvae are carried to the liver. Some remain there, developing into hydatid cysts; others may form cysts in the lungs, or occasionally elsewhere, such as the spleen, kidney, marrow cavity of a bone, or even the brain. Inside the cysts brood capsules, containing the infective heads of the tapeworm, develop, and after five or six months can infest any dog eating meat from the infected grazing animal's carcase.

On a farm, dead sheep have to be found before they can be buried or otherwise disposed of, and hungry sheepdogs often have to rely for some of their food upon scavenging. Hounds may become infested through being fed the carcases of animals found dead.

Several other dog tapeworms have their cystic, 'bladder-worm' stage in farm animals, and dogs become infested in a similar way.

Rabbits, hares, rats and mice are the intermediate hosts to other dog tapeworms; dog fleas and lice carry the cystic stage of a dog tapeworm called *Dipylidium*. This is one which has several rows of hooks on its head, and tends to injure mucous membrane more than less well-armed tapeworms. The gravid segments escaping from the anus may cause irritation, and are capable of movement.

Segments of some tapeworms are easy to see, but this does not apply to every species. Fresh segments are whitish, flat, and almost rectangular; but they soon turn yellowish and shrink, assuming an appearance of rice grains.

Removal of tapeworms requires anthelmintics formulated for that purpose.

FLUKES

These are flattish, unsegmented worms, of which the common liver-fluke of sheep and cattle is the most familiar U.K. example. This leaf-shaped parasite, *Fasciola hepatica*, may also infest dogs. Other flukes are also found in the liver of dogs in Europe and North America, while in America and Asia, *Paragonimus* flukes are found in canine lungs. Outside the tropics, fluke disease in the dog is not generally considered important, since – with one exception – severe symptoms such as anaemia, jaundice, wasting and oedema, so often seen in sheep and cattle, are rarely observed in the dog. The exception is a fluke called *Troglotrema* which, on the Pacific coast of the U.S.A. is a well-recognised cause of so-called 'salmon poisoning' in dogs which eat raw fish (especially salmon and trout). Such flukes often carry a rickettsial infection and it is this, rather than the fluke itself, which gives rise to the often fatal illness characterised by vomiting and diarrhoea.

See the chapter 'In the Tropics' and the Table for information on other worms.

REFERENCE
1 Turner, T. *Vet. Record* 100 (1977), 284
See also papers on hyatid disease by T. M. H. Walters and M. J. Clarkson given at the 1977 B.V.A. Congress

7 Common Illnesses

This chapter deals mainly with canine distemper, canine viral hepatitis, and leptospirosis – all potential killers. Vaccines are available for protection against them.

CANINE DISTEMPER

While mainly a disease of young dogs, distemper can occur at any age. A naturally occurring attack, or vaccination, will lead to a useful degree of immunity, but as this wanes the animal will again become susceptible. This explains how it is that a dog which has already had distemper can die from a second attack in later life, and why booster doses of vaccine are recommended to reinforce waning immunity and give continuing protection.

At the height of a local outbreak the virus (of which there are various strains) may have become very virulent and able to overcome the natural resistance of a dog which could have withstood a less virulent virus and not become ill.

Distemper: technicians preparing a culture of virus for vaccine production

Infection may lead – after an incubation period varying from 3 to 21 days – to the mildest of illnesses (so that the owner does not realise that it is distemper), to a moderately severe illness, or to a very severe one and death.

Symptoms of distemper vary greatly, depending on what organs of the body are involved, and what complications are caused by secondary bacterial invaders. As mentioned at the beginning of chapter 2, the distemper virus can suppress or impair the normal responses of the body's natural defence mechanisms, and this has a bearing on possible complications.

The dog may be unwell for a day or two, with a temperature of 103°F (39.5°C) or more, and then, in many instances, the temperature falls and may remain normal for a couple of days before it rises again. It may be as much as ten days or a fortnight before obvious and characteristic symptoms of distemper are shown.

Symptoms. In the classical type of distemper there is fever, and a discharge from eyes and nose. The eyelids become swollen and inflamed on their inner surface (conjunctivitis), and they may sometimes be almost glued together by the sticky discharge, which is yellowish or greenish. The dog may avoid bright light, as this can be hurtful.

As the illness progresses, either the digestive system or the respiratory system may become involved. In the latter case, there is likely to be laryngitis, and bronchitis. The nostrils may become caked with discharge and blocked, so that the dog has to breathe through the mouth. This breathing may become rapid and laboured. Broncho-pneumonia often follows the bronchitis.

Vomiting and diarrhoea are characteristic when the digestive system is affected, and there is usually a complete loss of appetite. In severe cases, blood may be passed.

A skin rash occurs in some cases, when red spots are seen on the hairless areas of the body, and soon resemble small human boils which discharge.

Occasionally, a fit is the first intimation of distemper (apart from the dog being noticeably unwell), but more often the nervous form of distemper is seen after the dog has been ill for a fortnight or so and appears to be on the road to recovery. Convulsions may occur with increasing frequency, and the outlook is then grave. Encephalitis may result in the dog becoming very restless, occasionally aggressive, and the animal may bump into furniture as though blind.

Spinal cord involvement may result in gradual loss of power in the hindquarters, a staggering gait, and paralysis of the hind legs.

Chorea may appear in a dog which had seemed well on the way to recovery from distemper, and often it is a sequel to an apparently mild attack. Chorea is usually a progressive condition which begins with muscular twitchings affecting a limb or the head. In the early stages, the dog appears to suffer no discomfort, but later the muscular contractions become more frequent and more violent, so that the dog is unable to rest, and becomes exhausted, with accompanying loss of condition and weakness. The skin is likely to become abraded owing to the constant friction between a jerking limb and the floor. Euthanasia is the only humane course where chorea is becoming progressively worse. In a few cases, however, the chorea never proceeds beyond a slight twitch, and the dog may have this for the remainder of his life without any serious consequences.

So-called '**hard-pad disease**' is one form of distemper, and takes its name from the fact that the pads of the feet become hardened and horny, and make a tapping sound as the dog walks across a floor. With this type of distemper the discharge from eyes and nose is not seen as a rule; but diarrhoea is a common symptom, and there may be pneumonia.

This brief outline of canine distemper shows how very variable the disease can be, how numerous the complications, and sometimes how disappointing the outcome can be when recovery had seemed assured. On the other hand, some cases are mild, and a brownish discolouration of the teeth may be the only (unfortunately permanent) evidence that the dog's illness was, in fact, distemper.

One cannot emphasise too strongly the need for a long period of convalescence after apparent recovery, with the dog given the very minimum of exercise and protected from chilling or any form of stress.

If you suspect that your dog has distemper, it is wise to request a visit by your veterinary surgeon in the early stages. It is then that appropriate antibiotics, for example, can be given to control secondary bacterial invaders, such as *Bordetella bronchiseptica* – a frequent cause of bronchitis. If antiserum is to be used in treatment, it too must be given early.

Home nursing is all-important, and can make a most valuable contribution to recovery.

Immunisation against Distemper. A transient natural immunity against distemper is commonly acquired by the newborn puppy through antibodies present in the dam's colostrum (first milk). While these antibodies will protect a puppy against distemper for a limited period, they will also interfere with the normal response to vaccine, so rendering vaccination ineffective *if carried out at too early an age*.

With several vaccines, the ideal age for their administration is 12 weeks. However, if local circumstances render it likely that a puppy will be exposed to infection at an earlier age, then risk may be reduced by inoculating the puppy when 8 weeks old, with a second injection at 12 weeks, by which time the effect of any maternal antibodies will have disappeared.

A measles vaccine is available to protect puppies of three weeks old and upwards against distemper, and so tide the animal over a possible danger period; immunity normally being established in 72 hours and lasting perhaps five months. There is, however, a limitation on the use of measles vaccine, in that puppies born to a dam herself inoculated with measles vaccine will pass on to her puppies antibodies against it, so rendering measles vaccine ineffective in her puppies.

It is best to consult your veterinary surgeon as to the age at which he prefers to vaccinate against distemper.

A puppy should be isolated for a fortnight before inoculation. In practice this means confining the animal to the house and garden, avoiding contact with other dogs or places where they have been. Vaccination should not be carried out if the animal is not well.

If buying a puppy said to have been vaccinated against distemper, ask for the certificate of vaccination. As already explained, if the inoculation was carried out at 8 weeks, a second inoculation will be needed at 11 or 12 weeks; remember to have this done.

Multiple vaccines are available to protect not only against distemper, but also against canine viral hepatitis and leptospirosis simultaneously. Such protection is well worthwhile.

Other noteworthy points concerning distemper. (1) the disease is transmissible to and from ferrets, foxes, otters and badgers; (2) after an outbreak in kennels, or following death of a dog from distemper at home, an interval of about a month should be allowed before other dogs are introduced into the premises. Disinfection of kennels should be carried out, and any blankets, towels, collars etc., used by distemper patients should be burned.

KLEBSIELLA

Infection with the bacterium *Klebsiella pneumoniae* may cause illness clinically indistinguishable from distemper in the dog, and may therefore account for some of the suspected 'breakdowns' following the use of distemper vaccines.

TOXOPLASMOSIS

This is a common *infection* rather than a common *illness*, for many dogs become infected, show no symptoms at all or only mild ones, and develop a subsequent immunity. The reason for mentioning toxoplasmosis in this chapter is that it often coincides with distemper; in fact, the ability of the distemper virus to depress or impair the body's defence mechanisms may result in a latent infection with toxoplasmosis becoming an active one.

Caused by a coccidian parasite (i.e. one classified in the order Coccidia), *Toxoplasma gondii*, of which cats are the principal hosts, toxoplasmosis can very seldom be diagnosed except by laboratory methods. When the parasite does cause illness in the dog, a variety of organs may be affected. The central nervous system (brain and spinal cord) may be attacked, when nervous symptoms already described above under distemper will be seen. The liver may be involved, giving rise to jaundice. Pneumonia may occur, or the heart be affected. A pregnant bitch may abort, or her puppies may be stillborn.

In the early stages, and when diagnosis is possible, toxoplasmosis can be successfully treated with sulphonamides and pyrimethamine.

CANINE VIRAL HEPATITIS

This illness, also known as infectious canine hepatitis or Rubarth's disease, can affect dogs of any age, even puppies a few days old, but it is perhaps most common in young dogs of three to nine months.

C.V.H., to use a convenient abbreviation, is one cause of so-called 'fading' in newborn puppies, and may result in the loss of an entire litter.

In the very acute form of the disease, an adult dog, apparently well the night before, may be found dead in the morning. Usually, however, preliminary symptoms are noticed by the owner. Fever (a temperature rise of about 4°F (2°C) above normal is common) cause the animal to appear dull and listless, and probably thirsty. The abdomen is usually tender owing to inflammation of the liver (hepatitis), and there may be jaundice. Vomiting and diarrhoea soon show that the dog is indeed ill. An alarming symptom in severe cases of C.V.H. is the presence of blood in the vomit or in the faeces, as internal haemorrhages are a feature of the disease and contribute to a fatal outcome. Restlessness, convulsions and coma may precede death. Dogs which survive for five days or so usually recover.

Often the C.V.H. virus causes little more than malaise, so far as the owner can tell; the dog is dull and off his food for a few days. It is often this mild form which is followed by keratitis (inflammation of the cornea), or what is popularly known as 'blue eye'. This condition has also been known to follow vaccination against C.V.H.

Dogs which have recovered from C.V.H. may remain 'carriers' of the virus; ceasing to show symptoms, but excreting the virus in their urine and so infecting other dogs.

Antiserum can be used in treatment, and good home nursing helps.

C.V.H. is identical with fox encephalitis, and cross-infections between dogs and foxes probably occur.

Finally, remember that C.V.H. is preventable, and worth vaccinating against.

LEPTOSPIROSIS

A leptospira is a bacterium shaped rather like a corkscrew and able to penetrate intact mucous membrane, and also the skin if broken in any way, such as by cuts, abrasions, insect bites. Leptospirosis is the name give to illnesses caused by leptospirae. There are many different serotypes of these, but two are of most importance in the dog. First is *Leptospira*

Leptospirae as seen under the microscope (× 1,000 approx.)

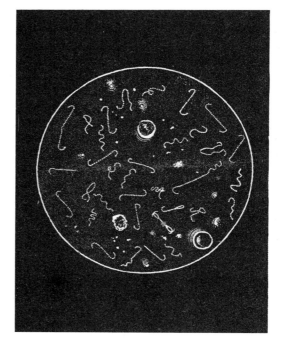

icterohaemorrhagiae which causes Weil's disease in man and jaundice in the dog. (The symptoms of Weil's disease are sudden high fever, shivering, vomiting, muscle cramps and jaundice, with the possibility of liver and kidney, and occasionally, brain damage. It is an occupational hazard of sewer-men as well as of people working on refuse dumps.) Secondly, *L. canicola*, which causes canicola fever in man and is a major cause of nephritis and kidney failure in the dog.

L. canicola infection. As this is the more common, let us consider it first. Although *L. canicola* can be transmitted via the urine of farm animals, it is mainly a 'tree or lamp-post infection' so far as dogs are concerned, one male passing it to another through his urine.

This type of leptospirosis is extremely common, accounting for much nephritis in younger and middle-aged dogs; repeated attacks can lead in the elderly dog to kidney failure and uraemia, as described in the chapter 'Urinary System Disorders'.

In the acute case of *L. canicola* infection, there is thirst, vomiting, and dejection. These symptoms may subside after a couple of days or so, when the owner may assume that the illness was a 'chill'. A loss of weight occurs if the illness continues, when there may be a foul odour from the breath, sometimes ulcers on the tongue; *occasionally* jaundice and diarrhoea. Kidney pain may cause the dog to assume an unnatural posture.

First-aid measures include keeping the animal warm, allowing only the very minimum of exercise, and offering barley-water if ordinary water is vomited almost as soon as drunk. Professional treatment is advisable when this is occurring. Treatment includes the use of penicillin, to which *L. canicola* is susceptible, and, equally important, any tendency to dehydration must be overcome.

Leptospirosis of the Weil's disease type. This, due to *L. icterohaemorrhagiae*, has jaundice as its main symptom. Appetite is lost and the dog becomes dull and dejected, and may vomit. A yellowish tinge appears discolouring the white of the eye and the mucous membrane lining the eyelids and mouth. Within two or three days the discolouration becomes more pronounced and may be of a canary yellow. The dog rapidly loses condition, and the abdomen becomes tucked up and tender. Food is refused and even water may be vomited. At first there is constipation; later, diarrhoea is not uncommon.

While fever is present at first, the temperature may drop below normal later. In severe cases there may be rapid collapse, the dog dying after convulsions. This is a very serious illness, in fact, and professional help should be sought at the outset. Antibiotics can help to overcome the infection, and antiserum or gamma-globulin may be used as well.

In the days before the advent of penicillin, I found that large daily doses of glucose-saline kept the animal alive, despite its eating nothing, and enabled recovery – aided by good home nursing – to take place in a matter of two or three weeks.

As regards prevention, vaccination has already been referred to, and can obviate losses in those localities where enzootic (i.e. regional or seasonal) jaundice, as it is sometimes called, is present. Kennel-owners should make every effort to keep their premises free from rats, since they are the main source of infection, and their urine may contaminate dog food.

Finally, a note of caution. Since both forms of leptospirosis are communicable to people, it is essential to wash one's hands thoroughly after attending to the dog or handling soiled bedding, etc.; and with this form of leptospirosis, too, a dog which has recovered may excrete the organism in his urine for months or even a year; so that this can be a dog-to-dog infection as well as a rat-to-dog infection. (Contaminated water and the urine of farm animals are less common sources.)

NOTES ON TERMS USED

An *anti-serum* may be used to treat an already-infected animal, or to give temporary protection, lasting 10 to a maximum of 21 days, against a specific infection, e.g., leptospirosis, or against a snake venom. An antiserum is produced by inoculating a susceptible animal with a sub-lethal dose of the infecting organism (or venom) and gradually increasing the dose until large amounts can safely be administered. The inoculated animal develops in its blood serum an antibody to the antigen which has been injected, and some of this protective serum is withdrawn from the donor animal for use in other animals.

Gamma-globulin is a protein fraction of blood serum containing antibodies (e.g. against specified bacteria or viruses). More concentrated, it is used like an anti-serum.

An *anti-toxin* is prepared in the same way as an anti-serum against a bacterial toxin, such as tetanus toxin.

A *vaccine* may consist of live, dead, inactivated, attenuated or modified viruses or bacteria, or parts of them. Some vaccines also contain toxoids (toxins which have been rendered non-poisonous by physical or chemical means). There are instances in which vaccines are used in treatment, but nearly always they are used as preventatives. In immunisation against some diseases, a second dose of vaccine will be necessary, and the interval between them must be the correct one, or protection may not be afforded.

CANINE PARVOVIRUS (CPV)

This infection appeared as a new disease in Europe, America, and Australia in 1978–79. Not having encountered this virus previously, dogs proved highly susceptible to it, and serious outbreaks occurred with a high mortality. However, by 1981 many dogs had acquired a useful degree of immunity against the virus following either recovery from a naturally occurring attack or vaccination. The virus is thought to be a mutation of the feline enteritis virus or the mink enteritis virus.

Symptoms. The illness takes the form of a severe gastro-enteritis, and diarrhoea is the main symptom; but puppies may die suddenly, within minutes of eating or playing, as a result of the virus having infected the heart muscle and caused myocarditis.

Treatment must include measures to overcome the severe dehydration which results from the diarrhoea. As implied above, a puppy may die before the owner is aware of the existence of any illness.

Prevention is therefore all the more important, and vaccines are available. A first vaccination may be carried out when a puppy is eight weeks old, but a second dose will be required a few weeks later. This is something which you should discuss with your own veterinary surgeon.

Thirty out of forty cases of canine parvovirus infection were found by Dr Simon Gretillat to be complicated by the presence of a blood parasite, *Haemobartonella canis*. This is transmitted by the brown dog tick, and usually causes little harm by itself; but in conjunction with the virus it can cause severe anaemia, laboured breathing, fever, and sometimes pain in the joints. The extent to which the blood parasite is present in Britain is not yet known.[1]

REFERENCE
1 Gretillat, S. *J. Small Animal Practice* **22** (1981) 647.

8 Nursing an Ill Dog at Home

The nursing of a sick dog at home is a task which can be prolonged, messy, time-consuming, sometimes disheartening; but it can influence recovery and prove rewarding. If your dog has an infectious disease such as distemper, nursing will have to be undertaken at home, since veterinary hospitals cannot admit cases owing to the risk to other dogs.

In nursing a dog, one has to bear in mind two things: the natural recuperative powers of the body, and the 'will to live'. The latter is important, and the dog is less likely to lose it if he is at home rather than in strange surroundings among strange people; to put it another way, the stress of being sent away could tip the balance and is best avoided. (I am thinking here of illnesses, as opposed to recovery from surgical operations.)

An animal which is ill seeks solitude and requires peace. Continual fussing and interference, however well meant, are to be avoided. Good nursing implies the minimum of interference, and handling – as opposed to being with – at fairly long intervals. (This is something which has to be impressed upon children. Young children should be kept away.) Fresh air, dryness, warmth, and an absence of bright lights and noise – these are points to consider when choosing a place to put the dog. (A patient with eye inflammation, or tetanus or other illness in which nervous symptoms occur, needs protection from strong light.)

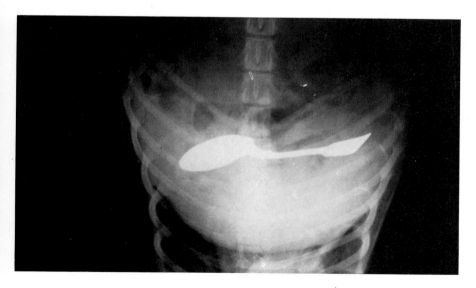

When dosing a dog, don't let him swallow the spoon! This happened when an owner was giving her dog cod-liver oil. The spoon, lodged in the stomach, shows up clearly on this radiograph

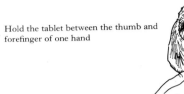

Hold the tablet between the thumb and forefinger of one hand

Open the animal's mouth, using the free hand and the middle finger of the hand holding the tablet. Pressure from the thumb of the free hand on the dog's palate will prevent the animal closing its mouth

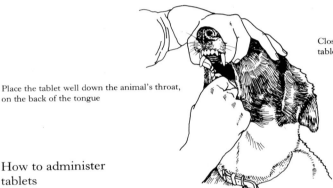

Place the tablet well down the animal's throat, on the back of the tongue

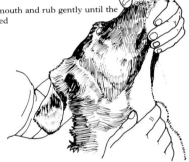

Close the dog's mouth and rub gently until the tablet is swallowed

How to administer tablets

It is helpful to put down sheets of newspaper, which can be burnt after use; if the weather is too cold or wet, or the dog cannot go outside for any other reason, a box of earth or ashes, or the material sold for cat litter, may be useful too.

Drink. Provide fresh drinking water; nevertheless, if vomiting is a problem, barley-water (which will be refused at first) may be preferable. A dog which is losing large quantities of water and salts as a result of persistent diarrhoea urgently needs this loss making good. An injection of glucose saline, which a veterinary surgeon will give, is the best way of achieving this; in countries where there are difficulties in obtaining veterinary help, a glucose saline preparation can be given the dog to drink (see the chapter 'In the Tropics'). If it is refused, dosing with it may be attempted, provided that this does not cause the dog to resist or choke. An ice cube out of a refrigerator can be given the dog to lick if there is haemorrhage from the digestive system or if it is the only successful method of getting some water into a dehydrated dog.

Forcible feeding exhausts and nauseates a dog. Offer food in very small

Hold the dog in a comfortable position (on a non-slippery table if possible), with one hand round the chest and the other holding the muzzle closed

Hold out the pouch of the animal's cheeck and pour in the medicine. (It is a help to have an assistant)

Keeping the dog's mouth closed and the head slightly raised, gently massage its throat until the medicine is swallowed

How to administer liquid medicine

quantities, and if it is refused, take it away. Human invalid foods can be tried; or small pieces of rabbit or chicken, a little meat jelly, or glucose in milk.

Constipation may be a problem. A little 'sardine oil' may be taken voluntarily. Liquid paraffin may have to be forced upon the dog and, if so, is best avoided.

Temperature-taking often forms a necessary part of animal nursing. Buy a clinical thermometer with a specially stout end. (The human type with a long mercury reservoir is not suitable for inserting into the rectum of a dog, being too easily broken.) Before use, lubricate the end of the thermometer well with Vaseline or liquid paraffin. The normal temperature of a dog varies from 100.9 to about 101.7°F (38.3 to 38.7°C). A subnormal temperature is a danger sign.

Bedding. A dog which is obliged to be prostrate for long periods needs fairly soft bedding – and periodic turning over on to his other side. By these means bed-sores may be avoided. A further safeguard is occasionally to swab danger spots with surgical spirit.

A jacket of some sort, with holes for the front legs, is useful in cases of bronchitis and pneumonia.

If the nostrils become caked with discharge, most of this can be wiped away with pieces of cotton-wool soaked in saline (a teaspoonful of common salt in a pint of water). A little olive oil may be used on an excessively dry nose.

Bathing discharge from the eyelids is also a worthwhile procedure, but do *not* use any antiseptic solution on the cotton wool or it will make the eyes smart – saline is best. Boracic acid is not to be recommended.

Saline is useful too as a mouth-wash and may bring a welcome freshness when gums and teeth are coated as the result of the dog's illness.

It is difficult to keep an ill animal clean. It is essential to cut away any hair which becomes soiled, and to wash with an antiseptic solution (TCP, Milton, or Cetrimide).

The dog's pulse can be conveniently felt on the inside of the thigh, where the femoral artery runs.

Convalescence is a matter of common sense; of not expecting a dog to go out for walks again before he can barely stand; of keeping him on nourishing food given in small meals.

Further reference to nursing is made in the chapter headed 'The Paralysed Dog'.

This is a convenient place to pay tribute to those animal nurses who assist many veterinary surgeons, and who have passed – or are studying for – the necessary examinations to qualify as R.A.N.A. These letters stand for Registered Animal Nursing Auxiliary, and the names of holders of this qualification are entered in a register maintained by the Royal College of Veterinary Surgeons. Duties include nursing of animals, the care of instruments, and help with the administration of anaesthetics, radiography, and the carrying out of certain laboratory tests. In 1984 RANA became Animal Nurse.

9 Accidents and Other Emergencies

A dog which has been hurt in an accident must always be approached with caution, and examined with the utmost gentleness, for pain may cause him to bite the very person most anxious to help, his owner. For this reason, it is advisable to apply a bandage muzzle, or improvise with his lead.

Pain (and shock) can be increased by well-intentioned but impetuous handling. It is best to stand back for a moment and look carefully at the dog, in an attempt to discover any unnatural shape or position of a limb (e.g. a bend where no bend should be, suggesting a fracture).

An improvised muzzle. Although not visible in the right-hand picture because of the dog's long hair, the lead ends pass down the side of each jaw, cross under and knot behind the neck

Fractures

If there is fracture of a limb, the dog must be handled in such a way that the ends of the broken bones do not grate against each other or cause further damage to surrounding tissues. In practice, this means keeping the limb as still and straight as possible. (Dog-owners who are doctors, nurses, or experienced in first-aid will, I hope, forgive what is elementary in this section.)

In theory, it may be possible to immobilise a fracture, but in practice, if one is out for a walk, materials such as a flat strip of wood or fibreboard, and cotton-wool and bandage will obviously not be to hand; moreover an owner inexperienced in first-aid might distress both dog and self more by attempts at splinting than by leaving the limb unsplinted. It is accordingly

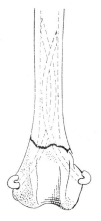

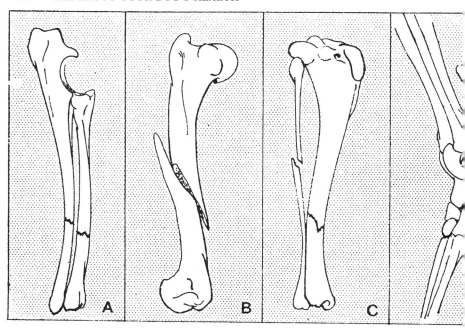

Right: Types of fractures. (A) Transverse fracture, which will be stable after reduction (reduction is the term applied to the restoring of a displaced part to its proper position). (B) Oblique fracture: little stability after reduction. (C) Irregular fracture line gives usable stability after reduction. (D) A 'distracted' fracture (one in which the parts are drawn apart). Pins may be used to assist stability, as in the diagram above

suggested that the best policy is to put down a coat or, if one has a car at the scene of the accident, a rug, and gently draw the dog on to this. The coat or rug, with dog on top, can then be lifted and put on the back seat of a car for transport to a veterinary surgery.

As in children, so in puppies a greenstick fracture may occur. The bone,

With a suspected fracture, draw the dog gently onto a rug or coat for lifting into a car

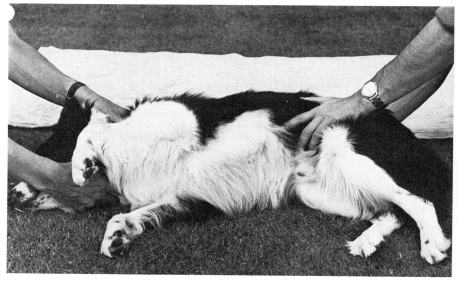

not yet being fully calcified, still has some pliability, and bends rather like a slender shoot of a growing tree. The fracture is incomplete.

Another type of injury may occur when the main shaft of a long bone is not damaged, but instead the 'growth plate' of cartilage (from which the shaft grows in length and which later in life becomes calcified and fused with the shaft).

Case history. A 3-month-old puppy was kicked by a horse. The end of the radius, the carpus (corresponding to our wrist) and the foot were all bent sideways after a week, during which there had been tenderness of the part, though the puppy was able to use the limb. Bone-stapling overcame the deformity, and three months later both fore-limbs were of equal length and there was no bend in the injured limb.[1]

Dogs Struck by Cars, etc.

A dog struck by a car may be very frightened and run away, if there is no leg injury to prevent him doing so. In other instances, there may be concussion, the animal regaining consciousness perhaps after several minutes, perhaps after many hours.

Sometimes the spine and not the head is struck, and the animal loses the use of his hind legs. Such paralysis may be temporary or permanent (see chapter 18). The animal should not be lifted, but drawn on to a rug or coat as described above. Fracture of the jaw is another accident which can occur after being hit by a car (or a fall); and so is rupture of the diaphragm, which gives rise to symptoms of laboured breathing and a tendency to assume an upright position. Haemorrhage and shock may be present to a variable degree, the gums being pale.

A dog struck a glancing blow may yelp and run away though there may be extensive bruising of both skin and underlying muscle, which shows itself only after a few hours. A graze can be extensive, and loss of skin made worse by penetration of road grit. The part should be washed clean with a warm antiseptic solution or saline. A dry dressing of a powder containing sulphanilamide may be used, or Acriflex ointment. Grazes should never be dismissed as trivial: they may be infected, or give rise to an ulcer.

Bleeding from the mouth may indicate that the dog bit his tongue at the moment of impact. Tongues heal readily as a rule, but the bleeding may seem alarming. Sutures (stitches) are needed occasionally, especially if the bleeding does not stop. Bleeding from the mouth may also indicate injuries to the jaw or teeth.

Internal haemorrhage may follow damage to the liver or spleen, for example, or to a major blood vessel, and gives rise to shock. This is characterised by an abrupt fall in blood pressure; breathing becomes shallow and the pulse weak. On examining the gums, they will be found very pale – almost white in some instances. While awaiting veterinary aid, keep the dog warm, and do not attempt to dose with brandy or whisky – alcohol may increase the bleeding. Professional treatment will involve use of a heart stimulant such as coramine or adrenalin, and perhaps a blood transfusion.

All this talk of fractures and haemorrhage may alarm or depress the reader, so let me at this point introduce a cheerful note. Consider, for example, the case of Hare Spy, a racing Greyhound which had the scaphoid (a bone in the hock) shattered in an accident. This small bone was replaced by a plastic replica, and Hare Spy not only raced again but won! Then again, dogs with one leg almost or completely severed by farm machinery have recovered, learned to adapt themselves to their infirmity, and herded cattle or sheep again with skill and obvious enjoyment. And even a pregnant bitch, struck by a car causing a tear in her uterus, has given birth to pups and had a subsequent litter, as related in chapter 22.

Bleeding

When the tiniest blood vessels are cut, bleeding soon stops owing to the clot formation – Nature's own way of arresting haemorrhage. When a vein is cut, crimson blood will *flow*. From a cut artery, scarlet blood will *spurt*, or issue in jets corresponding with the heart beats. In either of these circumstances (unless the artery is a very small one), normal clotting will not save the situation and the first-aider must take prompt action; otherwise the injured dog could suffer severe shock and even die as a result of loss of blood.

Again, apply a tape-muzzle if the dog shows signs of biting when approached at close quarters. Try to stop the bleeding by applying a pressure pad – a folded clean handkerchief will do – to the wound, and hold the pad there, pressing gently. A first attempt may be unsuccessful and a larger pad be required.

When a large vessel is cut, serious bleeding may persist; pressure should be applied above the wound if the bleeding is arterial, below it if blood is coming from a vein. In practice, this means pressing with the finger-tips, and maintaining the pressure.

If the wound involves a limb, and a major vessel is cut, serious bleeding may persist unless a tourniquet is applied. A double loop of bandage, or a handkerchief, should be placed above the wound (assuming the bleeding is arterial) and can be tightened with a pencil until the bleeding is seen to stop. Release it very gingerly after five to ten minutes, by which time sufficient clotting may have taken place. If not, re-tighten the tourniquet, *which must not be left on for a total of more than 20 minutes* otherwise permanent damage to the limb is likely to occur. Obtain veterinary help with the minimum of delay.

Case history. A night telephone call requested a visit to see a dog which had lost a lot of blood. On arrival, this new patient was found lying on his side on a cold stone floor of the scullery. Some brandy had been poured into the dog's mouth, and the owners wanted to administer more. The scullery floor was covered in blood, and there was more in the yard outside where the dog – a large crossbred – had put his foot through a rusty enamelled washing-up bowl. When a none-too-clean piece of towel had been removed from the injured hind leg, a small artery was still sending out a fine spray of blood.

The artery and wound were attended to, and measures taken to combat shock and loss of blood. 'Will he die?' the white-faced husband asked. 'He will have a swollen leg tomorrow, and he'll need a lot of care, but he is not likely to die,' he was told. The dog did indeed have a swollen leg, but made an uneventful recovery. This case is mentioned to show where the owners went wrong: giving alcohol, leaving the animal on a cold floor, and draping rather than bandaging the wound.

Before leaving the subject of bleeding, it should be mentioned that clotting of the blood is inhibited by anticoagulants such as warfarin, the rat poison; and also by rare congenital diseases of the blood, e.g. haemophilia and thrombasthenia. Even small knocks and minor injuries can then lead to subcutaneous haemorrhages and anaemia.

Wounds

These vary from an abrasion such as a graze, to a deep gash extending down to the bone or its periosteum; from punctures made by sharp-pointed objects, to lacerated wounds such as may result from dog fights.

A gaping wound is going to need stitches. This means professional help, and the sooner the better, for after several hours it may be impossible to draw the lips of the wound together.

With the exception of a cut foot, which obviously needs protection (one cannot rely on a dog walking on three legs), most wounds in dogs are best left uncovered – unless the dog is continually licking them. In that event a covering may be essential, or else use of an 'Elizabethan collar' to prevent the dog turning its head to reach the wound. The padding and bandaging of a cut foot are referred to under 'Injuries to the Pads' in chapter 3.

As regards first-aid for wounds, when the dog is home, first wash the hands; then with blunt-pointed scissors cut the hair away for half an inch around the margins of the wound. The cut hair must not be allowed to fall into the wound, and to prevent this, a piece of cotton wool wrung out of warm water may be used as a temporary plug or cover for the wound. When it is removed, any cut hair will come away with it.

Examine a wound twice a day, but if it looks clean and *pink*, there will be no need to interfere with it the second time, nor to repeat a wet dressing. On the other hand, if there is a greenish discharge at the lips or margins of the wound, it must be gently bathed away.

Any yellowish-green scab must always be removed and not mistaken for a healed surface. The wound must heal from below upwards, and not be covered over by a scab. This will merely delay healing, since pus may form below the scab.

In treating wounds, avoid tincture of iodine, lysol, or carbolic acid.

How Wounds Heal

First the blood clots. The clot consists of minute threads of the protein fibrin, in which are enmeshed red blood corpuscles and white blood cells. The threads of fibrin bridge the gap between the cut surfaces at the base of the wound, forming a scaffolding under which tissue repair takes place. From neighbouring capillaries come neutrophils (a type of white cell) which engulf dirt, bacteria, and dead tissue cells. Other white cells, monocytes, arrive later, especially if the wound has become infected, and engulf any dead or disintegrated neutrophils as well as bacteria. Multiplication of surrounding tissue cells, e.g. of the corium and epidermis, gradually restores the skin surface.

'Proud flesh' is the popular name for excessive granulation tissue which sometimes arises around an ulcer or badly infected wound. The granulations consist of masses of 'construction' cells with newly formed loops of capillaries. Treatment may be required if the 'proud flesh' persists.

Ulcer

This may follow a graze or abscess and, as the result of tissue destruction, has its surface below that of the surrounding healthy skin. Normal wound first-aid treatment applies, but should the ulcer be seen to be spreading, obtain professional aid.

Puncture Wounds

Deep puncture-type wounds are always serious, because bacteria are likely to be carried down on the point of whatever has caused the wound; e.g. another animal's tooth, a nail. Moreover, the opening of such a wound will be too small to allow of the type of wound cleaning described above, and it favours the growth of *Clostridium tetani* – the cause of tetanus – should this organism have been introduced into the wound. Antiseptics cannot reach the base of many puncture-type wounds, and so reliance must be placed upon antibiotics given by injection, and perhaps an anti-tetanus injection.

Multiple Small Wounds

These can be more dangerous than one large, clean gash.

Case history. The question 'Will he die?' was not one which the owner of a Border Terrier asked when he brought the animal to the surgery. The immediate reason for the consultation was that the animal was not eating anything, rather than the mass of small bites about the body. After three nights in a cold kennel, the Terrier was now in a state of shock, gums pale, temperature subnormal. The shock was probably due to a toxaemia resulting from the infection of the multiple bites, inflicted by some unknown small wild animal which the Terrier had encountered. The client was warned: 'You may, I am afraid, be going to lose him.' He expressed astonishment. 'Why, I thought nothing of it,' he said. 'I've seen a dog with a gash to the bone running about next day. My Peter's not got a bad bite among 'em.'

It was the number of bites – the multiple injuries – which killed Peter, for whom treatment arrived too late.

STAKE WOUNDS

One of the most serious, but fortunately rare, accidents is penetration of the abdominal wall by the spike on top of a railing, or a pointed stake in a fence which a dog tries unsuccessfully to jump. Sometimes a fall from an upstairs window has the same effect. The intestines may be exposed and escape from the wound, and if they do they must be gently tucked in and protected from further contamination and damage. First-aid: Wring a clean piece of sheet out of warm saline and use this to cover the abdomen, supporting its contents. Fasten the ends of the sheet over the back with safety pins or by other means. Keep the animal warm, and obtain professional help without delay.

DOG FIGHTS

These can be the cause of severe, lacerated wounds as well as of puncture-type wounds.

Case history 1. A Bedlington was attacked in the dark by a strange dog which, before running off, tore one ear very badly. Following a telephone call, the dog was brought to the surgery, bleeding in the car having been well controlled by a pad of cotton wool out of the first-aid kit. It was explained that the cartilage as well as the skin was torn, and undoubtedly infected by the other dog's teeth, and consequently necrosis of the cartilage was likely and a troublesome wound which would be very slow to heal and need much attention. It was suggested that the damaged portion should be removed, leaving a curved healthy edge instead of the ragged one. The owner agreeing, the ear was trimmed under local anaesthesia, bandaged, and taken back home. When next seen, the wound had healed perfectly, and gave no further trouble.

During a fight a dog may be bitten in the throat region. Sometimes the rings of cartilage which form the trachea are damaged, and may become infected; another possible sequel is an obstruction to breathing.

Case history 2. Half an hour after being attacked by another, a dog was taken to a veterinary surgery in a very distressed condition, the breathing being both noisy and laboured. Some impressive surgery repaired a completely severed trachea. This dog made an excellent recovery.[2]

Scalds and Burns

In order to relieve the pain and to minimise shock, hold the affected part of the body under a slowly-running cold tap. The cold or cool water will quickly reduce the temperature of the overheated skin. If the scalded or burnt area is small, apply either a dry sulphanilamide dressing, or tannic acid jelly, or Acriflex ointment. Do *not* apply tannic acid jelly over a large area. Scalded or burnt animals will need veterinary treatment to counter both shock and subsequent infection (which very commonly follows). Pain-relievers or sedatives may also be needed.

With chemical burns, washing off the offensive material is a preliminary to applying the antidote; e.g. use bicarbonate of soda in a little water to any area burnt by car-battery acid.

Electric Shock

I am indebted to a former Bishop of St Helena, the Rt Rev Harold Beardmore O.B.E., for a less usual example of electric shock in the dog. His Bulldog, Bill, was ship's mascot of H.M.S. *Hood*, and on returning on board with his master after leave Bill found the ship undergoing a refit, with dock workmen everywhere and, on the quarter-deck, new dynamos humming. Bill investigated one of these and lifted his leg over it. There was an immediate yelp, as the Bulldog bounded into the air; having discovered, the painful way, that water is a good conductor of electricity.

A recent incident of the same sort involved a dog which lifted his leg over bare live wires in a street lamp-standard, of which vandals had removed the safety cover. In both these incidents, the dogs apparently escaped serious harm.

Probably the most usual case of electric shock in the dog is the chewing (by a puppy) of the flex of some electric appliance in the home, such as a vacuum-cleaner, lamp, or electric fire. There may be burns in the mouth, loss of consciousness – and sometimes death.

If the dog has stopped breathing, lay the dog on its side and apply artificial respiration by placing one hand on the rib-cage and alternately pressing and releasing at intervals of two or three seconds. With a drowned dog, first hold the dog head-downwards and swing to and fro a few times.

Shooting Accidents

Sporting dogs may inadvertently be shot, and dogs chasing sheep may intentionally (and legally) be fired on. In either case, lead shot may cause multiple wounds in the skin and underlying muscle. Cases of eye damage from lead shot are described in chapter 5; and a 0.22 air rifle pellet has on one occasion obstructed the urethra at the *Os penis*, causing acute pain from distension of the bladder. In another dog, a radiograph revealed that a suspected foreign body in the frontal sinus was a bullet.

Bites

Snakes. In Britain dogs are bitten more often than some other animals, since they may disturb basking adders; cats may be more agile, and slower-moving cattle and horses cause enough vibration to warn the snake.

A snake bite may not be suspected by an owner who has not witnessed the occurrence. The dog may appear frightened or excited at first, but later becomes dull. A painful swelling is likely to appear, and if the hair be parted the skin can be seen to be reddened. Fang marks may be visible.

Nowadays, neither use of a tourniquet nor heroic measures such as incising the wound and inserting crystals of potassium permanganate is recommended. What the dog needs is a full dose of antivenin (an antiserum). This should be administered by a veterinary surgeon as soon as possible.

In the U.S.A., dogs are often bitten by the black widow spider. A very painful swelling results, breathing becomes laboured, and paralysis follows. Coma and death may occur within hours or days, unless the appropriate antivenin has been administered in time.

Other Emergencies

Heat exhaustion. This may occur in a dog left in a car not parked in the shade. A test[3] made on a day in May showed that, even with two windows left open to the extent of one inch, the temperature inside the car had risen after three hours to 92°F (as compared with a shade temperature outside the car of 65°F). At this or higher temperatures, a dog may be found in great distress or even unconscious, due to hyperthermia. For first-aid, see chapter 27.

Toad venom. The toad has no means of defence except its venom, which is secreted by glands in its skin and is called *bufotalin*. If a dog takes a toad into his mouth, he may soon come rushing indoors, salivating profusely. Vomiting may follow, rarely unconsciousness lasting an hour or two; the animal seldom if ever dies from toad venom in Britain.

Porcupines. In the U.S.A. and Canada, among other countries, dogs frequently need veterinary treatment after rash encounters with porcupines. The possibility of such encounters now exists in Britain, since there are free-living porcupines in both Devon and Staffordshire; these animals have escaped from human custody and bred in the wild.

Removal of porcupine quills must be a very painful process, for they are barbed. Dog-owners who live in porcupine country in North America often carry with them on walks a pair of pliers, for it is advisable to remove quills as soon as possible (dog permitting!); especially from tongue, chest and abdomen. If this is not done, deep penetration may follow, with possibly fatal injury to internal organs.

Quill removal should be completed under a general anaesthetic by a veterinary surgeon. If there is much delay, some of the quills may already have disappeared from view and, as they are not opaque to X-rays, he could not guarantee 100-per-cent removal.

Poisoning is dealt with in a separate chapter (pages 95–102); likewise fits and heart attacks, which can sometimes be mistaken for each other. *Tail fractures* may result from being caught in a door, and need veterinary help. *Dislocation of the eyeball* in breeds of dog with protruberant eyeballs is not uncommon – first-aid is described in chapter 5. *Inability to pass urine* should always be regarded as an emergency. Mishaps concerning the penis are referred to in chapter 22. Dogs rescued from *fires* may need both artificial respiration and the administration of oxygen. Rapid enlargement of the abdomen, as a result of an accumulation of gas in the stomach, is referred to in chapter 15. For a personal rabies emergency, see page 194.

REFERENCES
1 Duffel, S. J. *Vet. Record* 93 (1973), 655
2 Hill, F. W. G. *Vet. Record* 95 (1974), 265
3 Rohrbach, J. A. *Vet. Record* 102 (1978), 534

10 Accidental Poisoning

How it occurs

The purpose of this chapter is to point out circumstances in which accidental poisoning of dogs often occurs so that, forewarned, the owner may perhaps be able to avoid at least some of the hazards.

In suggesting simple first-aid measures, it must be emphasised that they necessarily differ from – and are likely to be less effective than – those measures the veterinary surgeon will take. So when it is known that a dog has taken a particular poison, the sooner professional aid is sought the better. If it is a chemical compound with either a proprietory name, or a long, barely pronounceable chemical name given on the label of a packet, can or bottle, take it or the label to your veterinarian; or jot down name and manufacturer of the product.

In most instances, however, there will be no can, no bottle; no certainty, even, that he has been poisoned – merely the fact that he is ill. Diagnosis is then all-important, especially since the symptoms of some illnesses are the same as those of some poisons; and *vice versa*. For example, not only vomiting and diarrhoea, but also cramp, fever, rapid breathing, convulsions, hysteria, jaundice, salivation, are common to both. One could add deafness and blindness.

In the Home

Medicines

It has to be said at the outset that sometimes people unintentionally poison their dogs through giving over-doses of medicines, or by dosing with unsuitable ones. In this connection, advice from neighbours, however well-meaning and reputedly 'good with animals' they are, should be treated with the utmost caution. For example, a neighbour recommended the use of that well-known tonic Easton's Syrup for some puppies which did not seem to be thriving. All of them died. Easton's Syrup contains strychnine, a poison to which the dog is highly susceptible; a safe human dose is potentially lethal especially when repeated.

Even aspirin must be used in moderation. While better tolerated by the dog than the cat, aspirin – and also sodium salicylate – can cause gastritis, nausea and vomiting in excessive doses, and is best reserved for acute muscular rheumatism or neuritis.

The inside of a veterinary surgery. Of course, medicines in the home are stored on rather a different scale, but the same principles of well-organised storage should apply. Be careful to keep human medicines well separated from ones intended for dogs. What is safe for one is not necessarily safe for the other

Not only may a dog be dosed with a medicine not intended for canine use, but puppies, especially, may poison themselves with capsules, pills or tablets left lying about. For example, a Terrier died within hours of eating a packet of 'pep' pills containing caffeine. Paracetamol is another bathroom cupboard medicine which has similarly caused poisoning in dogs; barbiturates, too.

Poisoning may occur not only from something swallowed but also from a chemical compound absorbed through the skin. Puppies may suffer in this way if too strong a concentration of a BHC shampoo is used. In days gone by, lysol, carbolic acid, and mercury dressings were often used as skin or wound dressings; they sometimes resulted in poisoning.

INHALATION

In the kitchen a puppy may find and eat non-safety matches, but in this room of the house poisoning is mainly through inhalation. Fat left to heat in a frying pan may be forgotten if the housewife is called to the telephone, with the result that the kitchen becomes filled with a harmful vapour. Professor E. G. C. Clarke, formerly head of the toxicology department at the Royal Veterinary College, London, gave an instance of this – a Poodle shut in a kitchen with a smoking chip pan for half an hour. When the owner returned, the dog was breathing with considerable distress, there was a bluish discoloration of the mouth, and death followed.[1]

Many an owner has come down in the morning to find the dog dead from asphyxia. This may occur where there is a solid-fuel stove if ventilation is inadequate, or with a gas stove.

Dr G. S. Venables, writing in *The Lancet* on the dangers of human poisoning by carbon monoxide, mentioned the content of this in various gases. In Britain, until the late 1960s, town gas contained 10 to 20 per cent carbon monoxide. Natural and oil-based gas contain less than 1 per cent. Natural gas (methane) normally burns leaving carbon dioxide and water, but with 'inadequate ventilation and poor escape for exhaust gases, incomplete combustion to carbon monoxide may occur.' This lethal gas accumulates rapidly and, in man, 'a 1-per-cent concentration in the atmosphere may result in 70 per cent saturation of haemoglobin, a level which may be fatal.'

LEAD

Beware of lead poisoning in your dog when a room is being re-decorated, for the animal may eat paint scrapings. A more common source of lead poisoning is old, flaking paintwork. For example, a litter of puppies and their dam were put in a pen improvised from old doors; the pups ate the paint flaking off these.

Other sources of lead are spilt paint; red lead left behind by a plumber; putty; linoleum; tarpaulins; golf balls; and lead shot.

Symptoms of lead poisoning include loss of appetite, vomiting, abdominal pain, and diarrhoea. Lead affects the central nervous system in many cases, giving rise to hysteria, convulsions, blindness, and occasionally partial paralysis. (A blue line may be seen along the gums in cases of *chronic* lead poisoning.)

As regards first-aid, Epsom salts may be given in sweetened milk if vomiting has not already started. Treatment of lead poisoning has in recent years been revolutionised by the antidote calcium disodium versenate, given by slow intravenous injection.

In the Garage

There have been cases of puppies gaining access to car battery **acid**; if this should happen it is necessary to counteract the corrosive effects of the acid by means of an alkali, e.g. sodium bicarbonate (baking powder) given in milk. This needs to be given immediately.

A far more common source of poisoning in the garage is **ethylene glycol** (anti-freeze), which has a sweetish taste which dogs evidently find palatable. Many dogs are killed by this every year. The symptoms of poisoning include depression, a staggering gait, convulsions, and coma. The only first-aid measure is to give an emetic, e.g. a crystal of washing soda in water, or salt in water. Professional treatment may require injections every six hours for up to three days, and is not always successful.

In the Garden

Dogs like the taste of anti-slug pellets containing **metaldehyde** or a related compound, methiocarb, and eat them readily. Since successful gardening and slugs are incompatible, and if no hedgehog is resident, the best course to adopt is to continue using these pellets, but to fix a piece of wire netting over the soil where they have been put, so that the dog cannot get at them.

Do not overlook the potting shed – often a poison store in all but name, with **nicotine** solution and many horticultural insecticides on the shelves. Packets of anti-slug pellets are easily overturned and their contents spilled.

Metaldehyde poisoning gives rise to convulsions, often preceded by muscular twitching, excitement, and vomiting. Partial paralysis and coma are later symptoms. The animal shows an exaggerated response (hyperaesthesia) to stimuli such as touch, noise, and bright light; it should therefore be kept quiet in semi-darkness until veterinary aid can be obtained. An anaesthetic may be given by intravenous injection as treatment. An unusual sequel to recovery from metaldehyde poisoning has been reported: blindness, which gradually disappeared after three weeks.

Some of the most attractive garden plants are poisonous, but dogs seldom eat the leaves or flowers, unless their scent is unusually attractive to an individual dog; poisonous berries are sometimes eaten.

Case history. One of the most unusual cases of plant poisoning ever recorded involved a 5-year-old Fox Terrier. He was taken for a walk and had a stick thrown for him to retrieve. Within an hour the dog was dead.

The Terrier had chewed the stick, as dogs will, and about a quarter of an hour later was seen to stagger, and soon afterwards was violently sick. The dog's owner sought immediate veterinary advice. At the surgery the Terrier had a mild fit, then wagged his tail, and did not appear to be seriously ill. Taken back home, however, he died twenty minutes later.[2]

Laboratory methods established the cause of death – **laburnum** poisoning. It was from a laburnum tree that the stick had been cut, three months earlier, and the alkaloid cytisine was isolated from both stick and stomach contents. Unusual features of this case were the comparative mildness of the symptoms yet the rapidity of death. Laburnum often causes vomiting before a fatal dose of the alkaloid has had time to be absorbed, but not in this instance. Twigs, seeds, and leaves of laburnum. are all poisonous.

Stored seeds of garden plants should be kept out of reach of puppies.

Treatment of the weedy areas in a lawn with the herbicide **paraquat** led to the death of a Terrier. The symptoms of poisoning by paraquat and diquat (a related compound) are vomiting and rapid breathing. This later becomes, to use a colloquial expression, 'fighting for breath'. There may be cyanosis, the blueness of the gums mentioned earlier. Paraquat causes oedema of the lungs, and the victim consequently 'drowns' in his own exudate. Unfortunately, there is no effective antidote.

Country Walks

Paraquat is sometimes applied by local authority workmen to roadside verges as an economical method of controlling rank growth. Within a week of such an application, a Scottish veterinary surgeon saw three poisoned dogs with these symptoms. At autopsy, lung changes were consistent with paraquat poisoning.

Paraquat is used on the widest scale, of course, by farmers as a herbicide, and dogs in several parts of Britain have been poisoned by this chemical near farmland. It is sometimes used in sheep carcases as a poison intended to kill foxes.

Another herbicide which has caused poisoning is **Trioxone 100**, applied to the cut stumps of coppices to prevent regrowth before replanting. A high concentration of this chemical was found in the stomach of a dog, regularly exercised in a wood, within four days of such an application. The dog began vomiting at 11 a.m. and was dead by the next morning.

On Farmland

Poison under snow is, to say the least, unexpected, but a Labrador playing in a snow-covered farm field collapsed within ten minutes, with symptoms of salivation, vomiting and diarrhoea. It later transpired that the field had been sown on the previous day with chemically dressed sugar-beet seed, and sprayed with a pre-emergence weedkiller. This dog's life was saved by veterinary treatment.[3]

Organochlorine compounds are widely used as farm insecticides and include DDT, BHC, aldrin, dieldrin, endrin, toxaphene, and many others. It is probably true to say that as many, or more, dogs are poisoned indirectly than directly by these compounds – through eating dead or moribund birds which have themselves been poisoned after feeding on farm crops. However, **dieldrin** was found in a batch of dog meal which poisoned several dogs in a breeding kennel. It was concluded that dressed seed corn had been used.

Symptoms of poisoning by this group of compounds vary somewhat but, generally speaking, they include excitement (which may amount to hysteria or aggressiveness), salivation, a staggering gait, aimless wandering, convulsions, and a raised body temperature. In other instances, dullness, loss of appetite and emaciation result.

First-aid consists of giving an emetic and a saline laxative such as Epsom salts, if this is practicable. Professional treatment involves the use of barbiturates or other drugs to control convulsions, etc.

Another large group of farm chemicals are the **organophosphorus compounds**. Dichlorvos, schradan, parathion, dimefox, and malathion are some of their names. Poisoning by them may give rise to loss of appetite, abdominal pain, salivation, vomiting and diarrhoea, rapid breathing, convulsions and paralysis; not all these symptoms necessarily being shown in any one case.

Poisoned Bait

Reference has already been made to the use of paraquat as a fox poison.

Strychnine is a poison commonly used against moles and, illicitly, sometimes against foxes. The laying of poison above ground for the destruction of rats and mice is illegal in Britain, but the law is frequently broken. In my own practice I treated a dog poisoned with strychnine within days of a rumour that pieces of poisoned sausage had been put down as bait by local council workmen. A dog may be poisoned not only by eating bait, but also through eating an animal which itself has taken poison bait.

Strychnine is a very violent poison. After perhaps some excitement and muscular twitching, convulsions occur, along with the hyperaesthesia seen in tetanus. Opisthotonus – the arching of the back like a bow – is another symptom common to both conditions. Vomiting is sometimes seen.

Veterinary advice was sought for one dog which the owner thought had suddenly gone blind; the characteristic symptoms of strychnine poisoning did not appear until the following day.

The animal should be kept as quiet and undisturbed as possible in semi-darkness until veterinary treatment can begin; this requires volatile anaesthetics, or barbiturates by injection.

Alphachloralose is a hypnotic or stupefying agent used against both wood-pigeons and mice. Against the former it is mixed with beans as bait. Dogs have been poisoned by eating eggs treated with alphachloralose as a bait for crows. Symptoms of poisoning include a staggering gait, and coma. First-aid: give an emetic, unless the dog is unconscious, and keep him warm, as hypothermia is one of the effects of the poison.

Warfarin is one of a group of compounds which are all anticoagulants, acting as a rodenticide by inhibiting normal clotting of the blood, and so producing internal haemorrhage. Dogs may eat warfarin bait – ready mixed to put around a piggery, for example, and left unguarded for a few minutes, or illegally laid above ground. They may also be poisoned by eating food contaminated by the urine of rats and mice containing warfarin. Some years ago the Animal Health Trust investigated an outbreak of warfarin poisoning in greyhound kennels, and traced the source to stored biscuit meal contaminated in this way.

Symptoms of warfarin poisoning include a suggestion of cramp, swellings due to subcutaneous haemorrhages, pale gums, and rapid breathing. The dog may collapse while being exercised. The antidote is vitamin K, which a veterinary surgeon can inject. Chances of recovery are good.

Thallium is a rodenticide sometimes used where local rats and mice have acquired resistance to warfarin. It is painful in its effects.

Case history. A farm dog became ill with frequent vomiting, fever, and diarrhoea. After an interval of two or three days, the vomiting began again, and the dog was obviously in pain – lying on his back and groaning. Semi-consciousness alternated with intermittent activity. A brick-red discoloration of the skin of the groin was noticed, and the paws were painful and swollen. Before death, the hair was beginning to fall out.[4]

Treatment is very rarely successful in cases of thallium poisoning. An emetic should be given if it is known that a dog has eaten a poison bait containing this substance.

Other Hazards

In Britain the use of certain poisons has been banned under the Animals (Cruel Poisons) Act, 1962, following representations by U.F.A.W. and other bodies. Nevertheless, not everyone obeys the law, and there may be overseas readers who encounter poisoning by the following:

Antu. This is an abbreviation for alphanaphylthiourea, sometimes referred to as thiourea, an effective rat-killer. Difficult breathing, vomiting and diarrhoea are produced, with death from oedema of the lungs.

Sodium monofluoroacetate (1080). A poisoned dog may yelp, vomit, and have convulsions. First-aid: give an emetic.

Red squill is prepared from the sea onion, and its unpleasant taste and smell – unless masked by an attractive bait – would probably tempt few dogs, but they might eat an animal already poisoned by it. Excitement, a staggering gait, sometimes vomiting, and convulsions are the symptoms.

Barium salts (usually barium chloride) cause the dog to salivate and have convulsions. Epsom salts are useful as a first-aid antidote.

Yellow **phosphorus**, in non-safety matches eaten by puppies, or in rat poisons, causes great thirst, severe abdominal pain, vomiting, diarrhoea, and great dejection. Vomited material may be greenish in colour and luminous in the dark.

Zinc phosphide poisoning is characterised by symptoms similar to those of phosphorus itself.

In Kennels (bedding)

Some thought needs to be given to choice of bedding material for dogs in kennels. Building regulations in Britain now require timber to be treated with a fungicide, e.g. **pentachlorphenol**. This is readily absorbed through the skin and has caused fatal poisoning in dogs bedded on sawdust originating from treated timber.

Dogs have died also after being bedded on shavings from the red African hardwood *Mansonia altissima*.

In Food

Of interest are three outbreaks of poisoning in kennels due to contamination of biscuit meal. Reference has been made above to warfarin-containing rats' urine.

A second outbreak of poisoning, characterised by gastro-enteritis with the passing of blood, was caused by dangerously high levels of **aflatoxin** in the meal. The toxin is produced by the fungus *Aspergillus fumigatus*, which contaminates some samples of groundnut meal, etc.

Case history 1. Several hounds of a kennel had died by the time a veterinary investigation was requested. Symptoms included loss of appetite, depression, thirst, the passing of more urine than normal, jaundice and, towards the end, haemorrhages. Autopsy findings: hepatitis plus gastro-enteritis.[5]

Case history 2. The third outbreak, in gundog breeding kennels, was found by the State Veterinary Service to be due to contamination by dieldrin, suggesting that dressed seed corn had been used as an ingredient of the dog meal. Nervous symptoms were shown, and two dogs had to be put down.[6]

REFERENCES
1 Clarke, E. G. C. B.S.A.V.A. Conference Proceedings
2 Clarke, Myra *et al. Vet. Record* 88 (1971), 199
3 Lloyd, J. R. *et al. Vet. Record* 96 (1975), 366
4 Withers, A. R. *Vet. Record* 90 (1972), 429
5 Greene, C. E. *et al. Cornell Veterinarian* 67 (1977), 29
6 Brown, M. E. *State Vet. J.* 32 (1977), 111

11 'Lumps' and Swellings

'He's got a lump on his back', a dog-owner will say on coming into the consulting room. Very often that word 'lump' is an apt description and could not be bettered. The nature of the 'lump' is something for the veterinarian to ascertain.

RETENTION CYST

Swellings beneath the skin can be of many and various kinds. For example, the duct leading from one of the sebaceous glands may have become blocked, leading to what is called a retention cyst; the normal secretion of the oily substance which gives the coat its natural gloss is unable to escape to the surface of the skin. This is not at all a serious condition, but as there is often slight discomfort or tenderness, due to the stretching of the skin and its nerves – and as it may be injured by a comb during grooming – the cyst usually needs opening and its contents evacuating.

ABSCESS

Whereas the retention cyst develops slowly and is not painful, an acute abscess quickly increases in size and is hot and painful. Formation of an abscess may follow a dog-bite, or an injury from barbed wire, or following penetration of a grass seed or thorn; bacteria such as staphylococci and streptococci enter through the breach in the skin.

These bacteria multiply, produce poisonous substances (toxins) which affect adjacent cells; white blood cells (leucocytes) migrate from the local tiny blood vessels and engulf the bacteria. The area becomes congested

A small abscess below the skin. (A) Centre of abscess, undergoing liquefaction. (B) The surrounding ring of white blood cells. (C) Subcutaneous tissue. (D) Skin. (E) Blood vessels in the vicinity of the abscess are enlarged

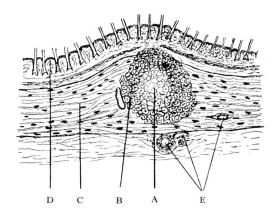

D   C   B   A   E

with dead or dying bacteria, dead or dying leucocytes, dead tissue cells which formerly occupied the site, and other debris. All this constitutes the pus. Pressure inside the cavity increases, and overlying tissue (the skin, in the case of external abscesses) loses its blood supply and dies. This is the stage of 'pointing' when the skin over a superficial abscess is dead, thin, and bulging.

What goes on beneath the surface is as described, whether the abscess be large or smaller than a human 'boil'.

First-aid. Hot fomentations are well worth the trouble of carrying them out. The technique is simple: merely soak a large pad of cotton wool, or a piece of old sheet, in hot water, wring out the excess of water, and apply the pad to the swelling, holding it there for two or three minutes, and then repeat the process. (The temperature of the water should not be higher than can comfortably be borne by the point of one's elbow.) Fomentations can be applied three or four times a day. They will reduce pain and hasten 'pointing'. If the abscess bursts, it is important that the cavity be syringed out with warm antiseptic solution or saline, and kept open, unbandaged, for as long as possible, so that healing takes place from the bottom; if it heals across the top while infection is still present, the abscess will persist.

Veterinary treatment consists in lancing an abscess so that, as far as possible, drainage can proceed by gravity, with the opening large enough to facilitate this and prevent premature healing of the edges. Antibiotics or sulpha drugs may be used.

GAS GANGRENE

This is very rare in the dog, but may follow a compound fracture or deep puncture wound. The swelling resembles that of an acute abscess, but the skin may crackle when touched and any escaping pus will be frothy – due to the gas. Do not waste time with first-aid measures – professional treatment is urgently needed.

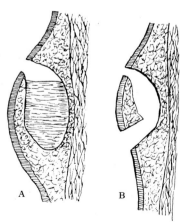

In (A) the abscess cannot drain away the pus, although it has burst. After lancing, as in (B), drainage can proceed by gravity

HAEMATOMA

This is a swelling containing blood or blood-clot, and results from injury (e.g. being struck by a car). It may occur anywhere on the body, below the skin or deep in muscle. The dog's ear-flap (pinna) is a not uncommon site for a haematoma, following a cat-scratch or repeated shaking of the head due to ear-mange, etc.; veterinary treatment is advisable, as otherwise the ear may become permanently distorted in shape. The contents of the swelling are removed, and precautions taken to prevent the swelling recurring. In other situations treatment is not necessary.

Swellings of this type beneath the skin also occur in dogs suffering from warfarin poisoning, and in two rare blood diseases – haemophilia and thrombasthenia – both congenital and resulting in a failure of the normal clotting of the blood at the site of an injury. Large subcutaneous swellings may occur in a dog infested with parasitic worms (*Angiostrongylus*) which live in blood vessels; but this too is rare.

HERNIA

A cold, painless swelling at a puppy's navel is likely to be a hernia or 'rupture'. Gentle pressure with the fingers will usually cause it momentarily to disappear. The opening in the abdominal wall involved in an **umbilical hernia** is a natural one which, however, should normally have closed at birth. If allowed time, it may still do so. Only a persistent or irreducible umbilical hernia will need surgical intervention, owing to the risk of a piece of omentum having its blood supply interfered with, or a piece of bowel becoming obstructed or strangulated – both serious conditions necessitating surgery without delay.

Hernias may also occur in other situations but are much less common than umbilical hernia. **Inguinal hernia** is hardly ever seen in the male, but occasionally in the bitch. Normally the inguinal canal, which leads from the interior of the abdominal cavity to the inguinal region, is occupied by the spermatic cords or by the mammary blood vessels, according to sex; but it may become sufficiently enlarged to allow a portion of omentum or intestine to descend and cause a visible swelling. A part of the uterus or bladder may, even more rarely, become trapped.

Intestine and bladder may protrude through the pelvic cavity into the perineal region, forming a swelling there. This **perineal hernia** is very occasionally seen in old dogs. The short-tailed, or docked, male is particularly susceptible, owing to under-development of the coccygeal muscles.

A swelling on the inside of the thigh – **femoral hernia** – was virtually restricted to circus dogs trained to walk on their hind legs, and is rarely seen nowadays.

A so-called **ventral hernia** may result from an accident which has damaged the muscular wall of the abdomen, but has left the skin intact though usually bruised. It is, so to speak, one stage removed from the type of accident which results in protrusion of some of the abdominal organs.

TICKS

An engorged tick, with its legs concealed under its bloated body, hardly looks like a parasite to anyone seeing it for the first time, and may be mistaken for a small tumour – or just another 'lump'.

Various stages (clockwise from centre left) in the engorgement of a female tick. When engorged, mouth parts and legs are concealed, so that the tick may not be recognised as a parasite at all

TUBERCULOSIS

Flat, oval 'lumps' on the surface of the body may be the result of tuberculosis, and a veterinary surgeon should always be consulted if these appear; the more urgently so if they are beginning to ulcerate and discharge pus.

SNAKE BITE

A red, swollen area on the skin of a dog which has *suddenly become frightened or excited*, may be the result of a snake bite. (Adder bites and spider bites are referred to in the chapter on 'Accidents and Other Emergencies'.)

TUMOURS

'Growths' or tumours vary greatly in appearance, rate of growth, type and importance. Hollow swellings containing fluid are known as cysts.

A benign tumour grows slowly, presses neighbouring parts aside but neither invades nor destroys them (though pressure may have an adverse effect upon adjacent organs and tissues). Unlike a cancerous growth, a benign tumour does not spread to distant tissues and, once removed surgically, is unlikely to recur. Some do not need to be removed at all.

Warts are small solid tumours and are very common on many parts of the dog's body. A wart may have a flat top, or a cauliflower-like top, or be irregular in shape, Eyelids, lips, paws, and ears are among the sites for warts. They usually grow to a small size and then do not get any bigger, and may be present for years without causing pain or discomfort. Warts in the mouth, however, may grow very quickly in clusters, and prove troublesome. They may disappear spontaneously after a while, but usually some advice is needed, as they tend to bleed, ulcerate, or become offensive.

Venereal tumours, a contagious condition caused by a virus, affect the vagina and penis or prepuce. These tumours may be wart-like or have relatively long stalks.

This chapter is concerned mainly with external swellings, but should not omit enlargement of the abdomen. Apart from pregnancy and ascites (dropsy), pyometra or torsion of the stomach, such enlargement may of course be due to an internal tumour.

Case history. Veterinary advice was sought concerning a 4-year-old Pointer bitch on account of enlargement of the abdomen, a capricious appetite, digestive disturbances, and lassitude. Symptoms had first appeared four months previously. A laparotomy was performed, and a tumour involving the spleen was found. The growth had a diameter of $11\frac{1}{2}$ inches and weighed 12 lb. After its removal the patient made an uneventful recovery.[1]

MALIGNANT TUMOURS

Owners sometimes express surprise when informed that dogs are subject to cancer, but unfortunately this is so. Veterinary surgeons encounter many cases of it over the years, and veterinary pathologists are constantly being sent specimens for identification in the laboratories.

Malignant tumours differ from benign ones in that they are, as a rule, faster growing. They invade and destroy normal tissues, and frequently they give rise to secondary growths in other parts of the body. Unlike a benign tumour, which is often enclosed in a fibrous capsule, a cancerous growth is often of irregular shape and its margins indeterminate. Separation of such a growth from the organ it has invaded may be impossible, so that the whole organ has to be removed.

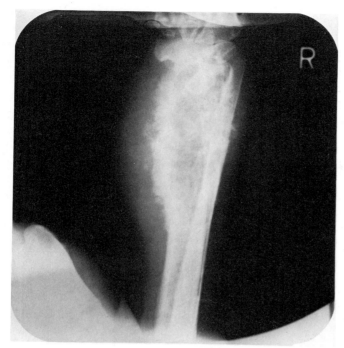

Malignant tumours.
This radiograph
shows a case of cancer
affecting the bone, an
osteo-sarcoma

Case history. A 9-month-old black Labrador dog was brought to the surgery on account of a painful swelling on one leg. The animal had appeared dejected for some little time. On palpation, one could feel that this swelling was deep and immoveable. The dog showed signs of pain when the swelling was handled. A tentative diagnosis of an osteo-sarcoma of the radius was made. A radiograph confirmed the diagnosis. It was a case of inoperable cancer. Euthanasia was suggested to the owner as the only course open, and the owner agreed.

Leukaemia. Out of 10,000 dogs admitted to the University of Glasgow's veterinary hospital over a certain period of time, 200 were suffering from leukaemia; while out of 630 dogs with fatal cancer, 22 per cent had leukaemia.

This disease takes its name from the presence in the bloodstream of an abnormally large number of leucocytes (white blood-cells), but in the domestic animals – as opposed to man – this symptom is often lacking, and the alternative name of *lympho-sarcoma* is preferable, if less familiar to dog-owners.

The disease is one of the lymphoid system concerned with bodily defence against infections through the action of cells called lymphocytes. Lymph nodes, spleen, bone marrow, and thymus gland are the organs associated with the function of lymphocytes.

In lympho-sarcoma, a large tumour may form at the site of the thymus gland in the chest. Enlargement of the spleen and infiltration of the liver may accompany enlargement of lymph nodes, both near the surface and deep. Tumours may occur in almost any organ.

Most cases of this disease occur in dogs aged between five and eleven years. In the early stages the animal may be bright and active, with the lymph-node enlargement as the only danger signal. The veterinary surgeon may be able to feel an enlargement of the spleen, and may be disbelieved if he suggests that the dog may have only a matter of weeks to live. Soon, however, the dog becomes progressively thinner, and there are usually digestive upsets such as diarrhoea. Later the appetite is lost, and the animal becomes depressed and very ill.

In one form of the disease the superficial lymph nodes do not show a characteristic symmetrical enlargement, and the illness is more gradual in onset; revealing itself first with digestive upsets and, later, persistent diarrhoea and loss of weight.

The veterinary diagnosis may be aided by detection of a large tumour in the abdomen. Blood examination is not a reliable guide. Treatment is not practicable, and euthanasia the best course.

MUMPS

It should be emphasised here that enlargement of the lymph nodes occurs during the course of many infections – some of them mild and transient – and not only with lympho-sarcoma. For example, mumps can be transmitted from a human patient to a dog. A 1956 survey carried out in Pennsylvania showed that 38 out of 209 apparently healthy country dogs had antibodies against the mumps virus.

Case history. A bitch lost her appetite and seemed depressed. Her submaxillary lymph nodes were enlarged and painful. The owner's daughter was ill with mumps, and blood samples taken from the dog by her veterinary surgeon confirmed that she too had mumps.

There is no mention in this case report of enlargement of the parotid salivary gland, which is a symptom common in mumps.[2] Any salivary gland may become swollen as a result of an abscess due to other infections. A swelling under the tongue, as a result of a blocked salivary duct, is referred to in the chapter on 'Digestive System Disorders'.

A reddish 'lump' on the dog's third eyelid is referred to in the chapter on 'The Dog's Face'.

REFERENCES
1 Walsh, F. B. and Schneck, G. W. *Vet. Record* 95 (1974), 352
2 Smith, R. E. *Vet. Record* 96 (1975), 296

12 The Coughing Dog

Generally speaking, dogs cough for the same reasons that people do. The cough reflex could be likened to a protective mechanism, its trigger being any irritation of the mucous membrane lining the larynx, trachea, and bronchi; its function is to rid the air passages of anything which tends to block or irritate them. Dust or smoke, for example, can cause coughing, as we all know from personal experience; so will fluids or solids accidentally entering from the mouth and 'going the wrong way'. A blade of grass, or a grass seed lodged behind the soft palate, may cause coughing and retching; so may tonsillitis.

A far more common cause is catarrhal inflammation of the mucous membrane lining the air passages. The membrane's goblet cells normally secrete a lubricant, but when there is inflammation, extra mucus is produced. To this becomes added white blood cells, tissue debris, and – if infection is present, as it usually is – dead bacteria and viruses. The exudate or discharge may then be described as muco-purulent.

A cough is, of course, one symptom of canine distemper.

Acute Attacks

Kennel Cough

This is no more than a convenient term for those outbreaks of respiratory disease, distinct from distemper, which are troublesome in boarding kennels and animal pounds. Whereas the distemper virus causes respiratory disease but may also involve the digestive and nervous systems, kennel cough, in the majority of instances, involves the upper air passages only. There is a harsh, dry cough, heard especially after exercise or excitement.

One cause of kennel cough is the bacterium *Bordetella bronchiseptica* already referred to in the chapter dealing with distemper. Five different viruses have also been isolated from dogs suffering from kennel cough, and it appears that there is often a mixed infection. 'It is possible to find two or even three different viruses in the same dog on the same day', Dr H. Thompson and Professor W. G. Wright of the University of Glasgow Veterinary School have stated.

One is sometimes asked: Can dogs become infected with influenza? The answer is Yes. For example, it has been shown that dogs are susceptible to the Hong Kong human influenza virus Type A; and a survey of 271 canine blood samples obtained after human epidemics, from different parts of the U.S.A and the U.K. showed that 5 per cent of the samples were positive. Para-influenza virus 5 is a common pathogen of the dog.

In puppies, and even in the adult, a cough may result from the migration of roundworm larvae through the lungs.

Coughing can be a symptom of an allergy of the hay-fever type; the dog also having conjunctivitis and sometimes skin irritation.

ACUTE BRONCHITIS

This may occur during the course of distemper, or follow a chill, or result from an allergy. The symptoms include fever, loss of appetite, a cough, and breathing which is faster than normal. The dog may wheeze as it breathes. (For first-aid, see chapter 8.)

PNEUMONIA

This is a not infrequent sequel to bronchitis in a dog already ill with a viral disease. Symptoms include shivering, fever (103° to 105°F or higher) and a rapid pulse. The breathing is laboured, and the lips may be alternately blown out and sucked in. A short, moist cough may become very troublesome. In some instances, coughing fits are so severe as to prove exhausting.

In broncho-pneumonia there may be a copious discharge from the nostrils during recovery, and finally a 'cast' may be expelled. (These 'casts' are formed of exudate, moulded to the inside of a bronchial tube.) Broncho-pneumonia can prove fatal in three to four days, or may persist for a matter of weeks before recovery takes place.

OEDEMA OF THE LUNGS

This condition is the result of the passage of blood serum (and cells) from engorged capillaries into the alveoli (air-cells) of the lungs. Gradually the fluid collects and fills what are normally air spaces for the exchange of oxygen and carbon dioxide, so that the dog, in effect, 'drowns' in its own effusions, and dies from lack of oxygen, plus shock.

Oedema of the lungs is seen in dogs which have been exposed to smoke and rescued from burning buildings, in cases of paraquat poisoning, and can occasionally result from an allergy. Treatment may include the use of oxygen in an attempt to save life.

PLEURISY

A short, sharp 'hacking' cough may be a later symptom of pleurisy which, in its acute form, often begins with shivering, fever, dullness, and evidence of pain when slight pressure is applied to the chest. Breathing becomes rapid and altered in character, giving the impression that the abdominal, rather than the chest, muscles are doing all the work. After twenty-four to

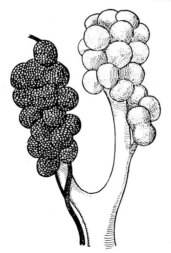

Air-sacs (alveoli) of the lungs. The left group has the blood supply superimposed (×25 approx.)

forty-eight hours there is an effusion of exudate into the pleural cavity. Pain is then reduced, but breathing becomes more difficult. Urgent veterinary attention is needed.

Persistent Coughs

So far, this chapter has been concerned with fits of coughing which extend only over a short period. Now we must turn to something rather different: persistent coughs.

CHRONIC BRONCHITIS

In dogs five years old and upwards, this is probably the most common cause of a persistent cough. It is one of those canine ills about which the dog-owner readily seeks professional advice, but sometimes comes, mind already made up, requesting euthanasia. In many instances this decision is taken because of the possible suffering on the part of the dog; but occasionally the persistent coughing becomes a source of irritation to another member of the household, or visitors to the house raise their eyebrows and ask 'Is it healthy to have a dog like that around?' The owner then starts worrying.

The veterinary surgeon will examine the dog, elicit its history from the owner, listen to the cough, apply a stethoscope to the chest, perhaps make use of X-rays, and decide what, in his opinion is causing the cough.

Assuming for a moment that his diagnosis *is* chronic bronchitis, how does it arise, and is it likely to clear up? Many cases follow an acute attack of bronchitis or kennel cough, and are due to the already mentioned *Bordetella* organism. The coughing arises from excessive secretion of mucus in the trachea and bronchi. The trouble often clears up for a while, but is liable to flare up again at any time, resulting in another acute attack – sometimes with a slight degree of pneumonia. Coughing may persist over weeks or months, and recur in subsequent years. In between times, the dog, while never fully fit or capable of strenuous exercise, appears to find life tolerable enough.

Chronic bronchitis may be followed by what is technically known as destructive (vesicular) **emphysema**. This is characterised by an abnormal enlargement of the air spaces in the lungs, accompanied by destructive changes in the walls of the tiny air sacs (alveoli). The main symptom is laboured breathing, with a special effort for breathing *out*, after exercise.

Since the advent of almost universally pasteurised milk in Britain, tuberculosis in the dog is a far less common disease than it once was. It is, however, an infection which must be borne in mind in cases of chronic bronchitis, pleurisy, and pneumonia.

HEART DISEASE

Far more common than tuberculosis as a cause of a persistent cough, especially in elderly and rather fat dogs, is heart disease, which may co-exist with chronic bronchitis.

There are, of course, numerous different diseases of the heart, some of which are discovered only when a veterinarian, examining a dog, applies his stethoscope to the chest and hears a tell-tale murmur or other abnormal sound.

Some cases are suspected and looked for, since they may attract the owner's attention through symptoms such as fainting, or a dropsical swelling (oedema) affecting the lowest part of the chest and abdomen; occasionally the legs, too. A defective mitral valve, which may give rise to an asthmatic type of cough, is not confined to old dogs, but may be present in very young ones. In dogs less than four years old, suffering from heart disease, the principal cause is said to be congenital abnormalities.

In an overseas survey, it was found that mitral valve defects were present in 42 per cent of 550 dogs of both sexes and 42 breeds, examined after death and not selected with any particular disease in mind. (See also the Appendix).

In an American survey autopsy of over 4,800 dogs revealed heart disease of one kind or another in over 11 per cent of them. In a Swiss survey of 421 dogs examined for suspected heart disease, chronic valvular disease was diagnosed in 32 per cent of them, and disease of the heart muscle in 41 per cent. (See Canine Parvovirus infection on page 80.)

If all this sounds rather alarming to the reader, remember that a great many dogs with imperfect heart action live to a ripe old age. Despite the heart's beating 90 or 100 times per minute, and the fact that it never completely rests from the time of its formation before birth until death, it is remarkable that heart disease does not incapacitate dogs to a greater extent that it does. Compare the exertions of a racing Greyhound, an Alsatian running at 30 m.p.h., or a sheepdog working all day on hill land, with the performance and fallibility of man-made pumps!

PARASITIC WORMS

A persistent cough may be due to the heartworm (see the chapter 'In the Tropics'), or to another worm *Oslerus* which is present in Britain, and infests the dog's trachea. Retching may be a symptom, as well as coughing. In *severe* infestations there may be emaciation despite a good appetite, laboured breathing, and death.

Case history. A Terrier aged 1½ years had had a persistent cough since the age of six months. Antibiotics had been tried, without success. Examination under anaesthesia was carried out at the Royal Veterinary College's hospital, where an endoscope revealed pink nodules in the trachea, some of them almost completely obstructing the airway. Fluid on the end of the endoscope contained larvae of this filarial worm. Treatment with thiabendazole, an anthelmintic, proved effective.

DYSPNOEA

Breathing with difficulty or distress (dyspnoea) may follow several conditions of which coughing is one symptom. Among causes not already mentioned is the presence of a tumour.

Case history. Veterinary advice was sought concerning a 7-year-old bitch of one of the larger breeds. Her breathing had been rather laboured over a 4-month period, and during exercise it always became worse, with cyanosis – blue discolouration of the tongue, gums, etc. Radiography showed the presence of a tumour which had pushed the heart slightly out of position and put pressure on the main blood vessels. A thoracotomy was performed, revealing a non-malignant fatty tumour (lipoma) weighing over 8 lb.[1]

SNEEZING

An irritant such as pepper, an allergy (canine hay-fever), and distemper, are all causes of sneezing, which may also indicate the presence of a foreign body in the nose or sinuses – for example a grass seed, or rarely a stone or parasite (leeches in the tropics; *Linguatula serratica* – the 'tongue-worm' – in Europe, including Britain). A thick muco-purulent discharge from *one* nostril only may be noticed with sinusitis – without sneezing – when the cause may be a fungal infection, e.g. aspergillosis. (See also the chapter 'The Dog's Face'.)

REFERENCE
1 Teunissen, G. H. B. *Tijdschr. Diergeneesk* 102 (1977), 113

13 The Thirsty Dog

A feverish dog is likely to be a thirsty dog, though thirst will be only one of the symptoms; so if he seems unwell, take his temperature. If it is raised, look for other signs of ill-health.

Inflammation of the kidneys gives rise to thirst and, along with cystitis, is described in chapter 16. Among other ailments associated with drinking more water than usual are the following. **Diabetes insipidus** is characterised by the passing of large quantities of urine (polyuria) as well as by thirst. The cause is generally regarded as a deficiency of vasopressin, the anti-diuretic hormone secreted by the pituitary gland, and may be treated by your veterinary surgeon accordingly.

In human medicine **compulsive polydipsia**, meaning the urge to drink excessive quantities of water, is recognised, and is attributed to psychological disturbance. It is likely that it occurs in dogs also, as a result of stress.

A case history of polydipsia. A large dog attacked a smaller one, which remained cowed and frightened for several hours afterwards, and took to drinking as much as 12 pints of water in 24 hours. This obviously meant that more urine had to be passed, and led at night-time to urinary incontinence – which, so far as the dog-owner is concerned, means puddles on the floor to clear up in the morning. The dog's coat became dull and the appetite poor. Veterinary treatment succeeded in reducing the water intake and restoring lustre to the coat. After a few months, however, the drug used in treatment had to be abandoned owing to the onset of cystitis (inflammation of the bladder), and the puddle nuisance returned. Fortunately, it was found by experience that feeding the dog in the mornings only reduced the intake of water later in the day, and the incontinence ceased.[1]

DIABETES

True diabetes (**Diabetes mellitus**), as opposed to diabetes insipidus, gives rise to similar symptoms.

In human medicine diabetes is now regarded as a group of diseases rather than as a single disease entity, and has been related to auto-immune defects running in families, to the presence of an insulin-antagonist circulating in the bloodstream, as well as to the classical deficiency of the hormone insulin, secreted by cells of the Islets of Langerhans in the pancreas. It is recognised, too, that human diabetes may arise from excessive dosage of cortisone or similar compounds, and that viruses – such as that of mumps – may adversely affect the insulin-secreting cells.

All such causes may be relevant in canine medicine, too. The main point to bear in mind concerning diabetes in the dog is that the animal becomes unable to control the use and storage of glucose (blood sugar) derived from the carbohydrate part of the diet. Normally, when blood sugar rises above a certain level, the hormone insulin is released by the pancreas and rectifies the situation. If this fails to occur, as in diabetes, an excess of glucose in the blood persists and is removed by the kidneys and excreted in the urine.

The symptoms of diabetes in the dog are often rather vague. The animal drinks more and passes more urine, as already mentioned; he tends to lose weight despite a fairly good appetite; he becomes rather sluggish. Vision may be impaired by the appearance of a cataract in one or both eyes. Long-term deterioration may involve the liver and kidneys.

Case history. A 7 year-old Airedale dog was brought to the surgery. 'He hasn't seemed well for some time', the owner's sister remarked. 'I know that sounds vague, but apart from a few spots there is really nothing more than I can tell you about him. Except,' she added, 'that *I* think he's getting rather fat. He doesn't seem to have the energy he used to,' she continued, 'and he's only seven.'

She was wrong about the dog being fat – perhaps misled by a pendulous abdomen which perhaps suggested 'middle-aged spread'. However, the dog's ribs and vertebrae were sadly prominent; in reality the animal was *losing* flesh, although the abdomen was enlarged – due to ascites (dropsy).

'Is he thirsty?' she was asked.

'Yes, come to think of it, he does drink more than he used to.'

There was a slight cataract in one eye – suggestive, no more, but a urine test revealed a high level of sugar present, and also protein.

'He has diabetes,' she was told, 'and there seems to be some kidney derangement, too.'

Her brother, a doctor, came in the next day, having decided on euthanasia, as he had no wish for the dog to have insulin injections.

Today, insulin does not necessarily have to be given by injection; it, or sulphonylureas or other drugs, can be given in tablet form, which is satisfactory in many cases.

Thirst is a symptom common in cases of pyometra, in the maiden bitch especially. Cushing's disease also gives rise to thirst, often accompanied by a ravenous appetite, lethargy, and hair loss.

URINARY INCONTINENCE

An example of this has aleady been given at the beginning of this chapter. Another cause is an enlarged prostate gland. In old dogs with failing kidneys, incontinence is a common symptom, since the animal has to drink

REFERENCE
1 Potter, W. R. and Fraser, T. W. *Vet Record* 76 (1964), 488 and 543

more water than usual, and has to pass urine during the night. Inflammation of the bladder (cystitis) – sometimes associated with brucellosis – is another cause of urinary incontinence; and this occurs too in the dog suffering from paraplegia (paralysis of the hind legs). See also end of chapter 16.

14 The Vomiting Dog

Vomiting is a complex act involving a contraction not merely of the stomach muscles and a dilation of the oesophagus, but also contraction of the abdominal muscles, the diaphragm, and muscles of the chest. Before vomiting occurs, there is usually a profuse secretion of watery saliva which serves as a lubricant for the passage of material from stomach to mouth.

A dog about to vomit may appear uneasy and sometimes seek a secluded place; but dogs, like cats, often vomit with the minimum of fuss, and often deliberately induce the act by eating couch grass.

Sometimes all that is vomited is a little yellowish froth; in other instances the last meal, or part of it, is returned.

Regurgitation is a word which might conveniently be reserved for the vomiting of partly digested food by the nursing bitch, shortly before her puppies are weaned. This is a natural means of providing them with some semi-solid food.

Undoubtedly a simple error of diet accounts for much vomiting in dogs – they sometimes eat infected, decomposing, or contaminated food; or they eat too much, or drink too much water. Highly seasoned table scraps may upset some dogs, while the stomachs of others are not upset by curry. The fact that a few dogs are allergic to a certain food or foods has already been mentioned in chapter 2, and these may give rise to vomiting. So, it seems, may stress of some kind.

GASTRITIS

Inflammation of the mucous membrane lining the stomach may result from some of the causes mentioned above; yet it is probably true to say that vomiting occurs more often as a result of enteritis (inflammation of the intestine) than of gastritis.

Naturally, vomiting often gives rise to the question: 'Has my dog been poisoned?' In only a small proportion of cases does the answer turn out to be 'Yes'; even then it may not be a violent poison such as arsenic. Repeated or excessive doses of salicylates, notably aspirin, may result in tiny haemorrhages from the stomach lining, and vomiting. (For poisoning, see chapter 10.)

Repeated vomiting, usually accompanied by other symptoms, may occur during the course of a generalised illness such as distemper, canine viral hepatitis, leptospirosis, or rabies.

The presence of a foreign body may inflame the stomach lining. If a sharp-pointed object has been swallowed, the dog may salivate, arch his back and become very miserable. If vomiting occurs, a little blood may be seen, either in the form of easily recognised blood clots or having the appearance of coffee grounds. In such circumstances, professional advice should be sought.

A chronic, as opposed to an acute, gastritis may result from foreign bodies. Even smooth ones such as sea-washed pebbles tend to set up inflammation sufficient to cause the dog to retch or vomit at frequent intervals.

Case history. A Labrador bitch swallowed 89 such pebbles – and rattled as she walked. Major surgery was necessitated for, although other measures produced from either end of the animal a total of 30, the remaining 59 pebbles had to be removed through an incision into the stomach wall.[1]

Small balls, pieces of carpet, coal, nails, corks – these are some of the other foreign bodies which have been found in dogs' stomachs.

In long-haired breeds, a hairball may give rise to vomiting. Dogs rarely have stomach ulcers. Vomiting, sometimes of a little blood, is a symptom.

PYLORIC STENOSIS

What is called projectile vomiting – in which the stomach contents are ejected for a greater distance than normal – is a symptom of pyloric stenosis. This is a constriction of the pylorus, the muscular valve which controls the exit of food from the stomach into the duodenum, the first part of the small intestine. Not a common condition, it is seen both in puppies (when there may be a congenital defect) and in adult dogs. It can often be relieved by means of an abdominal operation, should this prove necessary.

Sometimes there is muscular spasm of the pylorus, and not an anatomical abnormality. Projectile vomiting occurs also when there is spasm at the entrance to the stomach. Dilation of the oesophagus often accompanies this, and food may be returned within minutes of being swallowed.

OTHER CAUSES

Among less common causes of vomiting is *hiatus hernia*, in which a part of the stomach protrudes through an opening in the diaphragm into the chest cavity. In a case involving incomplete closure of the cardia (the upper opening of the stomach where the oesophagus ends) and dilation at the lower end of the oesophagus, stomach contents may almost *flow* out – without force.

Even rarer is torsion (twisting) of the stomach (see chapter 15), blockage of the bile duct, and vomiting due to a disease of pigs, referred to at the end of chapter 20.

Vomiting is not always due to a stomach disorder but, as already mentioned, is a common symptom of inflammation of the intestines, enteritis. It is also a symptom of blockage of the oesophagus or intestine by a foreign body. Retching and vomiting are sometimes associated with a **parasitic worm** of the oesophagus, and occasionally of the stomach, *Spirocerca*. Retching may occur as a result of another worm infestation of the trachea, and in tonsillitis.

Vomiting is a common symptom of **nephritis** (inflammation of the kidneys) and kidney failure; of **pyometra** – in which the uterus becomes chronically infected with abundant pus formation; of inflammation of the pancreas; and of the liver.

Persistent vomiting was a symptom in a case of **blastomycosis**, a fungal infection, affecting the liver and kidneys and at first mistaken for canine viral hepatitis. Rare in the U.K., blastomycosis is relatively common in the U.S.A.

Another uncommon cause of vomiting is *myasthenia gravis*, described in chapter 17.

Travel Sickness

This may be associated with fear of a car, or with the balancing mechanism of the ear, and affects many young dogs. Some motorists try to prevent it by fitting an earthing chain to the car. Success is more likely to follow stopping periodically to let the dog out during the journey, especially if he is beginning to look anxious or to salivate. If this, too, fails, ask your veterinary surgeon to prescribe a sedative or tranquilliser which can be given well in advance of the start of the car journey. Fortunately, most dogs grow out of a tendency to travel sickness.

Finally, do not be alarmed if your dog vomits a little froth at a fixed time each day, or if he vomits once or even twice during a short period but *otherwise seems well*. It is, as a rule, only repeated vomiting, with or without other symptoms, which requires professional aid – and that urgently.

A tendency to lie in cold places, or an unusual posture, is often an indication of abdominal pain. Restlessness and arching of the back are other signs that all is not well.

When it seems likely that non-repeated vomiting is the result of an error of diet, the dog will be best without food for some hours; then offer a little milk, if that is liked.

REFERENCE
1 Wilson, Margaret E. M. *Vet. Record* 76 (1964), 1213

15 Disorders of the Digestive System

The digestive system of the dog could be described as a tube, some 16 to 18 feet long, extending from the mouth, passing back through the chest into the abdomen through a special opening in the diaphragm, continuing with stomach, small and large intestines, and ending at the anus; also included are the salivary glands, the liver and gall-bladder and the pancreas.

Of course, this tube is not permanently continuous with the mouth, since there is a cross-over to be negotiated. As we all know, we can breathe through the mouth which is then, via the pharynx, continuous with the trachea. However, as soon as food is ready for swallowing, and enters the pharynx, it touches areas supplied with nerves which automatically inhibit breathing, in order to prevent food 'going the wrong way'; this closes the larynx, which is pulled upwards and forwards; the base of the tongue folds the epiglottis over the opening of the larynx. The pharynx is shortened and its muscles force the food into the oesophagus. In this tube, alternate muscular relaxation and contraction, occurring in waves and called peristalsis, move the food onwards to the stomach.

Swallowing is one-third voluntary and two-thirds reflex ('automatic'). The voluntary part is placing the food on the upper surface of the tongue, which is raised – tip first – against the hard palate towards the rear. At the same time the soft palate is raised, closing the gateway to the nose. The base of the tongue forces the food into the pharynx. The next two stages of swallowing are involuntary, reflex actions.

The epiglottis, it should be added, is a leaf-like piece of cartilage covered with mucous membrane, which stands between the back of the tongue and the glottis (entrance to the larynx).

The palate is the partition between the cavity of the mouth below and that of the nose above. It consists of the hard palate, formed by the bony floor of the nasal cavity and having those well-marked ridges with which we are all familiar; and the soft palate, which is a continuation of the hard palate but formed of muscle with the usual covering of mucous membrane which lines all these cavities. The soft palate acts as sort of curtain between mouth and pharynx.

Cleft palate is a congenital deformity of the hard palate. This defect varies in extent and is often associated with 'hare-lip'. Puppies with a cleft palate may be unable to suck at all and die soon after birth; others can obtain some milk from the bitch but seldom thrive.

Cleft palate in the adult dog results from an accident, such as falling from a height, but is uncommon. Surgical repair can be achieved in some cases.

Hare-lip in a young Bulldog puppy. The complete cleft in the upper lip would prevent successful sucking

Prolonged soft palate is another inherited abnormality, occurring in some dogs of the short-nosed breeds, e.g. Pekingese, Boxers, Bulldogs. It makes breathing difficult at times, with snoring or even loss of consciousness resulting. An operation to correct the condition is often very successful.

Like the eyes, the mouth offers the dog-owner some helpful pointers to the state of the dog's health. Note the pink colour of the gums and tongue when the dog is well. (The Chow's tongue is black, of course.) It is in the mouth that the owner might notice a tinge of yellow, indicating jaundice; or whitish gums, indicating shock or internal haemorrhage.

GLOSSITIS

Inflammation of the tongue (glossitis) often draws attention to itself through excessive salivation, and may result from injuries, infections, vitamin deficiencies, and poisons. Ulcers may occur at the margins of the tongue if in contact with diseased teeth.

Foreign bodies in the tongue include needles and fish-hooks. These and a bone wedged across the roof of the mouth between the teeth, cause much distress. Indeed, the dog may become almost frantic, crying out and pawing the face violently, and may bite anyone trying to afford relief. Saliva usually drips from the mouth.

Bleeding from the tongue may be profuse if bitten during a fight or an accident. Normally wounds of the tongue in a healthy dog heal very readily, but a deep gash will require stitches. A pad of cotton-wool soaked in water chilled in a refrigerator, and held in place for a minute or two, may reduce the haemorrhage.

Warts may appear inside the mouth, especially inside the cheeks. Occasionally they are so numerous as to interfere with eating, or they ulcerate; but if not, they seldom need treatment and usually disappear spontaneously. However, they are caused by a virus, and so the dog might transmit the infection to others in the same household or encountered outside.

So-called '**black-tongue**' is caused by a vitamin deficiency – a lack of nicotinic acid, a constituent of vitamin B_2 – in the diet. It can easily be prevented by feeding a diet containing egg, meat and yeast. If untreated, this canine equivalent of human pellagra can prove fatal; if treated in time it responds to a vitamin supplement or to proper feeding. Apart from the discolouration of the tongue, the latter may have ulcers on it, and a foul odour.

So-called '**brown mouth**' is a syndrome characterised by necrosis (cell death) of the gums and the passing of blood in the faeces. It may be an accompaniment of viral infections. While antibiotics are useless against viruses, they may control the secondary bacterial invaders; in fact antibiotic treatment is often successful. A vitamin supplement is perhaps even more useful.

Brown discolouration of the mouth, accompanied by halitosis, is also seen in dogs with kidney failure and uraemia. (See chapter 16.)

A cyst, popularly known as a **ranula**, may develop below the tongue, which it may push to one side, interfering with eating. This is a simple retention cyst due to blockage of a duct leading from one of the salivary glands. It has been known for a grass seed to block the duct. It is not a serious disorder, but needs relieving by incision or excision.

Salivary glands. There are three pairs of salivary glands: a pair at the sides of the tongue; the parotid glands below the ears and behind the borders of the lower jaw; and the third pair below the parotids.

Most dogs bolt their food, giving little or no time for salivary digestion of starches which, in man, begins in the mouth. Moreover, the dog's saliva contains very little of the necessary enzyme for this, ptyalin, and probably performs mainly the function of lubrication for the swallowing of food. Like all glands, they are subject to inflammation, infection, blockage of their ducts, and to tumour formation. Swelling of one or more glands may be seen accordingly. Infections of the salivary glands include rabies and mumps.

Pharyngitis

Inflammation of the pharynx occurs as an extension of catarrhal inflammation elsewhere, as in distemper, for example, and may give rise to discomfort or difficulty in swallowing (dysphagia). In itself it is not an important condition as a rule.

Tonsillitis

The tonsils are, in health, not conspicuous, being situated in a depression. When inflamed, they appear as two bright red lumps. Tonsillitis may cause the dog to retch or cough, and the animal is often slightly feverish and dejected as a result of the infection which has led to the inflammation.

CHOKING AND 'CHOKING'

Sometimes a lump of gristly meat, a dangerously small rubber ball, or a child's toy becomes lodged and blocks the air passageway, so that the dog is in immediate danger of choking. The dog will fall over and the tongue become a bluish-purple colour. A sharp blow to the back while the dog is held up by the hind legs may succeed in dislodging the object. Otherwise, the owner must open the mouth and try to locate and remove the obstruction. Sometimes it is easier to push it down – if a piece of meat, for example – so that it is swallowed and the airway automatically unblocked, as explained earlier.

The word 'choking' – through long use by farmers – has another meaning in veterinary practice: an obstruction not to breathing but to the passage of food through the oesophagus. For example, part of a chop bone may be swallowed, pass some way along the oesophagus, and then become stuck there.

'Choking' in this sense gives rise to vomiting of all solid food very shortly after swallowing it, and the dog may 'have a wet mouth', i.e. salivate. The dog's owner may suspect poisoning as the cause of the vomiting, which ceases to be a symptom after a time, as the dog refuses all solid food. Dejection is apparent, and loss of weight follows.

Case history 1. When operated upon at the Royal Veterinary College, London, an 8-month-old Scottish Terrier had had part of a chop bone obstructing the oesophagus for eight days, having meanwhile lost much weight and been in poor condition. Removal of the bone – the size and position of which were ascertained with the aid of X-rays – necessitated surgical opening of the chest (thoracotomy) after removal of part of one rib. Complete recovery followed.

It is surprising what large objects can be swallowed. Mathematically, $11\frac{1}{2}$ will go into 16 easily, but biologically, so to speak, one would have thought it impossible. Sixteen inches, from angle of jaw to tail, was the length of a 10-week-old Bulldog puppy; $11\frac{1}{2}$ inches was the length of a steel poker which he completely swallowed.

Case history 2. Seeing that the puppy was vomiting, the owners called their veterinary surgeon, who was informed on arrival that the poker, which the puppy had been playing with, was missing. On examination, the point of the poker could be felt and also, in the abdomen, the knob on the end of the poker. The puppy was anaesthetised and, with relaxation of the muscles, the point of the poker entered the mouth. The monster foreign body was then gently withdrawn, without recourse to surgery at all, and the puppy appeared to be none the worse afterwards.[1]

Overseas, if not in Britain, the dog's oesophagus is sometimes affected by a parasitic worm found in nodules, which may cause partial obstruction and give rise to vomiting or retching. The worm (*Spirocerca*), which may also be found in the stomach, occasionally causes fatal haemorrhage, and the nodules may become the site of a malignant tumour.

GASTRITIS

Inflammation of the stomach and pyloric stenosis are described in the chapter on 'The Vomiting Dog'.

Except in the giant breeds, torsion or twisting of the stomach is rare. Gas collects and distends the stomach. The abdomen becomes painful to the touch, swelling may be apparent, and vomiting is likely to occur. The dog is soon in a very distressed condition, and this is an emergency.

DIARRHOEA

This is not, of course, a disease in itself but merely a symptom which may indicate nothing more than an 'error of diet'. The eating of mouldy, decomposing or otherwise unsuitable food may cause diarrhoea, as may also food contaminated with *Salmonella* or coliform bacteria. In a puppy, a sudden change of diet or the presence of worms may be possible causes.
First-aid. Measures include withholding food for a few hours and then offering white of egg in milk, milky rice pudding, or other light foods. Do not give preparations sold for human use to treat 'traveller's diarrhoea', but one containing kaolin or charcoal may be suitable for canine use.

As implied above, diarrhoea may be a very transient disorder. If it does not spontaneously disappear quickly, veterinary advice should be obtained. The causes are many and varied, and it is important to ascertain the underlying cause if possible.

Persistent diarrhoea may result from stress in the 'worried' dog which has been lost, moved to a new home or sent to boarding kennels, etc. Parasitic worms are another possible cause, but less often than many dog-owners might imagine. Allergies may result in alarming cases of gastro-enteritis, with vomiting and sometimes the passing of blood in the faeces. The same is true of some poisons.

Disease of the pancreas and a tumour may both cause diarrhoea, which may also occur during the course of an illness such as distemper, canine viral hepatitis, tuberculosis, or leukaemia. It will be appreciated that a differential diagnosis is important.

Dehydration is a serious consequence of diarrhoea occurring for any length of time; water and also salts being lost. In an attempt to conserve body fluids the kidneys diminish the quantity of urine, so that there is likely to be an added complication of waste products circulating in the bloodstream. Dehydration is a potential cause of death, and needs treatment. For dog-owners living overseas, a prescription for UNICEF's 'Oral Rehydration Salts' (intended for human use) is given in the chapter 'In the Tropics'. Professional treatment involves the administration of glucose-saline by injection, though it may be necessary first to overcome defects in the circulation due to the high viscosity of the blood, and its reduced alkalinity, by giving blood plasma or dextran.

CONSTIPATION

Inadequate exercise and too much food may predispose to constipation. Some bulk is needed in the food in order to assist peristalsis, referred to earlier in this chapter. The dog's digestive system is not well adapted for coping with much fibre, but inclusion of some cooked vegetables in the diet is helpful. Constipation is seldom serious, and can be relieved by offering some oil out of a tin of sardines. Laxatives should never be given regularly; and this applies to medicinal liquid paraffin, prolonged use of which can lead to a deficiency of fat-soluble vitamins.

When a hard mass of bone particles or dry faeces are present in the rectum and cannot be passed, the term **impaction** is often used. A couple of doses of liquid paraffin may relieve this impaction, or the 'sardine oil' may be tried; but often an enema is necessary to soften the hard mass sufficiently for it to be removed. A tablespoonful of glycerine in a pint of warm water is useful, administered slowly by means of a Higginson's type of enema as sold for human use.

In order to prevent impaction as far as possible, elderly dogs should *not* be given bones to gnaw.

Constipation may be evident not merely from an absence of faeces but from unsuccessful efforts to pass them; i.e. straining. Painful anal glands may deter the dog from defaecating, while in long-haired breeds, matted hair across the anus may act as a physical barrier. An enlarged prostate gland may also interfere with defaecation.

Prolonged straining occasionally results in **prolapse of the rectum**, when the inverted portion is seen outside the anus as a sausage-shaped projection, red or bluish-red in colour. As there is risk of gangrene if the condition persists, professional help should be obtained.

INTESTINAL OBSTRUCTION

One form of this has already been mentioned – the impacted rectum – but the obstruction may be present higher up. Sometimes, for instance, a loop of small intestine becomes trapped in a hernia. There may be a foreign body causing the obstruction, e.g. a hair-ball, some object or material which has been swallowed. Obstruction may also be due to a tumour.

Sometimes a portion of intestine becomes turned in upon itself, a condition known as **intussusception**, or becomes twisted – **volvulus**. These are serious conditions which can lead to a fatal peritonitis.

With intussusception, a sausage-like swelling can sometimes be felt through the abdominal wall. There is usually great pain, and the dog may assume a crouching position or stand on the hind legs with the forelegs extended forwards on the ground. With volvulus, the twist involves the blood vessels as well as the intestine, and necrosis (death of cells) sooner or later follows the failure of blood supply and may be complicated by infection – as with intussusception. Surgery offers the only hope of recovery.

Peritonitis, inflammation of the peritoneum – the membrane lining the abdominal cavity and forming a covering for the various organs – occurs not only as mentioned above, but following stake wounds, penetration of the wall of the intestine by a sharp-pointed foreign body, and during the course of some infectious diseases.

Vomit may resemble coffee-grounds if partly digested blood is present; while in cases of intestinal obstruction the vomit resembles faeces and is foul-smelling.

THE LIVER

In the dog, the liver is relatively large and accounts for about one-twentieth of total body-weight. It lies in the front of the abdomen, close to the diaphragm, and receives – via the portal vein – blood from the stomach, intestines, spleen and pancreas. Substances in this blood are chemically changed in the liver, and harmful ones detoxified, if possible, before entering the venous circulation *en route* to the heart. Blood to nourish the liver cells comes from the hepatic artery.

The functions of the liver include the storage of glycogen (the starch readily convertible into blood sugar, glucose) and of iron salts, the breakdown of old red blood corpuscles, and the secretion of bile. The conversion of many compounds present in the blood of the portal vein is assisted by enzymes – catalysts produced by living cells.

Bile, a greenish-yellow fluid secreted by liver cells and stored in the gall-bladder, is important in the digestion of fats and in the absorption of these and fat-soluble vitamins.

Acute **hepatitis**, or inflammation of the liver, can be produced by viruses (e.g. that of canine viral hepatitis); bacteria and their toxins; and by poisons of many kinds. The liver is a common site for abscesses, and its tissues may suffer damage through the migration of liver flukes.

Symptoms of hepatitis include fever, signs of pain when pressure is applied to the abdomen, loss of appetite, a disinclination to move, and either constipation or diarrhoea.

Symptoms of disease of the liver other than in its most acute form may include a gradual loss of condition, capricious appetite, a staring coat, jaundice, and sometimes ascites (dropsy).

Jaundice is a symptom seen in leptospirosis, sometimes in canine distemper, canine viral hepatitis; in obstruction of the bile duct and in liver damage; in tropical diseases involving destruction of red blood cells by parasites; in some cases of tuberculosis, or a tumour, involving the liver. The white of the eyes, the lining of the eyelids, and the gums become tinged with yellow.

The liver is subject to fatty and other forms of degeneration, including cirrhosis – in which many of the liver cells are replaced by fibrous tissue cells. Jaundice and ascites (dropsy) are symptoms commonly seen in cases of cirrhosis of the liver.

THE GALL-BLADDER

Simple inflammation of the gall-bladder, technically known as cholecystitis, is seldom diagnosed; the only symptom may be pain. In rare instances, however, the gall-bladder may rupture, giving rise to repeated vomiting.

Blockage of the bile duct may be caused either by worms or by gall-stones. The latter are not all opaque to X-rays. Jaundice and vomiting are likely symptoms.

Case history. A 7-year-old male Boxer had, a year previously, had jaundice, and was now suffering progressively worsening bouts of vomiting; between which appetite was normal. Faeces were pale and evil-smelling. A laparotomy revealed a gall-stone (which X-rays had not shown) blocking the bile duct. When the stone was removed, the dog became well again.[2]

THE PANCREAS

Situated near the kidneys, the pancreas is an endocrine gland, secreting hormones such as insulin and glucagon directly into the bloodstream. Disease of the cells known as the Islets of Langerhans can result in diabetes.

The pancreas is also an exocrine gland (i.e. one which has a duct through which it secretes a juice). The juice's function is digestive; the duct enters the first part of the small intestine, the duodenum, close to where the bile duct enters. Pancreatic juice contains several enzymes, including trypsin which continues the digestion of proteins already begun in the stomach; and lipase which aids digestion of fats.

Acute necrotic inflammation of the pancreas occurs in obese dogs, with symptoms which may include increased tension of the abdominal wall, tenderness or severe pain, and sometimes a later rise in blood sugar, and shock.

Malodorous fatty faeces may be passed in chronic inflammation of the pancreas; other symptoms are thirst and passing of large volumes of urine. Atrophy of the pancreas gives rise to a ravenous appetite, an enlarged abdomen, and fatty faeces (pale in colour).

REFERENCES
1 Wilkinson, I. S. *Vet. Record* 77 (1965), 770
2 Binns, R. M. *Vet. Record* 76 (1964), 239

16 Urinary System Disorders

The Kidney

Your veterinary surgeon may speak of **nephrosis**, or of the nephrotic syndrome. This may be a stage in nephritis (inflammation of the kidneys), and it involves damage to the tiny tubes which filter off waste products from the bloodstream. Such damage may result in protein being excreted in the urine, to the detriment of protein levels in the blood. Nephrosis may be caused by various toxins or poisoning by metallic salts, but more commonly it follows certain diseases.

In acute **nephritis** there is inflammation of the kidney tissues as a whole, or of the glomeruli (small knots of blood vessels about the size of a grain of sand, from which excretion of fluid out of the blood into the tubules of the kidney takes place), and of the tubules only.

Acute or sub-acute nephritis is often associated with leptospirosis, and especially with *Leptospira canicola* infection. Protection against this infection is afforded by vaccination – combined distemper, canine viral hepatitis, and leptospirosis vaccine is commonly used. The acute nephritis may follow the nephrotic syndrome, and may co-exist with distemper or canine viral hepatitis in the absence of vaccination or following the waning of immunity in a dog vaccinated years previously.

Experience in practice suggests that a sudden cold spell – with an east wind, for example – may act as a predisposing cause, by lowering the animal's resistance and enabling a subclinical infection to give rise to symptoms of illness.

Such symptoms include depression, loss of appetite, thirst, and vomiting. The back may be arched slightly, and the dog may appear to be stiff. The temperature is raised. Sometimes ulcers appear in the mouth.

First-aid measures consist of keeping the animal warm and out of draughts. If water is vomited almost as soon as drunk, try offering barley-water instead. The amount of protein in the diet should be reduced. Your veterinary surgeon may suggest use of a proprietary canned food formulated specially for dogs with nephritis. Veterinary treatment may include the use of antibiotics.

In the bitch, nephritis may be a sequel to infection spreading from vagina to bladder, and along the ureters to the kidneys.

A chronic form of nephritis may develop insidiously or follow repeated attacks of the acute form. The dog becomes thin, vaguely unwell, vomits now and then, may appear stiff. An unpleasant odour from the mouth may be associated with ulcers there. There may be dropsy.

Many elderly or old dogs are able to cope with chronic nephritis; but in order to enable waste products to be got rid of from a diminishing area of functioning kidney, they may need to drink more than they used to do. This may result in the dog being unable to avoid passing some urine during the night, so allowance must be made for any incontinence.

A small proportion of dogs with chronic nephritis suffer a sudden flare-up of illness and may die from **uraemia** – a condition in which poisonous waste products which should have been excreted in the urine are retained in the bloodstream. Symptoms may include vomiting of coffee-coloured material, a brownish tongue with an ulcerated tip, sometimes diarrhoea, and later convulsions.

Hydronephrosis is a condition in which the capsule of the kidney, or even the kidney itself, becomes distended with urine. It may result from an obstruction of the ureter by a stone, tumour, or an infection. If the obstruction, sometimes due to a mere kink in the ureter, cannot be corrected, the kidney may have to be removed, in which event the other kidney will gradually enlarge to cope with the additional work.

An inoperable tumour is another reason for nephrectomy, as the operation for removal of a kidney is called.

Case history. A Collie, only two years old, had been unwell for two days, her owner reported. Palpation of the abdomen revealed the presence of a hard mass, the size of an orange. The following day an exploratory laparotomy was carried out, when a tumour was found adherent to, and partly enclosing, the left kidney. It was impossible to separate tumour from kidney, and this was accordingly removed. The bitch made an excellent recovery.[1]

In some parts of Asia, Europe, and the U.S.A., dogs may become infested with a kidney worm, *Dioctophyma renale*, as a result of eating infested raw fish. This worm, also known as *Eustrongylus gigas*, is indeed a giant, attaining a length of up to 1 metre and having a thickness of up to 1 cm. It gradually destroys the kidney tissue, leaving that organ as little more than a shell containing purulent fluid. A survey of 500 dogs in Iran showed that $1\frac{1}{2}$ per cent were infested.

The Ureter and Bladder

CYSTITIS

Inflammation of the urinary bladder is a common condition, and usually the result of infection. Cystitis may be mild, and clear up without any treatment, or it may need professional help if the following symptoms are

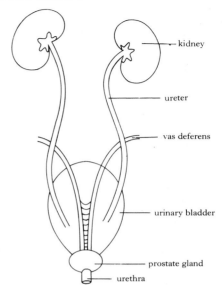

kidney

ureter

vas deferens

urinary bladder

prostate gland

urethra

The male urinary
system

at all severe. The frequent passing of small quantities of urine may be noticed, sometimes accompanied by straining. A drop or two of blood, or blood-tinged urine is a further indication. Bitches may lick the vulva more than usual, and there may be a discharge.

The inflammation may result in the most punctilious of house-trained animals leaving small quantities of urine on the floor during the night, and so it is a good plan to put down sheets of old newspaper.

Cystitis may occur during the course of brucellosis. (See chapter 20.)

Inflammation of the bladder may also be caused by the presence of urinary calculi – 'stones' – or by sand-like material formed in the same way. A blockage of the urethra may result, often just behind the *Os penis*. The animal will strain, pass only a few drops of urine or blood, and stand with legs wide apart.

Case history 1. At about ten o'clock one night, a $3\frac{1}{2}$-months-old puppy began to show signs of discomfort, and before long was yelping periodically and straining to pass urine. By the following morning the animal was in a distressed condition, and veterinary advice was sought. A sedative was given intravenously, after which it was easier to palpate the distended bladder through the abdominal wall. A catheter was passed, and thick, darkish urine drawn off. A subsequent X-ray examination revealed one large stone and several smaller ones. A laparotomy was carried out, the bladder incised, and the stones removed. By the time the stitches were taken out a few days later, the puppy had recovered, and the trouble (unusual in so young an animal) did not recur.[2]

Sometimes it is necessary to open the urethra to remove an obstruction there.

Case history 2. A sheepdog was known to have been shot at, and six weeks later was seen to be in pain. On veterinary examination, the urinary bladder was found to be distended. A foreign body could be detected in the urethra just behind the *Os penis*, and proved to be a 0.22 air rifle pellet. From previous symptoms and history of the case, it seemed that the pellet had passed through the prostate gland before becoming lodged in the bladder and then passing out into the urethra. The patient made an uneventful recovery.[3]

Occasionally the bladder becomes trapped in a perineal hernia and becomes distended, with symptoms as already described; in the bitch this may happen with an inguinal hernia.

Pain or difficulty in passing urine, or inability to pass any at all, is always an emergency. To delay obtaining professional help may mean much pain for the animal, and even cost its life. Apart from pain and shock caused by over-distension of the bladder, there is the danger of its rupture. This can result, too, from falling from a height or being run over by a car.

The urinary system, like any other, is subject to congenital abnormalities. For example, in the U.S.A. a very few Beagles are born having only one kidney. An extremely rare defect was diagnosed in an incontinent bitch – she was found to have one ureter by-passing the bladder and opening directly into the vagina, as described below.

Case history 3. The owners of a 5-year-old Golden Retriever bitch revealed to their veterinary surgeon that for the past five years they had been patiently mopping up after her wherever she had been lying. She had been incontinent ever since they had acquired her as a puppy. This fact had not been mentioned previously, on the several occasions when she had been treated for an eczema-like 'scalding' of the skin around the vulva. Their veterinary surgeon suggested that this might possibly be a case of an ectopic ureter, and when the bitch was X-rayed this tentative diagnosis was confirmed. A laparotomy was performed, and the right ureter (the one by-passing the bladder) was dissected free at one point, severed and ligated; its other cut end was then transplanted into the wall of the bladder. This involved bringing the mucous membrane lining the ureter into apposition with that lining the bladder, and making a secure joint – highly skilful surgery, in fact.[4]

REFERENCES
1 Douch, J. M. *Vet. Record* 98 (1976), 89
2 Hogger, D. G. *Vet. Record* 77 (1965), 405
3 Evans, W. E. S. *et al. Vet. Record* 94 (1974), 525
4 Holt, P. E. *Vet. Record* 98 (1976), 299

17 Muscles, Joints and Bones

The man on the telephone said, in a surprised and aggrieved tone: 'Leo has just bitten me. He's been staying in one position, won't move, all stiff and peculiar-looking . . . and trembling. I don't know whether he's broken a bone, or what. It was as I went to touch him, to feel where the pain might be, that he snapped. Got his teeth right into a couple of my fingers.'

This was in May – rather late, you might think, for acute **muscular rheumatism**, but that was what it proved to be. The description on the telephone was almost enough in itself, even before the caller added that the Poodle had screamed earlier when his wife went within touching distance; although of course it would be wrong to assume that such symptoms invariably indicate acute rheumatism. A differential diagnosis is called for, and that cannot be made on the strength of a telephone conversation.

This condition always strikes me as one of the more dramatic canine ills. After all, screaming and biting the owner are unusual. Certainly, it is something which the owner never forgets. Fortunately the pain can be relieved, and the animal is usually back to normal within a few days.

First-aid. Measures include switching on a bowl-fire or other electric heater and positioning it near the dog, which will probably move so that the painful group of muscles receive the warmth. One 5-grain aspirin tablet (half a tablet for a very small dog) can be given, powdered and offered in chocolate so as to disguise the taste, rather than as a dose to be forced upon the dog if such an attempt is even permitted.

Rheumatism is, of course, a somewhat vague and unscientific term, but a convenient one, indicating diseases of muscles, tendons, joints, bones, or nerves, resulting in pain or disability. It is thought probable that the cause is, in some instances at least, the absorption of toxins produced by bacteria in the intestine, and that these toxins cause a local inflammation in some area of the body which is overworked, chilled, or affected adversely in some other way.

Especially in Alsatians, overdosage of vitamin D, given by the owner with the intention of preventing rickets, may lead to deposits of calcium salts within and between muscles.

Muscles

MYOSITIS
Inflammation of muscles may result also from injuries such as kicks, blows,

a fall, or a strain – in which over-stretching or tearing of muscle fibres occurs, causing pain and swelling. There may even be partial or complete rupture of a muscle, but this is rare. Bleeding into or from muscle tissue may cause a haematoma (a swelling containing blood clot).

Muscle pain may result from the formation of cysts by *Trichinella* worm larvae, but the condition is virtually impossible to diagnose, and is not of great importance. Eating raw pork or infested rats is how dogs and other carnivores acquire this muscle trouble, which is known as trichinosis and also occurs in man.

Disorders of jaw muscles are described in chapter 5.

ATROPHY

Wasting, or atrophy, of muscles occurs when there is a nerve injury, failure of blood supply, or disuse of a part, as well as in cases of starvation. One example of atrophy of muscles following a nerve injury is suprascapular paralysis, when two distinct hollows appear on either side of the spine of the scapula (shoulder blade).

CRAMP

This, as we all know from personal experience, is a painful involuntary contraction of a muscle. Cramp is especially noteworthy in the racing greyhound, which will slow down during a race and drag both hind legs or, in severe cases, may collapse and writhe on the ground. In other instances, the animal's gait and appearance seem 'wooden'. The muscles of the hind-quarters are hard to the touch. Sometimes the tongue and mucous membrane lining the mouth are bluish. This symptom, technically known as cyanosis, can result from an overworked heart, and is seen in animals that have been hunted. Possible causes, therefore, include fatigue, defective heart action, or perhaps some lack of training expertise. A dietary deficiency or bacterial toxins are suggested as other possible causes.

'Scottie Cramp' is a condition seen in the one breed of dog. It occurs for the first time at an age of between four and eight months, as a rule, and usually follows exercise; though sometimes excitement without exertion will bring it on. In mild cases the dog may be seen to be in difficulties when negotiating steps. In severe cases the symptoms resemble those in the racing greyhound. Mild attacks usually become worse, reaching a maximum severity when the Terrier is between 12 and 15 months old. By the age of two years or so, 'Scottie cramp' is usually outgrown. It would seem that breeders might be able to eliminate the susceptibility to this cramp. Professional treatment can alleviate the symptoms.

MYASTHENIA GRAVIS

This is a rare disease in the dog but, owing to its considerable importance in human beings, it is being studied at the Wellcome Laboratory for

Comparative Neurology, at the School of Veterinary Medicine, Cambridge University. The cause of this disease is believed to be a difficulty in the transmission of nerve impulses to the affected muscles, and it results in fatigue. In a paper given at a British Veterinary Association congress, Dr A. C. Palmer and Dr J. Baker described cases in gundogs, a Collie, a Jack Russell, Alsatians and a Dalmatian.

The symptoms which dog-owners notice are muscular weakness after exercise, and the taking of shorter steps. There may be difficulty in closing the jaws, holding up the head, and in swallowing.

Rest may lead to a complete disappearance of the symptoms for the time being. Drug treatment can effect dramatic improvement, but this is often only temporary, unfortunately.

Case history. Dr R. P. Johnson recorded a case of the disease in a litter of Springer Spaniels in which muscular weakness was shown when the puppies were 6 weeks old. They could walk normally only for short distances, but then shortened their stride and attempted to hop. One of them was still alive 16 months later, but needed twice-daily dosing to retain normality of gait.[1]

SEVERED TENDONS

Accidents occasionally result in the severing of one or more tendons. For example, a deep cut – caused by a piece of glass – in the pads of the paw may sever flexor tendons, so that the pads are raised off the ground. Surgical repair is feasible in many instances.

Joints

ARTHRITIS

Inflammation of a joint may involve any of its structures or tissues – the synovial membrane which lines the joint cavity and secretes a lubricating fluid; the cartilages; ligaments; and the ends of the bones forming the joint.

Arthritis may result from external violence, such as being struck a violent blow. A sharp-pointed object may penetrate into the joint cavity, causing the condition known as 'open joint'. The wound may be very small, even trivial-looking, but its effects can be very serious owing to the entry of bacteria which often complicate matters. Fortunately, antibiotics can help here. Pain, local swelling, a sticky discharge, shivering, loss of appetite, and fever are among the symptoms of 'open joint'. In a few cases septicaemia occurs and proves fatal.

An intact joint may also become infected during the course of an illness such as brucellosis or tuberculosis.

Besides inflammation, there are degenerative changes which can affect the mobility and efficiency of a joint. These occur in **rheumatoid arthritis**.

This may occur at any age, usually not before a dog is two years old. The symptoms may be vague at first, the animal appearing depressed, often with a poor appetite and some degree of fever, but with no lameness. This appears later, sometimes involving several joints simultaneously, sometimes affecting one limb and then shifting to another. There may be crepitus, a grating sound, when the limb is moved.

Diagnosis of rheumatoid arthritis, or its confirmation, depends on radiography and, as in human medicine, there are various laboratory tests.

Readers may have friends or relatives who had intractable arthritis of a hip-joint with pain and disability which were overcome by major surgery involving removal of the top of the femur and replacement of the ball part of the ball-and-socket joint by a plastic prosthesis. Such operations for the relief of painful arthritis have also been performed by veterinary surgeons.

In the dog, amputation of the head of the femur alone is often sufficient, most cases compensating well.

Hip Dysplasia

This is one of those convenient group names covering a number of abnormal conditions of the acetabulum (the cup-shaped depression on the pelvis) and head of the femur. A scheme drawn up by the British Veterinary Association (B.V.A.) and the Kennel Club in 1965, in an attempt to reduce the incidence of these defects, has shown that the number of dogs with less than perfect hips is much greater than had been realised. Indeed a 1977 B.V.A. report pointed out that in some breeds the majority of hip radiographs will not reach the scheme's accepted standard, and the general view is that breed societies should do more in the way of control.

Hip dysplasia includes **subluxation**, in which the head of the femur is no longer firmly seated within the acetabulum. Deformity of the former may then gradually develop. Symptoms include a reluctance to rise from a sitting position, and a 'sawing' gait, observed when the puppy (most often an Alsatian, sometimes a Golden Retriever or Boxer) is four or five months old.

Congenital dislocation in which the acetabulum is too shallow to retain the head of the femur. A false joint may form in time.

Osteochondritis is inflammation of bone and cartilage; and, in the context of hip dysplasia, this term has been used for a condition in which muscular wasting and lameness occur in one limb.

Osteochondrosis is similar, but perhaps a more accurate name for cases where there is no inflammation, but rather necrosis (local death) of bone cells and separation of splinters or flaps of joint cartilage. There is a hereditary basis for this, too, in the dog.

Under the B.V.A./K.C. scheme mentioned above, an expert veterinary panel assess the radiographs of the dog's hips, reporting back to the veterinary surgeon who submitted the radiographs to them; he in turn passes on the verdict to his client.

It can be argued that what the X-rays reveal is the result of both heredity and environment, and the question is: How much does each account for? However, from a practical point of view it was suggested that a dog with radiographically normal hips at the age of one or two years could be certified as such, and would be likely to remain normal.

DISLOCATIONS

A dislocation, or luxation, may be defined as displacement of a bone from its normal position in relation to a joint, producing a deformity; usually it is the result of violence, which often gives rise to bruising of the soft tissues around the joint. Intense pain may be caused if the limb is moved. Crepitus, the grating sound associated with fractures, is not present.

The most common dislocation in the canine species is undoubtedly that of the patella (knee-cap) since this – or a tendency to it – is an inherited condition in over twenty breeds. Such a patella has an abnormal freedom of movement, and can be readily slipped into and out of its normal position in many cases. Patellar dislocation may also, of course, be unconnected with any hereditary influence but occur, like any other, as a result of violence. Stifle-joint deformity is also sometimes due to congenital misalignment of the trochlea of the femur and the crest of the tibia.

Other dislocations commonly seen in the dog are those of the shoulder, hip-joint, and jaw. The last two may occur together with fractures.

RUPTURED LIGAMENTS

Among the many causes of lameness in the dog is rupture of one or both of the cruciate ligaments. These are arranged like the letter X, preventing over-extension of the stifle joint. The front ligament prevents forward movement of the tibia in relation to the femur. This accident is not uncommon in all breeds and sizes of dogs, but especially in gundogs, sheepdogs and police dogs. There may be discomfort rather than pain after the accident, and the lameness usually disappears after several weeks of rest.

Bones

RICKETS

Of all bone diseases rickets is probably the most widely known. In Britain it is no longer so common in dogs, perhaps for that very reason. It is essentially a disorder of puppies, caused by a deficiency of either vitamin D or of phosphorus, or both. An absence of sunlight is a contributory factor, and animals kept in dark buildings are prone to it, especially if inadequately fed. Swellings are visible at the ends of long bones, and where the ribs join

The skeleton of the dog

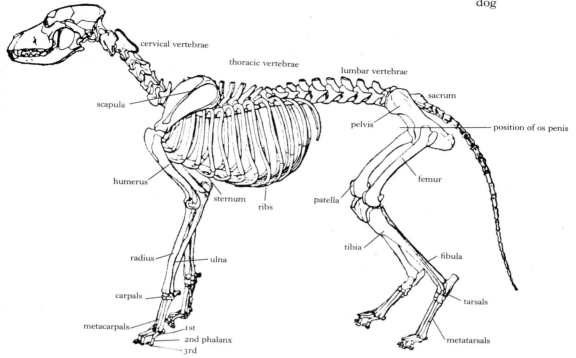

cervical vertebrae

thoracic vertebrae

lumbar vertebrae

sacrum

scapula

pelvis

position of os penis

humerus

femur

sternum

patella

ribs

radius

ulna

tibia

fibula

carpals

metacarpals

1st

2nd phalanx

3rd

tarsals

metatarsals

the sternum. There is also a tendency for the long bones to bend outwards, giving the animal a bow-legged appearance.

Best-quality cod-liver oil, or halibut-liver oil, is effective in both prevention and treatment. Avoid the continuous administration of yeast and medicinal liquid paraffin.

Rickets in the adult animal is known as **osteomalacia**. This is seen in the pregnant bitch, for example. The bones become softened owing to absorption of minerals. Deformity may result, and occasionally a fracture. Loss of mineral salts, resulting in bone fragility, is known as **osteoporosis**.

Canine Juvenile Osteodystrophy

This is known also by other names, such as nutritional secondary parathyroidism. It is the result of a calcium deficiency, which stimulates the release of parathyroid hormone, leading to resorption of bone. It is a preventable disease, since it is caused by feeding a muscle-meat diet (see chapter 17) containing little calcium but proportionately too much phosphorus. Symptoms include pain; and the animal may cry out in anticipation of being forced to move. Short, hesitant steps may be taken, and splaying of the toes is sometimes seen. Swelling at the elbow or carpus is another symptom.

INFLAMMATION OF BONE

Acute inflammation of a bone is known as **osteitis**, and that of its covering membrane, the periosteum, as **periostitis**. **Osteomyelitis** is the name for inflammation inside the marrow cavity of a bone. External violence usually leads to the first two conditions; bacterial infection to the last one. Pain and lameness are symptoms. A chronic infection sometimes occurs, with eventual discharge of pus through the surface of the skin. The wound will not heal if a small portion of dead bone remains, so this has to be removed surgically.

REFERENCE
1 Johnson, R. P. *et al. J. Small Anim. Pract.* 16 (1975), 641

18 The Paralysed Dog

In its widest sense, paralysis may mean loss of nerve control over any of the bodily functions, loss of feeling, and loss of senses, but for the purposes of this chapter it is intended to refer mainly to loss of muscular power as a result of injury to a nerve or to some part of the central nervous system (brain and spinal cord).

Paralysis may be temporary or permanent. When muscular power is merely weakened, without being lost altogether, the term **paresis** is used.

The causes of paralysis are many and include a brain haemorrhage, thrombosis, pressure on a nerve by a tumour, pressure on the spinal cord caused by protrusion of an intervertebral disc, some form of violence damaging a nerve, poisoning, and certain infections.

A few examples of paralysis are given below; it would be impracticable to list and describe every type of paralysis which might befall a dog.

Radial paralysis is not uncommon in the dog; and most cases result from fracture of the first rib – the broken ends of the bone lacerating or pressing upon the radial nerve. (Inflammation affecting this nerve or a tumour pressing upon it could similarly cause radial paralysis.) The effect is that the forelimb is held in the position assumed at the beginning of a stride, but the toe cannot be brought forward, since nerve impulses are no longer getting through to the muscles which extend the elbow, carpus and foot. The outlook in radial paralysis is good, though recovery will take months.

Injury to the brachial plexus usually results in complete paralysis of the forelimb – **brachial paralysis** – and recovery from it is so rare that amputation is usually advised. This course is, however, repugnant to most dog-owners. The following case suggests an alternative.

Case history. A crossbred Collie had been involved in an accident some months previously, and when seen by a veterinary surgeon the muscles of the paralysed leg showed considerable atrophy (wasting), and the upper surface of the paw was excoriated as a result of being dragged along the ground. As the owners did not favour amputation, an operation was devised to bring the radius close to the humerus, with the elbow permanently bent. After surgery, the paw was kept off the ground and healed rapidly, and the dog was enabled to remain active, getting around on three legs. The dog's owners were happy too, especially since the degree of deformity was far less than amputation would have involved.[1]

Another dog with brachial paralysis solved its problem in its own way – by taking its paw in its mouth and then hopping. There was no damage to the skin of the paw – so amputation was not advised.[2]

Suprascapular paralysis follows injury to the nerve of that name, and the muscles which act as ligaments to the shoulder-joint are affected so that the shoulder slips outwards each time the foot is placed upon the ground. The dog has difficulty in bringing the limb forward.

PARAPLEGIA

Paralysis of both hind legs is known as paraplegia, and its principal causes are given below.

Fracture of the spine may be caused by a fall from a height, but more commonly it results from a car accident. Blows and kicks are other possible causes. There is complete loss of use in the hind limbs, together with incontinence as a rule. Euthanasia is the only course, but first a diagnosis is important, as some cases of paraplegia from other causes recover in time.

First-aid. Where a fracture of the spine is suspected, gently slide or pull the dog on to a rug or coat, rather than lifting him, and carry him on the rug to the car for transport to a veterinary surgery.

Sometimes the spine is not fractured but injury to the spinal cord results in paraplegia. This may follow a day or two *after* the accident.

Case history 1. A Dachshund fell out of an upstairs window, injuring but not fracturing his spine. Paraplegia followed, and remained permanent. However, the dog was able to get about by means of a little trolley improvised to take his hind legs.

Another cause of paraplegia is **intervertebral disc protrusion**. Between each vertebra of the spine there is a disc which has a soft pulpy centre and a fibrous or gristly outer ring. The disc acts as a shock-absorber between the vertebrae and also supports the spinal cord at the gaps between the bones. Partial or complete rupture of the disc may occur, thereby exerting pressure on the spinal cord, as explained in the diagrams.

This type of spinal injury is most common in Dachshunds, Pekingese, Spaniels, and Sealyhams.

In some cases there is some form of violence to account for the injury; in other instances a sudden muscular effort, e.g. in jumping to catch a ball. However it is believed that a gradual wear and tear of the disc with age, and perhaps the extra strain on the spine of short-legged breeds, is the underlying cause in many instances.

Symptoms consist of pain and weakness (paresis) or paralysis (paraplegia). Sometimes, as already implied, they follow shortly after a jump, slip or fall which the owner may have seen; or a dog apparently normal at night may be found in the morning with both legs paralysed.

Natural recovery may take place within a fortnight, but if paraplegia

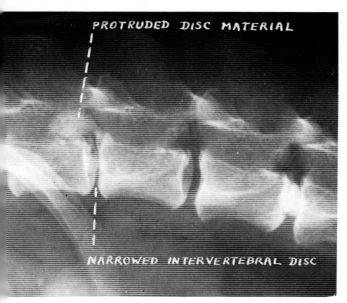

PROTRUDED DISC MATERIAL

NARROWED INTERVERTEBRAL DISC

persists the outlook becomes progressively less hopeful (though a complete recovery after 12 months is not unknown).

Occasionally a similar type of injury involves the neck vertebrae. Owing to the resultant pain, the dog avoids turning his head, which is kept pointing straight to the front.

A fenestration operation is occasionally performed to relieve severe pain (see diagram) but is not often recommended for relief of paralysis.

Case history 2. A 6-year-old dog jumped to greet his owner and immediately cried out with pain; then collapsed. The animal was paralysed in both hind legs and gave signs of intense pain when touched or moved. Five days after the accident, a fenestration operation was performed. It was apparent immediately after recovery from the anaesthetic that the pain was much reduced. However, paralysis remained and it was not until nearly eight months later that the dog could walk again without difficulty.[3]

Home nursing in such cases involves a great deal of patience, time, coping with weeks of incontinence, stiffish veterinary fees, and strength of mind on the part of the owner. One should add that it is never possible to forecast soon after the accident what the outcome will be. Some owners decide to have the dog put down immediately, or after a week or two; others persevere for longer. Even those who wait months may be disappointed. In other cases, such as the one above, perseverance is not in vain.

Thrombosis of the femoral arteries is a relatively rare cause of paraplegia. The muscles and nerves are deprived of their blood supply and paralysis may ensue quite suddenly. For example, a dog may be playing normally one minute, and the next minute may give a yelp, collapse, and be unable to rise. The complete absence of pulse in the femoral arteries assists in diagnosis. Euthanasia is usually the only course of action to take.

Above left: Intervertebral disc protrusion. Compare the apparent space between the central two vertebrae, and between those and the outer two
Above right: A Dachshund suffering from paraplegia following intervertebral disc protrusion

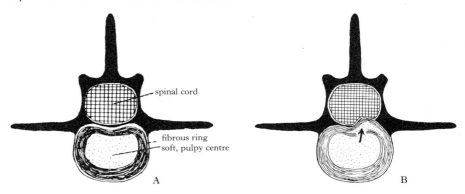

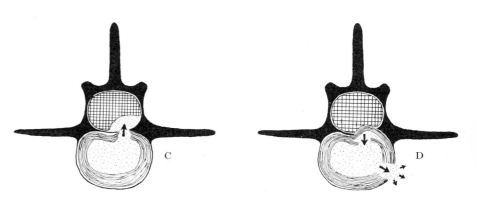

Rupture of the intervertebral disc, and fenestration. (A) The normal section. (B) Partial rupture. (C) Complete rupture. (D) Pressure on the spinal cord is relieved after the operation of fenestration

Paraplegia may be seen in the later stages of canine distemper and rabies. A third infection which may result in paralysis is botulism.

Case history 3. An outbreak of paralysis occurred in a pack of foxhounds, and a bitch was found prostrate one night, being attacked by others. The next day three more hounds were found unable to stand, though in response to calls they were able to lift their heads and tails. Later three more hounds showed stiffness when walking, and this symptom was observed in 10 others. Digestive upsets and difficulty in swallowing were other symptoms. There were two deaths. *Clostridium botulinum* type C was shown to be a bacterial contaminant of some of the meat left over from feeding hounds, and botulinal toxin was detected in the blood of one hound.[4]

Chronic ossifying pachymeningitis is a slowly developing condition in which bone tissue is laid down in the posterior part of the vertebral column, leading to difficulty in hind-limb control, and usually, ultimate paraplegia.

Poisoning as a cause of paralysis recalls to mind hemlock, from which Socrates died in 399 B.C., and curare, but neither of these poisons is likely to affect the dog. Partial paralysis may be caused, however, by lead and metaldehyde.

QUADRIPLEGIA

Quadriplegia, i.e. paralysis in all four legs, was a feature of the outbreak of botulism described above, and it also results (though not in Britain or the European mainland) from tick paralysis. This is seen both in the U.S.A. and in the tropics.

Case history 1. A dog began to show weakness of the hind legs, and within 48 hours the forelegs had become affected too. Seen by Dr Cheryl Chrisman at the veterinary hospital of Ohio State University five days later, the dog seemed alert and friendly, but unable to move legs or tail. Although more than one search of the dog's matted coat had already been made, an additional one was now made, and this time an engorged female tick (*Dermacentor variabilis*) was found on the neck. (The female tick produces a toxin which prevents nerve impulses from reaching muscle fibres.) Within 24 hours of removal of this single tick, the dog could move all four limbs and sit up. Within 48 hours it could stand and walk a little shakily, and by the end of the week it had recovered and was sent home.[5]

Although it has not yet been established exactly how the effect is produced, a bite from a racoon may also cause paralysis of all four legs. Dr Chrisman referred to a very sophisticated technique, electromyography, used to differentiate racoon bite paralysis from tick bite paralysis.

Case history 2. A 4-year-old male Coonhound became paralysed in all four legs, though remaining bright, alert, and 'responsive to affection'. Although several *Dermacentor* ticks were found and removed, the electromyography results indicated that this was probably not a case of tick paralysis, but the result of past contact with racoons. The dog died a few days later.[6]

REFERENCES
1 Peters, I. T. *Vet. Record* 96 (1975), 412
2 Hutton-Wilson, T. *Vet. Record* 96 (1975), 574
3 Tandy, J. *Vet. Record* 96 (1975), 63
4 Darke, P. G. *et al. Vet. Record* 99 (1976), 98
5,6 Chrisman, C. L. *J. Am. Anim. Hosp. Assoc.* 11 (1975), 455

19 Fits and Hysteria

Very alarming to the dog's owner, fits are convulsive seizures accompanied by a period of unconsciousness. They may occur when the dog is lying down; otherwise the animal falls to the ground, loses consciousness for a matter of seconds or minutes, and has convulsive movements of the limbs. There is first a spasm of voluntary muscle, and then 'galloping' movements of the legs. Salivation, or 'frothing at the mouth', is commonly seen. Afterwards the dog may get up almost immediately, or lie exhausted for a while. In some instances full consciousness is quickly restored, and the animal behaves normally; sometimes the dog may wander round, bumping into furniture, before regaining normality. After a fit a dog usually has a ravenous appetite.

In a puppy, fits may result from teething or the effects of intestinal worms. These occasionally cause fits in adult dogs, too. Other causes include disease of the ear and, even in puppies, a brain tumour. Brain damage following an accident may lead to fits; for example, in a dog struck by a car.

Convulsions may be associated with a viral disease, such as canine distemper, canine viral hepatitis, or rabies, when encephalitis or meningitis is present.

Encephalitis (inflammation of the brain) and **meningitis** (inflammation of the membranes covering the brain and spinal cord) may also have a bacterial origin, e.g. from a focus of infection elsewhere in the body, or as the result of a brain abscess following penetration of an object lodged in the dog's mouth. Erratic movements, falling over, bumping into objects, and turning in circles are other symptoms – which may precede convulsions.

A tumour of the pancreas, or too low a level of sugar in the blood – a condition known as **hypoglycaemia** – may result in a fit, especially, Dr A. C. Palmer has stated, in toy breeds and sporting dogs.[1] A gundog may have a fit after many hours' work in the field on an empty stomach.

Many **poisons** give rise to symptoms which include convulsions; for example, lead, strychnine, ethylene glycol (antifreeze), metaldehyde or a similar compound used to kill garden slugs, and insecticides such as BHC and DDT.

Epilepsy is characterised by fits. This is a chronic nervous disorder arising from brain damage. What is often called primary epilepsy is usually an inherited condition. In a series of 260 cases of suspected lesions of the central nervous system investigated by Dr Phyllis Croft, 167 were shown by electro-encephalogram to be epilepsy.[2]

A dog with epilepsy may not have his first fit until he is between one and three years old. It is not a condition which he can be expected to outgrow. However, epilepsy and a working dog's usefulness are not necessarily incompatible, as the fits may all occur when the dog is at home resting.

So-called secondary epilepsy may be the result of a head injury, and occurs whenever scar tissue is formed in the brain. Without recourse to the specialist's technique mentioned above, it is virtually impossible to differentiate 'epileptiform' convulsions from those of true epilepsy. The veterinary surgeon in general practice can, however, eliminate some of the causes of fits mentioned above when making his diagnosis. Where necessary, a drug can be used to ameliorate the severity of attacks, or even to suppress the fits altogether; drugs are not, however, the complete answer to fits, and at best should be used as little as practicable. There is often so much variation between individual dogs that the dose has to be adjusted; too large a dose may give rise to undesirable side-effects.

Is there ever a connection between fits in the dog and television? It is known that flickering lights can induce a fit in human epileptics, and possibly a badly adjusted television set might have a similar effect in dogs. A veterinary surgeon writing in 1971 suggested a possible connection and referred to fits in dogs whose only refuge in an overcrowded room was under the television set. It has also been suggested that some of the remote control units emit a subsonic note which may cause a dog to have a fit. However, proof is lacking and these are matters of speculation.

HYSTERIA

In the 1930s, canine hysteria was a common reason for an emergency visit to a client's house. One usually arrived to find the owners of the hysterical dog in a state of anxiety, if not of desperation. (It is certainly a nerve-racking experience to have a dog incessantly uttering shrill barks or yelps, rushing around the room in a frenzy, and then falling to the ground in a fit. The sudden change from a peaceful home to a temporary canine madhouse is traumatic.)

Hysteria is, in fact, a distressing condition in which a dog suddenly appears bereft of his reason. The animal has a fixed stare, races about, and his high-pitched barking or yelping is loud enough to disturb and then infuriate neighbours. Recovering consciousness, the dog appears somewhat dazed and exhausted.

Attacks of hysteria may last for a few minutes, or very much longer, and one attack may follow another after a brief interval. If one dog in kennels is hysterical, the other inmates are likely to be affected too.

Hysteria was formerly often encountered in greyhound and gundog kennels, but is now almost a thing of the past. Several theories were advanced to account for hysteria, and indeed there may be several causes. One theory concerned the agene process of bleaching flour with nitrogen trichloride; since that process was abandoned hysteria has ceased to be a common ailment in dogs in Britain.

Hysteria in a milder form may occur in a nervous dog subjected to stress. Always keep such an animal away from the storm-centre of a children's party. Perhaps already upset by the re-arrangement of furniture which such an occasion may entail, and by the presence of strangers, it may take no more than the pulling of crackers to provoke hysteria. Fireworks may have the same effect – the 5th of November is a bad day for nervous dogs in Britain. Some may need a tranquilliser well before dark.

Hysteria may be associated with lead poisoning. At one university veterinary hospital in the U.S.A. between 1963 and 1975, hysteria was a symptom in 11 out of 27 dogs suffering from this form of poisoning. Most of these dogs were under one year old, and had eaten paint scrapings when a room was being re-decorated.[3]

NARCOLEPSY

This is a very rare condition in the dog, and might be said to be the converse of hysteria. (In man, the condition is characterised by a tendency to fall asleep at any time, anywhere, even when the person is not tired; the causes are regarded as a brain infection, a brain tumour, or a head injury.) American veterinarians suggest that in the dog, narcolepsy may be partly genetic in origin; this, however, was apparently ruled out as a likely cause in the following case – the first to be recorded in the U.K.

Case history. A 3-year-old Corgi sometimes collapsed when taken for his first walk of the day, or offered food. Often, yawning, and a vacant expression, would precede a sudden drop from a standing position to a sitting one; or else the dog would fall on to his side or on to his brisket. At all other times he was active and mentally alert. There was no excitement, salivation, or convulsions. He was easily aroused and would then immediately get to his feet, though sometimes falling again. Following drug treatment over a period of six months, the frequency and depth of the attacks diminished, but they were not prevented from occurring.

The diagnosis of narcolepsy was made in this case after exhaustive tests at the department of veterinary medicine, University of Bristol. Electro-encephalograms recorded during periods of collapse revealed 'abrupt rather than progressive changes from normal to the very slow [brain] activity typical of deep sleep.'[4]

As a footnote to this case, it is interesting that the Corgi had, some nine months previously, shown signs of being unable to see objects at close range – a disability from which he had soon recovered. One cannot help wondering whether a head injury, or a virus infection, could have accounted for both the narcolepsy and the temporarily impaired vision.

REFERENCES
1 Palmer, A. C. *Vet. Record* 90 (1972), 167
2 Croft, Phyllis *Vet. Record* 77 (1965), 438
3 Kowalczyk, D. F. *J. Am. Vet. Med. Assoc.* 168 (1976), 428
4 Darke, P. G. and Jessen, V. *Vet. Record* 101 (1977), 117

20 Less-Common Infections

TETANUS

Tetanus appears to be much less common in the dog than it is in man or in the horse. Contamination of a wound, especially a deep puncture, with soil or manure is the usual preliminary to this illness. The bacterium which causes tetanus, *Clostridium tetani*, is found both in the gut of a healthy animal and in soil (especially that which has received heavy dressings of manure). A farm dog might consequently be expected to be at greater risk than a town dog owned by a non-gardener, though the soil of public parks is no doubt an abundant source.

The dog's owner may not be aware of the wound, or may disregard it since there will have been little bleeding; often the wound has healed by the time that the dog has become ill. It is thought that, in rare instances, the infection may also occur following not an *external* injury, but an *internal* one.

Multiplying in the tissues, the organism produces an extremely potent toxin which affects nerves so that they transmit impulses which result in involuntary contraction of muscles.

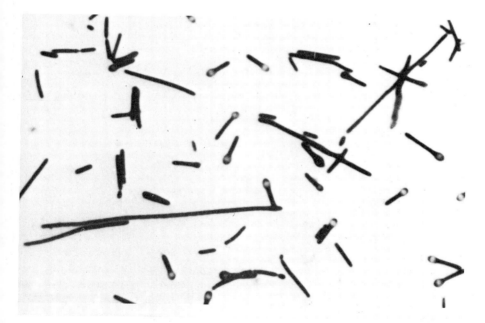

Clostridium tetani, the bacterium which causes tetanus ($\times 3,250$)

The early symptoms of tetanus are not alarming. The dog appears dull, some stiffness develops in the limbs, eating becomes difficult, and there *may* be a squint. Later there may be hyperaesthesia – an exaggerated reaction to noise such as the banging of a door, or to bright light, or to a touch.

In the later stages of the illness the symptoms may become very alarming indeed. Convulsions may occur at the slightest stimulus of the kind mentioned above. The dog may stand with the tail held rigid or quivering, and the hind legs extended backwards. A sardonic grin may appear on the unfortunate animal's face. A sudden spasm may cause the whole body to arch like a bow.

Case history. A farm dog went lame. His owner sought veterinary advice a fortnight later as there was 'something peculiar about the animal's eyes and mouth', and food had been rarely touched during the preceding three days.

Note that the owner did not say anything about clamped jaws, the symptom which gave tetanus its colloquial name of 'lockjaw'. Indeed, this symptom may not be in evidence, at any rate in the earlier stages. All that was noticed was stiffness, a failure to eat much, and a different look about the dog's face.[1]

Tetanus is always a very serious disease. Treatment consists in giving antiserum or anti-toxin, and a drug which will moderate the severity of the muscular contractions. An antibiotic may be given too, together with vitamin supplements. Injections of glucose saline will probably be needed to maintain the dog's strength at a time when he is unable to take food by mouth.

The chances of recovery should be discussed with your own veterinary surgeon. Much will obviously depend upon how far the infection and intoxication have advanced, the age of the dog, etc. The farm dog mentioned above made a complete recovery, though there was a period when he became worse before he improved. Devoted home nursing, with frequent visits by the veterinary surgeon, over a period of a fortnight or so will probably be necessary; or the patient may be admitted to a veterinary hospital and treated there.

TUBERCULOSIS

This is a contagious disease caused by *Mycobacterium tuberculosis* (bovine, human, or avian strains) and is characterised by the formation of nodules or tubercles in any of the organs or tissues of the body, including the skin.

A dog may become infected in one of several ways, for example, from a cat, or another dog, or a person in the same household, or as the result of being given raw or insufficiently cooked meat originating from a tubercular carcase, or, possibly, from catching and eating some small animal which had the disease. Many years ago, when T.B. was still rife in our dairy herds, milk was a common source of infection unless pasteurised, but now that the disease has been virtually eradicated from British dairy cattle, that risk is small – indeed non-existent if only pasteurised milk is given to the dog.

The disease is typically a chronic one, slowly progressive, and giving rise to abscesses in the liver, or to infection of bones or joints (resulting in arthritis), or to lesions in the lungs or in the lymph nodes. It sometimes happens that the infection remains circumscribed and dormant, until stress of some kind occurs, when it becomes progressive. Occasionally an established infection may become acute, producing the miliary form of tuberculosis, so called because, after invasion of the bloodstream, multiple small abscesses, each the size of a millet-seed, are formed in any or almost all the organs.

The symptoms of chronic tuberculosis are at first somewhat vague; the owner may find the dog's appetite capricious, and notice a slight loss of bodily condition and lack of energy. Like the appetite, body temperature varies; on some days it may be normal or only slightly raised, on others it may be 2 or 3°F above normal.

In the dog, tuberculosis often affects the abdominal organs, giving rise to alternating diarrhoea and constipation, paleness about the gums, and ascites (dropsy). The animal may accordingly begin to have a pot-bellied appearance, with simultaneous loss of flesh over the ribs and spine. There may be some vomiting or jaundice.

If the chest is affected, the first signs may be those of pleurisy. There is evidence of pain, particularly if the ribs are lightly pressed. The animal is dejected, reluctant to move, and it may seem that the abdominal muscles are more involved in breathing than those of the chest. There may be a short, sharp cough. Later, pain may subside as fluid collects.

In other cases symptoms are less definite. Lung involvement may be accompanied by a cough, and sometimes a discharge from the nostrils. The dog may show signs of fatigue when out for a walk.

When the skin is affected, small hard swellings may appear, or there may be flat oval lesions which ulcerate after a time.

Diagnosis is obviously important, not only for the dog's sake but because the illness is easily transmitted to people. On public health grounds, tuberculosis in the dog is seldom or never treated.

Preventive measures, such as the use of B.C.G. vaccine, can be taken to protect a dog in a household where the owner or another person is receiving medical treatment for tuberculosis and might infect the dog.

BRUCELLOSIS

This means infection with any one of the five important species of a genus of bacteria called *Brucella*, each of which can cause illness in man – the names Malta Fever or Undulant Fever may be more familiar.

One of the five species is *B. canis* which, in the U.S.A., has caused outbreaks of severe illness in laboratory Beagles. In Mexico City, testing of 203 human serum samples and 500 dog serum samples for canine brucellosis showed positive reactions for 13 per cent of the human samples and 28 per cent of the dog sera. *B. canis* was isolated from the blood of 8 dogs.

In Britain all reported cases of brucellosis in the dog appear (at the time of writing) to have been caused by *B. abortus*, an important cause of abortion in cattle. Dogs can be infected with this bacterium through being given raw milk straight from the cow, or any unpasteurised milk; or through eating the afterbirth of an infected cow. It will be appreciated, therefore, that brucellosis is more common in dogs on farms.

Arthritis and cystitis in both sexes are common sequels to this infection. In the male, orchitis (inflammation of the testicle) and prostate gland inflammation are common. In a pregnant bitch, abortion is likely to occur.

Case history 1. A dog, given raw milk on a farm where the dairy herd was known to be infected, became lame in one hind leg. Within a week the animal had become dull, feverish, and constipated. Treatment with an antibiotic had little effect on the dog's fluctuating temperature, but improvement in his general condition occurred after a few days. Then an elbow joint became painful, and although this too improved, yet another joint became involved within a matter of weeks, and the dog – still suffering intermittent bouts of fever – was put down.[2]

It will be appreciated from this case history that brucellosis in the dog, as in man, can be a cause of long-term disability.

Case history 2. Fever, loss of appetite, and stiffness were the symptoms in a Labrador which had access to fields grazed by cattle in a non-accredited herd. Treatment with penicillin appeared to overcome these symptoms, but three weeks later the dog was again unwell and incontinent at night on a few occasions. After a further three weeks veterinary advice was again sought as the original symptoms had returned, with additionally a painful inflammation of one testicle. As *Brucella abortus* was isolated from the dog's urine, euthanasia was recommended on public health grounds.[3]

ASPERGILLOSIS

This is a fungal disease of birds and mammals. The fungus *Aspergillus fumigatus* grows readily in baled straw or hay with too high a water content, and in many other situations. The fungus forms spores, and it is these which gain entry into the animal. If conditions are favourable, the fungus sends out filaments called *hyphae* which invade the tissues. The commonest site of infection in the dog is the nose and nasal sinuses. Symptoms include a purulent discharge from one nostril. Later there may be bleeding from that nostril and, if the infection progresses, a discharge from both nostrils. There may be pain, and sometimes the bridge of the nose becomes mis-shapen, indicating that the fungus has destroyed part of the turbinate bone(s). Thiabendazole has been found to be effective in treating some not-too-advanced cases.

Other fungi which occasionally or rarely cause disease in the dog include *Cryptococcus neoformans*, also found in the nose; *Candida albicans*, a yeast-like fungus which causes a disease called moniliasis, often characterised by fever, loss of weight, and oedema of the lungs, and sometimes associated with stomach ulcers; and *Blastomyces*, the cause of blastomycosis. This last infection is less rare in the U.S.A. than in the U.K., and may involve liver and kidneys, with vomiting as the main symptom.

PSITTACOSIS

This is the name for infection of birds of the parrot family with *Chlamydia psittaci*, a round or oval micro organism. The less familiar name ornithosis is often used for the illness in other birds, man, and domestic mammals. In the dog this infection is unlikely to occur unless his owner breeds budgerigars or imports parrots, etc. Apart from causing conjunctivitis, *Chlamydia* organisms have been isolated from dogs with enteritis and pneumonia. In one Edinburgh outbreak, 100 out of about 300 budgerigars in an aviary died. Human cases followed, and a dog was found to have a lung infection and to be excreting *Chlamydia*.

AUJESZKY'S DISEASE

This is mainly a disease of pigs and rats, and dogs become infected only after being fed on raw meat from infected pig or cow carcases, as a rule, although the eating of an infected rodent could theoretically lead to the disease. For all practical purposes, however, the disease is not one which the ordinary dog-owner is likely to encounter; in farm dogs, foxhounds, and dogs having access to piggeries or boarded in kennels where raw carcase meat is fed, the risk is however there.

In pigs, Aujeszky's disease often takes a subclinical form and, as symptoms are not evident for some time, the farmer may not be aware that he has this infection on his premises. In cattle the disease is rare and usually affects but a single individual in the herd.

The cause of Aujeszky's disease (sometimes known as pseudo-rabies) is a virus. In typical cases, it gives rise to intense irritation of some part of the body which the afflicted cow or dog rubs and bites, sometimes causing injuries which amount to self-mutilation.

Case history 1. A cow died on a farm after a short illness during which she rubbed away the skin over one hip. Before the carcase could be removed from the farm, a Collie chewed the raw area, and ate a considerable quantity of the flesh. Three days later the dog showed signs of intense irritation about the face, became unsteady on his legs, and then comatose, death following shortly afterwards.[4]

Besides the skin irritation, other symptoms of Aujeszky's disease may include dullness, fever (a temperature of up to about 106°F), vomiting, diarrhoea, salivation, rapid breathing, and whimpering.

Case history 2. In an outbreak resulting in the death of 11 out of a pack of 51 Harrier hounds, the first victim died after twenty-four hours' illness during which only dullness and 'heavy breathing' were noticed. The second hound to die also showed this rapid breathing and, after twelve hours, salivation and evidence of pain. Vomiting occurred in about half the other cases, diarrhoea in most. Itchiness was a symptom in only four hounds, which scratched their heads and necks and occasionally bit a foreleg.[5]

BOTULISM

This is a type of food-poisoning characterised by some degree of paralysis. It is caused by a bacterium, *Clostridium botulinum*, which belongs to the same genus as the organism causing tetanus, and likewise produces a very potent toxin. Decaying animal and vegetable matter is a source of infection, especially in the tropics, where dogs may become ill after eating carrion.

In Britain there have been outbreaks of botulism in foxhound kennels.

Case history. Some hounds were unable to stand and, in response to calls, could lift only their heads and tails. There were two deaths.[6] *Cl. botulinum* type C was isolated from remains of meat which had been used for feeding.

An ordinary pet or working dog could become infected through eating the carcase of a bird or rodent, or, rarely, through retrieving infected waterfowl. It should, however, be borne in mind that botulism is one of those types of human food-poisoning which sometimes occurs after eating ineffectively preserved food, such as smoked trout, or after eating re-heated cooked food. A dog is not immune from the latter hazard.

ANTHRAX

Carnivores being resistant to anthrax, dogs are seldom affected, even in the tropics where the disease is more common than in temperate regions. However, anthrax has occurred in kennels in Britain, after feeding meat from an animal dead from anthrax. Once again, hounds and farm dogs are the most likely victims; the common house fly and stable flies can transmit infection after feeding on an infected carcase.

Anthrax is characterised by a high fever, an enlarged spleen, sometimes swellings in the throat region (or involving both neck and head), and rapid breathing.

Comparable with the 'malignant pustule' of the disease in human beings, a skin form is occasionally seen in the dog, and may affect the lips. In cattle, death may occur so quickly that no symptoms are observed, and the farmer may assume that the animal was struck by lightning. This has some bearing on the offer of such a carcase for hound feeding.

ORF

Also known as contagious pustular dermatitis, this is a skin disease of sheep and goats chiefly, caused by a virus – aided and abetted, so to speak, by the bacterium *Fusiformis necrophorus*. The disease is transmissible to man and is, in fact, an occupational hazard of shepherds. In the dog, orf is likely to be seen only in sheepdogs, other farm dogs, or hounds given an unskinned sheep carcase as food.

The first recorded case of canine orf was reported in the *Veterinary Record* in 1970 following an investigation by Mr G. T. Wilkinson M.V.SC., of the Animal Health Trust, and by veterinarians of the Wellcome Research Laboratories. The outbreak involved hounds, which had acute inflammation of the skin on or near the head, with circular moist areas, ulceration, and scab formation.

TRANSMISSIBLE GASTRO-ENTERITIS (OF PIGS)

This was found to be the cause of an outbreak of vomiting and diarrhoea among 40 dogs in breeding kennels. The illness lasted on average about 48 hours, after which the dogs were soon fit again. The outbreak was investigated by research workers of M.A.F.F.'s Central Veterinary Laboratory, who were left with little doubt that the cause was t.g.e. Farm dogs, or those eating uncooked pig meat, would normally be the only ones at risk.[7]

REFERENCES

1 Hill, F. W. G. and Gibbons, R. W. *Vet. Record* 76 (1964), 642

2 McErlean, R. A. *Vet. Record* 79 (1966), 567

3 Hall, R. F. *Vet. Record* 94 (1974), 454

4 Dow, C. W. and McFerran, J. B. *Vet. Record* 97 (1975), 1100

5 Gore, R. *et al. Vet. Record* 101 (1977), 93

6 Darke, P. G. *et al. Vet. Record* 99 (1976), 98

7 Cartwright, Sheila and Lewis, Margaret *Vet. Record* 91 (1972), 571

21 To Breed-Or Not To Breed?

As a companion animal, many people prefer a bitch to a dog, on the assumption that the female of the species is likely to be more affectionate and less aggressive. A male which frequently involves himself in dog fights can be a source of worry and embarrassment to his owner, who often incurs thereby the displeasure, if not odium, of dog-owning neighbours. However, bitches may attack each other; the local postman may find their attitude towards human beings only a trifle less aggressive than that of male dogs.

Guide dogs for the blind are exclusively bitches, and all are spayed – but that is a topic for the end of the chapter. For the moment, let me assume that the reader decides to allow his or her bitch to have at least one litter of puppies, and offer information for the guidance only of those who have never owned a bitch before.

Canine puberty is reached in both sexes between the ages of 6 and 12 months. As a very rough guide, it can be said that the larger the breed, the later the puberty. In the U.S.A., Dr R. J. Garner found that in 1,500 Beagles kept at Colorado State University, the first heat occurred on average at the age of 9 months 3 weeks and 5 days.

OESTRUS ('HEAT')
Bitches of nearly all breeds of *Canis familiaris*, the domestic dog, come into oestrus twice a year; although there are always individual bitches which provide exceptions to the general rule. The Basenji is a breed in which oestrus occurs only once a year.

If an unwanted pregnancy is to be avoided, a close watch must be kept for signs of the bitch's first heat. As bleeding from the vulva is very slight in some bitches, especially on the first occasion, it can easily be missed by the owner, who should therefore watch for preliminary swelling of the vulva, slight at first, then becoming more noticeable. In small breeds, the swelling may be observed as early as the fifth month of age.

The duration of 'heat' is approximately three weeks, though here again there are differences between individuals of the same breed.

The 'heat' is divided into two stages: (1) *pre-oestrus*, which last from 7 to 10 days, and during which a bitch will flirt with a dog but not accept him; and (2) *oestrus*, during which blood-stained mucus continues, at first, to discharge from the vulva, and then usually becomes clear (blood-free). It is then that the bitch is usually ready for mating and will stand for the dog.

While no calamity will necessarily befall a mating at first heat, it is generally accepted that it is better not to breed at this time. However, the owner's decision not to mate the bitch may not be the final one — she may escape from home to search for a mate — and, of course, there may be a number of eager males already waiting outside!

Should mating take place under these circumstances, and the owner be aware of the fact — through seeing the mating or being told of it — a decision will have to be taken as to whether to allow the bitch to become pregnant or whether to have this averted by means of a hormone injection which a veterinary surgeon can give. This is best carried out within 24 hours — the sooner the better. If treatment is delayed for 48 hours the dose needed may be so large as to give rise to side-effects, and the chances of failure are increased.

It should perhaps be added here that attempts to separate dog and bitch during mating — pouring a bucket of cold water over them, or trying to drag them apart — are both inhumane and ineffective. It will be too late to prevent conception and, owing to the anatomy of the dog, harm may be done to both animals.

AGE AND MATING

Assuming that the owner wishes to breed from the bitch, at what age is a first mating recommended? Experienced breeders will have their own views on this subject, but for the novice it can be repeated that the first heat is probably better avoided. Veterinary opinion is not unanimous. Some favour mating at about 18 months of age, by which time the bitch will be fully grown and should have no difficulty so far as size of the genital passageway is concerned; moreover the strain of whelping will by then probably be less. Some veterinarians have no objections to mating at the first heat. Dr Garner, after experience with 1,500 Beagles, noticed no ill-effects on either bitches or puppies as a result of breeding then. However, what is safe and sound for laboratory Beagles is not necessarily relevant for bitches of all breeds (and Dr Garner did not suggest that it was).

One has to bear in mind that a bitch which is still growing will have the added stress of coping with this as well as providing for the growth of her puppies developing within the uterus. So one would still say: avoid the first heat. Choice between second and third heat is a decision called for mainly in the larger breeds, which mature late.

Ease of whelping is, generally speaking, probably greatest between the ages of 18 months and 6 years. After that age a bitch mated *for the first time* may have a difficult whelping. Some bitches — bred from regularly — continue into relatively old age; but that is not to say that all bitches can be expected to remain fertile as they grow older.

Mating, Pregnancy, and Whelping

MATING

The bitch is usually ready for mating between the 10th and 12th days of 'heat', but remember that *she* is always the best judge. (Occasionally, a bitch is ready slightly later, or slightly earlier, and will not stand for the dog on the date which her owner has written down in a diary. Canine mating and conception are matters of physiology, and not mathematics; it is that particular bitch's physiology which counts.)

It is a mistake not to allow dog and bitch – often total strangers to each other – to have enough time in which to become acquainted and to indulge in the preliminary play that is natural; and for this they need space!

A maiden bitch may be nervous and even aggressive, but one has to differentiate between true aggressiveness (a readiness to bite) and what Dr Eleanor Frankling has so well described as 'playful semi-snapping which is in effect a sort of token resistance and is well understood by both animals to be no more than this.' This 'token resistance' may be expressed by a bitch which has been mated before.

As regards the actual mating, the less human interference or 'assistance' the better, as a general rule. Any bitch may refuse to mate a particular dog, yet readily accept another. The dog, too, for one reason or another, may refuse; and he may be physically unable to mate if there is one of those obstructions in the bitch which are described in the next chapter.

When the bitch is ready for the dog, she will stand firmly, tail held aside. Copulation lasts for anything up to 40 minutes or so; usually less than 30 minutes. After mounting the bitch and clasping her with his forelegs, engorgement of part of his penis leads to what is known as the 'tie' –

Below left: 'It is a mistake not to allow dog and bitch . . . to become acquainted'
Below right: 'When the bitch is ready for the dog, she will stand firmly'

preventing separation of the two animals. The dog may turn and stand (on all four feet) so that he is back-to-back with the bitch.

Many breeders who come into the professional category have their bitches mated twice, and this seems a good practice for the owner of a single companion animal, too. If the bitch is mated twice with the chosen sire, she is likely to settle down more readily afterwards. If she is denied a second opportunity, she may try to escape, and her success in doing so could result in a mixed litter of pedigree and mongrel pups. (Of course, there is no truth whatsoever in that old belief that once mated with a mongrel, a pedigree bitch would in some way be 'tainted' for the rest of her breeding life. All the same a mixed litter may come as an unpleasant surprise to her owner.)

PREGNANCY

The period of gestation is about 63 days; but a bitch's first litter is often born a day early, so in her case the note in your diary should cover the 62nd day. Puppies of the giant breeds are often carried for less than 63 days. Puppies have been born alive as early as the 55th day, and as late as the 76th.

Is she in pup? Pregnancy in the bitch cannot be diagnosed in the early stages. From the 24th to the 32nd day of pregnancy is roughly the period during which foetuses can be palpated through the abdominal wall. After the 35th day it is usually impossible to detect pregnancy by palpation; although occasionally a foetal skeleton can be detected between days 45 to 55 or thereabouts; by which time the foetal bones will show on a radiograph – not that X-rays are to be recommended for pregnancy diagnosis. In the final week of pregnancy it should be possible to hear the foetal hearts beating, using a stethoscope. This can be useful in differentiating between pregnancy and false pregnancy.

Below left : The dog will mount the bitch and clasp her with his forelegs
Below right : The tie: dog and bitch can stand back-to-back during copulation

At this point one should perhaps describe **false pregnancy**, which may occur in either a maiden or a previously mated bitch, and may present an extremely convincing illusion of the real thing. The abdomen increases in size, there is often mammary development and even milk flow, and the bitch may make a 'bed' a few days before the time whelping might have been expected.

Soon, since no foetuses are present, the organs and tissues return to their normal state; the sexual cycle is resumed, heat returns, and successful breeding may take place subsequently. However, false pregnancy is apt to recur. If it does, it may be better to have the bitch spayed, though this is by no means essential.

Occasionally false pregnancy is followed by mastitis, in which the mammary glands become hard, hot and tense; or by pyometra – both these conditions are described in the next chapter.

Many dog-owners are probably under the impression that for a bitch which is truly in whelp, there are only two possibilities: either something goes wrong and abortion takes place, or else she has her litter in due course. There is, however, a third possibility – the foetuses may die, but instead of being expelled from the uterus as in abortion, they are retained there and undergo what is technically known as **foetal resorption**. In other words, they mummify. This is by no means an uncommon happening at mid-term.

Case history. A bitch was apparently already 10 days overdue, but seemingly in the best of health, when veterinary advice was sought. On examination it was found that normal foetal fluids were absent. A fortnight later the bitch was still eating well and in good health, but the foetuses were appreciably smaller. Gradually resorption took place. After the next mating, this bitch whelped normally.[1]

Infections which may produce **abortion** include toxoplasmosis, canine herpes virus, and brucellosis.

The bitch should have been wormed before she was due to come on heat, but if this was not carried out, ask your veterinary surgeon for a safe anthelmintic which can be given to her during *early* pregnancy.

During pregnancy the bitch must be well fed and kept exercised. While obviously there should be no violent or exhausting exercise, it is important that she is not allowed to become fat and flabby. Her muscular and circulatory systems need to be in first-class order if she is to have an easy whelping.

For the first month the bitch will not need more food than she usually receives, but it must be of high quality. Milk, meat, and eggs come into this category, with fish given occasionally, and dog biscuits abandoned for the time being.

After the first month, in order to meet both her own bodily

requirements, and those of the developing embryos within her, the bitch will require more food – rising to twice as much as she was having before. The extra food should be divided into extra meals, so that she is being fed four times a day and once during the night. A mineral/vitamin supplement can be obtained from, or prescribed by, your veterinary surgeon, to help with bone formation.

Failing this, a drop of halibut-liver oil may be given daily, and a teaspoonful of steamed bone-flour every other day. (On no account give unsterilised bone-meal intended as a garden fertiliser, since this can be a source of salmonella, anthrax, and other infections.) Lightly cooked liver, cut up small, is a useful item of diet once a week. Table-scraps containing any strong seasoning should not be offered. During the last three weeks, the bitch should be offered as much milk as she wishes; water should also be on offer as usual.

By the fifth week of pregnancy distension of the abdomen is usually obvious, and by the sixth week, nipple enlargement may be noticeable in the bitch pregnant for the first time. At any time during the last week she may make token efforts to form a bed or nest, though she is usually very near her time, or even in the first stage of parturition, before she makes a more determined effort.

Preparation for Whelping

If a bitch is to whelp in unfamiliar surroundings, she should be given a week to accustom herself to them; and not moved at the last moment, which may result in stress.

A dry, warm place with box or bed having sides and back high enough to prevent the puppies falling out, and to keep them out of any draught, is required. In the wild a bitch would have her litter in the privacy of a burrow; in your home she needs somewhere she can have a modicum of privacy, too – not somewhere where strangers, young children, and visiting tradesmen are likely to seem a threat. A room with bright lights and a television set going full blast for hours on end is obviously unsuitable. Remember, too, that when her time comes, the bitch may forsake her normal bed or box for the eiderdown on top of a bed or an expensively upholstered armchair; so the room should be one without such furniture.

As explained in the next chapter, for the first week of life outside the uterus the puppies need a temperature of not less than 75°F; otherwise they will run the risk of hypothermia, which can be fatal. There is, however, no need to heat a whole room to this temperature if a suitable whelping box is improvised along the lines indicated in the diagram. The lid is an important feature of the box, since it helps to retain warmth and to provide privacy for the bitch.

Newspaper, which can be burnt after soiling and easily replaced, is a

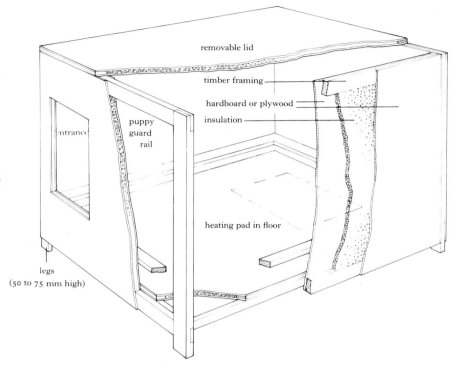

removable lid

timber framing

hardboard or plywood

insulation

entrance

puppy
guard
rail

heating pad in floor

legs
(50 to 75 mm high)

If whelping is likely to be more than a one-off event, it is worth constructing an insulated whelping box like this. Insulation material used must be inert and non-fibrous – there's no guarantee that it will not leak from the cavity, and there must be no risk to bitch or puppies

convenient bedding material. Those who have doubts about printer's ink can use a top layer of plain paper.

Some owners like to have their veterinary surgeon examine a bitch a week or so before she is due to whelp. In any case, it is a good plan to ensure that veterinary help will be forthcoming, should this prove necessary. It means choosing and meeting a veterinary surgeon before the whelping – assuming that you do not already have one, either because you have recently moved to a fresh district or have newly resumed or taken up dog-ownership. To telephone a veterinary surgeon who does not know you, or your bitch, and expect a visit at midnight or 5 a.m. is not the best way of going about things!

During the last week of pregnancy the bitch's temperature may be down to 100°F or 99°F; 12 to 24 hours before whelping begins it usually drops for a time to 98°F. This is mentioned as a matter of interest rather than as a suggestion that you should necessarily bother her with temperature-taking. There are other signs of imminent whelping. She will usually refuse food during the 12 to 24 hours beforehand; she will appear restless, and may pant, shiver or vomit shortly before labour begins; milk may be present at the nipples; and at this stage she may try to scratch out for herself some sort of nest.

WHELPING

A preliminary to whelping is relaxation of the pelvic ligaments, and a widening or dilation of the genital passageway. In the first stages of labour, contractions of the muscles of the uterus bring the first puppy from the horn into the body of the uterus towards the cervix which – if it has not already done so – has to relax before parturition can proceed.

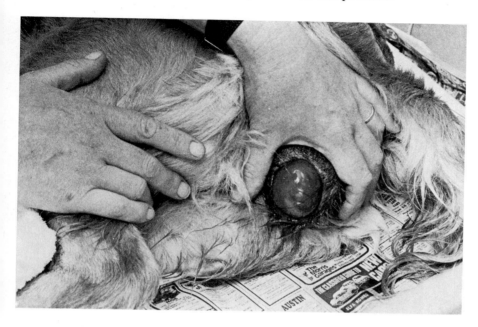

'Appearance at the vulva of a water-bag'

Onset of the second stage of labour is marked by contractions of abdominal muscles which in due course should lead to the appearance at the vulva of the black 'water-bag' – so-called because this foetal membrane, the *amnion*, contains fluid which has provided the foetus with a shock-proof water-bed while in the uterus, and has assisted in dilation of the cervix.

If labour is strong and sustained, the first puppy may be born within half an hour. The bitch will free and clean the puppy. If she does not do so, the owner must intervene and quickly open the membranous sac, or the puppy will suffocate. The puppy can be given back to the bitch to clean. If at this stage she appears uninterested, or uncertain of what to do, the owner should wipe away discharge from mouth and nostrils of the puppy, which can be held face downwards in a cloth to help clear the airway. If the puppy is not breathing, the puppy can be swung through a 45°-arc; taking care that the head is held as well as the body. The puppy should be dried with paper tissues, if the bitch is still not co-operating.

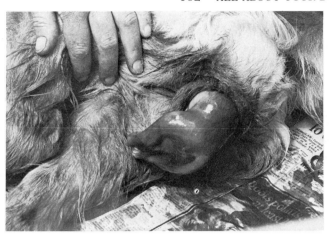 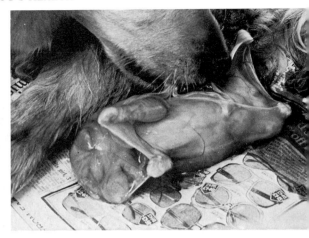

Parturition continues . . .

. . . and the bitch then frees the puppy from the sac

Sometimes the 'water-bag' ruptures inside the vagina, in which case a discharge may have been noticed, and the puppy's head may be visible at the mouth of the vulva or, if it is a breech presentation, hind legs may be seen.

The umbilical cord should *not* be immediately severed by the watching owner. The bitch will probably bite through it when she cleans the pup, but in any case there is no hurry, as it is best to allow time for blood to drain from the cord into the puppy, which may otherwise be deprived of it. If necessary, the cord can be cut with sterilised scissors, leaving about $1\frac{1}{2}$ inches attached to the puppy.

The afterbirth (placenta) may appear within a few minutes, and the bitch will eat it. Sometimes, however, the second puppy from the opposite horn of the uterus arrives first, and the first afterbirth may then precede the third puppy. The bitch should be allowed to eat two or three afterbirths, but subsequent ones can be disposed of before she does so.

Whelping can be a protracted process, with the first stage lasting 12 hours or more; or – as often happens with a large litter – it can be relatively quick. A point to bear in mind is that the first puppy cannot be expected to survive for more than six hours after the onset of second-stage labour. If there is an interval of three hours between puppies, ask for advice.

Problems. Many, perhaps most, whelpings proceed without the need for human assistance, but sometimes difficulties arise and delivery cannot be effected without human aid – circumstances conveniently summed up in one word – **dystokia.**

The bitch may have vigorous muscular contractions yet these may fail to achieve delivery because a puppy is awkwardly positioned. There are

A puppy an hour or so after birth. Note that a piece of the umbilical cord is still attached

several mal-presentations. In the simplest, where one leg is drawn back, it may be possible to hook a finger around the leg and draw it forward.

For any such manipulations, the hands should first be thoroughly washed. Long pointed nails are best sheathed; a finger cut from a rubber glove may be used.

Sometimes the legs are positioned correctly but it is the head of the puppy which seems too big for the opening. Lubrication with petroleum jelly (Vaseline), and gentle manipulation of the edges of the vulva, may succeed in allowing the head to pass. Otherwise it may be possible to grasp the puppy and ease it forwards and downwards at each contraction. A placenta may similarly be grasped and drawn out if it is obstructing the arrival of the next puppy.

In some instances, delivery fails not because of some mal-presentation of a puppy or other cause of obstruction, but because the muscular

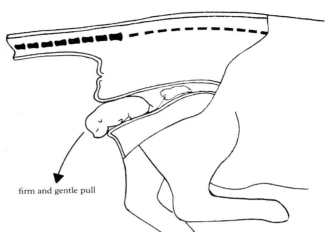

firm and gentle pull

If the puppy is visible, but whelping does not continue normally, a firm but gentle pull away from the spine (wrapping the hand in a clean dry towel) may assist

contractions are not powerful enough. This condition, known as **uterine inertia**, cannot be rectified by first-aid measures but requires an injection of the pituitary gland hormone oxytocin, which your veterinary surgeon will give if he diagnoses this inertia. He will also, of course, correct – so far as possible – any presentation which may be holding up whelping.

There are, however, situations in which normal birth is impossible; he may then advise **Caesarean section**. For example, continued failure of the cervix to dilate; a hopeless presentation; the presence of a 'monster' (grossly deformed foetus); torsion of the uterus; or some condition of the pelvis (perhaps following a fracture) which obstructs movement of the pups.

One type of veterinary anaesthetic equipment, consisting of oxygen cylinder, ether vaporiser, reservoir bag, and tube leading to the face mask

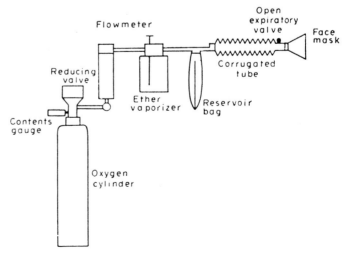

Unless the bitch is already in a state of exhaustion or shock, Caesarean section can be expected to be successful, major operation though it is.

The whelping bitch may welcome the presence of her owner, but all strangers and children are best kept away – even if they want to watch – as the bitch may fear for her puppies.

After whelping is completed, the bitch should be left in peace with her pups for a while. She may not want to leave them, and may have to be taken out on a lead to relieve herself.

A light diet, including plenty of milk and a beaten-up egg, is usually recommended for the first day or two after whelping. Meat or, for a change, fish can then be re-introduced, with egg and a drop of halibut-liver oil daily; in other words, a high-protein diet such as was recommended during pregnancy, maintained until the puppies are ready for weaning.

After whelping, the young pups suckle, while the bitch takes an intelligent – and contented – interest

An ailment to be on the lookout for between one and three weeks after whelping is **eclampsia**. Also known as 'milk fever' or lactation tetany, this is a metabolic illness in which the level of the calcium in the blood drops (hypocalcaemia). The bitch ignores her pups, becomes restless, may whine, pants and trembles; paresis or weakness of the legs, or stiffness, are followed – unless emergency treatment is obtained – by coma. She urgently needs an injection of a calcium preparation which your veterinary surgeon will administer.

Other illnesses which may follow more closely upon whelping are **mastitis** and **metritis** – both described in the next chapter.

The Avoidance of Mating

Owners of a pedigree bitch may naturally want to breed from her if she is a fine specimen of her breed with a good temperament. Who knows, might not one of her puppies one day become Supreme Champion at Crufts? For some people, the big dog shows have an irresistible appeal, and the dog fancy is an engrossing and sometimes lucrative occupation. Mainly financial considerations may motivate the professional breeders, who may have potential buyers in several countries. Then again, the owner of a first-class gundog or of a talented sheepdog may wish to breed, partly to use and preserve inherited skills and aptitudes, partly for the pleasure of being able to demonstrate first-class performances, and to accede to friends' requests for 'one of her next litter'.

Some of these considerations may weigh also with the owner of a companion animal which is neither the son or daughter of a star-performer nor has a conformation or pedigree likely to impress a judge or a wealthy buyer. Moreover, any owner may want her bitch to have at least one litter for the sake of the bitch herself, bearing in mind that pyometra is common in the maiden bitch, or merely because the animal is such a valued member of the household that it would seem a good idea to have a puppy to follow on.

In other instances the owner may feel that coping with a bitch on heat every six months is an unwelcome prospect, and that it is unkind to keep a bitch confined without opportunity to fulfil the very strong mating instinct. There may be the realisation, too, that there are times when even pups with a good pedigree are hard to sell, that strays are a problem locally, and that indeed the number of dogs being 'put down' by animal welfare organisations is greater than the demand for puppies.

Such reflections may influence a decision not to breed – or not to go on breeding. How can this best be achieved?

Chlorophyll preparations can be bought at pet stores with the object of masking the scent of a bitch on heat, and of her urine, but they cannot be fully relied on to keep all male dogs away from house or garden. They are certainly not contraceptive, nor do they diminish the bitch's desire for mating

Secondly, there are *plastic contraceptive devices*, which have come on to the American, if not the British, market; they are for insertion into the vagina. Their safety and success have yet to be evaluated, and they still leave the on-heat bitch unsatisfied.

Thirdly, there are *drugs to suppress oestrus* and in that way to act as contraceptives. Such drugs can spare the bitch the thwarting of her natural instincts which occurs at an oestrus without a mating, and may spare the owner some of the disagreeable aspects of having a bitch on heat in the home. However, one or two such drugs had to be withdrawn from the market because their side-effects proved harmful to bitches' health. It is accordingly pleasing to be able to report that a bitch treated with a (Glaxo) progestagen, megestrol acetate, had her first oestrus prevented, and all subsequent heat periods over an 8-year-period. Mr S. G. Lake B.VET.MED., M.R.C.V.S., who described this case in the *Veterinary Record*,[2] stated that the bitch received a total of 14 courses of this progestagen. Each course was started on the first day that both bleeding and swelling of the vulva were in evidence. The bitch was ultimately spayed at the age of nine; examination of uterus and ovaries showed no pathological changes. For advice on the use of such progestagens, timing and dosage, etc., consult your veterinary surgeon. One problem with such drugs may be increased appetite.

SPAYING

Fourthly, there is spaying. This involves a laparotomy and usually an **ovario-hysterectomy**; i.e. surgical removal of both ovaries as well as most of the uterus. This is the usual method of spaying, after which the bitch can neither come on heat nor become pregnant.

An ovario-hysterectomy is regarded by most veterinarians as preferable to half-measures, such as a hysterectomy with one or both ovaries left, or to ligation of the Fallopian tubes – a practice in vogue in the U.S.A. – which merely obstructs the passage of ova from ovary to uterus. Such 'half-measures', as I have called them, all leave oestrus unaffected. Some owners may feel that it is less traumatic for the bitch to undergo one of these lesser operations, that it is 'more natural' to leave one ovary, but they will not prevent the mental stress associated with heat periods unmatched by mating; nor will they prevent later pyometra.

Owners may be worried, too, that the full spay entails the animal becoming in some way diminished in terms of the canine equivalent of personality; but this is certainly not the experience of the vast majority of owners. The idea that the spayed bitch will become fat and lazy is something of a myth – some spayed bitches may be overfed! However, it has to be admitted that some do suffer from a tendency to alopecia and need hormone treatment for it; but unspayed bitches are subject to mammary tumours (occasionally malignant) and, as already mentioned, to pyometra – which usually, if not always, requires a hysterectomy.

On the whole, therefore, majority opinion favours the full spay – ovario-hysterectomy. There remains the question: When should the operation be performed? On this point veterinary opinion is far less nearly unanimous. It is easier to operate when the bitch is about five months old – before she has first come in oestrus and when the organs, and their blood supply, are less well developed. It is then less of a major operation, so to speak. Some veterinarians however, advocate spaying *after* one or more heat periods; one reason being that otherwise the vulva sometimes remains too small, and urine may cause inflammation of the skin in this region when she is adult.

Spaying is of potential value in reducing the problem of unwanted puppies, unwanted adult dogs, and strays; even if it is very seldom carried out for this reason.

CONTRACEPTION IN THE MALE

Another approach to the problem would be to sterilise the male rather than the female, and this has been advocated. It would not require castration, but the much less drastic operation of **vasectomy**. This involves cutting both spermatic cords and could be done under a local anaesthetic in a tranquillised dog. However, the owner of the dog would gain no personal advantage from vasectomy (comparable with the avoidance of heat in the spayed bitch) and so would have to be a very public-spirited person indeed in order to be willing to pay the fee. Consequently, were a mass campaign ever organised to reduce or limit the dog population, vasectomy would need to be subsidised by either central government or local authority.

Vasectomy does not diminish the dog's libido, nor alter his temperament; nor does it lead to obesity, which castration has a tendency to do. However, the operation does not render the dog immediately sterile, as viable sperms may be present in the ejaculate for as long as 21 days after the operation; and so within the first few weeks after the operation a vasectomised dog might still be able to sire a litter of puppies.[3]

Castration of a dog is usually requested by dog-owners because the animal has objectionable habits in the house. Unfortunately, the results of the operation are often disappointing in overcoming these habits; it is much less effective in the dog than in the cat, in this respect. Castration should not be regarded as a certain cure for aggressiveness – here again disappointment is likely.

Castration is probably best reserved for tumours of the testicle, enlarged prostate gland, and for intractable alopecia which has not responded to thryroid hormone treatment.

Sterilisation by immunisation against the lutenising hormone releasing hormone is a possibility in both male and female animals, according to a report following joint medical and veterinary study in Edinburgh and Dundee. It would prevent the bitch from coming on heat, and sterilise the male.

REFERENCES
1 Stockman, J. R. *Vet. Record* 75 (1963), 903
2 Lake, S. G. *Vet. Record* 101 (1977), 529
3 *J. Am. Vet. Med. Assoc.* 168 (1976), 502

22 Disorders of the Sex Organs

In the Female

A dog may be unable to mate a bitch because some condition of her vulva or vagina renders impossible, difficult, or painful the insertion of his penis. For example, the bitch may have an abnormally small vulva, or one the muscle of which does not relax at oestrus;[1] or there may be a constriction of the vagina, an unusually tough hymen, or blockage caused by a polyp (a tumour on a stalk) or by some other form of growth. Occasionally a polyp can be seen externally, having protruded from the vulva. A polyp can easily be removed; but some tumours in this region are either difficult to remove, malignant, or both.

Occasionally congenital defects of the female reproductive organs may be present – anatomical abnormalities which, while not preventing mating, nevertheless render the bitch sterile. Such defects may involve vagina, uterus, Fallopian tubes or ovaries.

The whole reproductive cycle is dependent on a delicate balance between the various hormones involved, and an excess of one or a deficiency of another account for some cases of infertility. Such an imbalance may be temporary and self-righting, or require treatment.

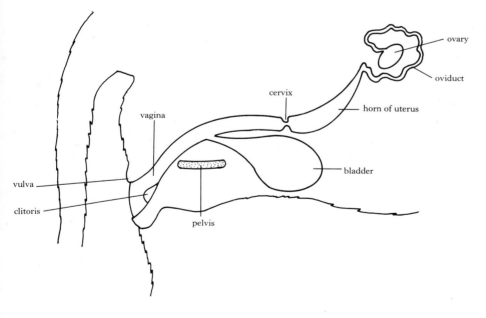

The female sex organs

Failure of the cervix to dilate so as to allow whelping to proceed has already been referred to in the last chapter; likewise uterine inertia and its correction by an injection of the hormone oxytocin.

A **cystic ovary** may result in nymphomania and infertility, and require professional attention; so may a tumour of the ovary which, by secreting an oestrogen hormone, may cause a bitch to come into oestrus several times in a year.

Infertility and abortion can both result from an **infection**. For example, the bitch may have brucellosis (see chapter 20); or toxoplasmosis or canine herpes virus infection.

Case history 1. The owner of breeding kennels sought veterinary advice as he had difficulty in getting his bitches in whelp, and there had been stillbirths and abortions. Examination of the bitches revealed vesicles and circular lesions on the mucous membrane of the genital tract; a finding which applied also to two dogs in the kennels. That it was a venereal infection was demonstrated at subsequent matings. Analysis of the breeding result over a period showed that the number of pregnancies in relation to matings had been halved, and litter size reduced on average from 9 to 5.7. There had been also two abortions of nearly full-term pups. Canine herpes virus was isolated.[2]

Abortion from a different cause occurred at other breeding kennels.

Case history 2. First a Collie and then a Bulldog bitch aborted, the latter on the 51st day of pregnancy. Laboratory tests indicated that the second bitch had brucellosis. She had used the kennel previously occupied by the Collie, which had aborted six weeks previously, and was found to have the same infection. Euthanasia was advised and carried out in both cases, owing to the risk to human health and because the bitches might have remained 'carriers' of brucellosis over a long period. The source of this infection was not proved, but the diet at these kennels included meat from stillborn calves.[3]

Another canine venereal infection is one in which wart-like growths appear in the vagina of the bitch and on the penis of the dog.

Acute **metritis** (inflammation of the uterus) may follow whelping if a placenta has been retained, if a dead puppy remains in the uterus, or if the lining mucous membrane of the latter has been injured during delivery, or bacteria introduced on fingers or anything else used to overcome dystokia.

A bitch suffering from acute metritis will be feverish, thirsty, depressed, and will show little interest in her puppies or in her food. Discharge from the vulva may be reddish or brownish with an unpleasant odour. Vomiting may occur; occasionally diarrhoea.

This illness is one requiring prompt veterinary help as, if severe or untreated, it can prove fatal. Fortunately, antibiotics or sulpha drugs, if given early, can be life-saving. (The puppies will have to be hand fed; the bitch may have little or no milk, and be unwilling to nurse them, and such milk as she has may not be good for them.)

Less acute cases of metritis, if untreated, may linger on, to become chronic.

Pyometra is a condition in which pus accumulates in the uterus, and is commonly seen in maiden bitches. In some instances the pus is discharged periodically and may be noticed by the bitch's owner. In other ('closed') cases, however, the cervix remains closed, there is no discharge to be seen, and the uterus gradually fills with pus. Such a 'closed' case of pyometra is always serious because it gives rise to toxaemia – the bitch is slowly poisoned by toxins produced by the bacteria in her uterus.

The symptoms may be a little vague at first. The bitch is not as bright as usual, may be feverish, is often very thirsty, may vomit, and her abdomen gradually becomes distended as though she were pregnant or had dropsy.

Case history 3. On the telephone a client explained that she had just returned from abroad to find one of her Dachshunds ill. 'It's Minty – you remember the one I took over from my sister? Minty's very off-colour, picks at her food, and brings back some of it – or water she has just drunk. I told my maid to ring you at the first sign of trouble if any of the dogs were ill while I was away; but she *would* go and listen to my gushing neighbour who *assured* her the trouble was only 'gastric' and would respond to milk of magnesia. Well, it hasn't. The only other thing I can tell you is that Minty has been getting rather large underneath. But, anyway, you'll see when you come.'

Minty was five years old, had never had pups – 'my sister was anxious to avoid all the bother' – and on examination proved to be suffering from pyometra.

Removal of the whole uterus and its offensive contents (the ovaries being removed at the same time) is the only treatment which is permanently effective, but the shock of an ovario-hysterectomy on top of an incipient toxaemia may render the operation extremely hazardous. In such instances it may be advisable to delay surgery *if* a hormone injection can open the cervix, allowing some of the pus to be evacuated. The use of antibiotics, perhaps uterine irrigation with a two-way catheter, may enable the bitch to become fit enough to withstand the operation later. In cases where the owner does not consent to an operation, or in 'open' cases, the above is a course which can be followed; it being explained that the condition is likely to recur.

Before leaving the subject of disorders of the reproductive organs of the bitch, it may be of interest to mention some rarer conditions of the uterus. For example, a part of it may become trapped in an inguinal hernia, or it may become twisted; or torn as the result of violence of some kind.

Case history 4. A 10-month-old bitch gave birth to three live pups without difficulty the day after being struck by a car and suffering external bruising and abrasions. Without any difficulty at whelping she later produced a second litter of eight. It was only after this second litter, when her owner decided to have her spayed, that – during the operation – the veterinary surgeon found a mummified full-term foetus *outside* the uterus, on which there was a scar. What had evidently happened was that the car accident had resulted in the uterus being torn; and one puppy had been displaced through the tear. A capsule of mainly fibrous tissue surrounded this ectopic foetus.[4]

In **torsion of the uterus**, which is very rare in the bitch, there is a complete or partial twist.

Case history 5. The owner of a 1-year-old Papillon bitch (believed to be six weeks' pregnant with her first litter) sought veterinary advice as, over the last fortnight, the animal's appetite had been decreasing while the abdomen had continued to swell. On examination the bitch seemed depressed and in poor condition. There was a clear discharge from the vulva. Palpation of the abdomen evinced no signs of pain but revealed a large swelling. When a laparotomy was performed, it was found that the gravid right horn of the uterus had twisted and then herniated through the broad ligament of the other (empty) horn. The bitch made an uneventful recovery after ovario-hysterectomy.[5]

Disorders in the Male

Under the rules of the Kennel Club only a dog which is 'entire', i.e. has both testicles in the scrotum, can compete in its shows; the **cryptorchid** which has either one or both testicles absent from the scrotum is disqualified from the show-ring. A similar rule has long applied to dog-shows in virtually all other countries.

It may be that the prospective purchaser of a puppy has no intention of showing; even so, he or she should never buy a cryptorchid – even if offered at a reduced price or, indeed, as a gift. The reason is that retained testicles are liable to tumour formation, and the purchaser who grows fond of the animal may later incur veterinary fees for surgery to remove the testicles or else see the dog in poor health.

Normally, both testicles descend through the inguinal canal into the scrotum shortly before or after birth, though sometimes descent of one may be delayed for weeks or even months. If it has not appeared by the age of six or seven months, it is unlikely ever to do so.

A bilateral cryptorchid, in which both testicles have failed to descend is likely to be sterile; the reason for testicles being lodged outside the body is

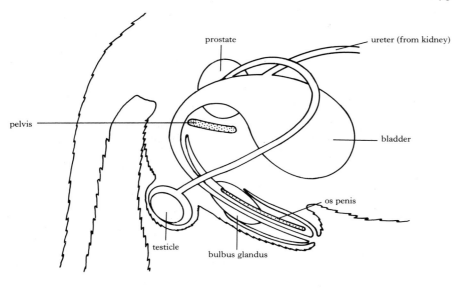

prostate

ureter (from kidney)

pelvis

bladder

os penis

testicle

bulbus glandus

The male sex organs

to obtain for them a slightly lower temperature than that of the interior of the body and one favourable to sperm production.

A unilateral cryptorchid is likely to be fertile, but should never be bred from; cryptorchidism is an inherited defect, associated with a recessive gene, hence the international rule disqualifying cryptorchids. The undescended testicle is best removed owing to the danger of its becoming the site of a **Sertoli-cell tumour**. This may give rise to persistent bleeding from the penis and cause the dog to develop female characteristics. For example, the nipples may become greatly enlarged, the dog may become less interested in bitches in oestrus, and the prepuce may become enlarged and pendulous. This type of tumour (and there are others which affect the testicle) commonly results in alopecia also.

Of 355 male dogs admitted over a period to the University of Glasgow's veterinary hospital, 31 had abnormalities of one or both testicles, and 10 Sertoli-cell tumours were identified. Seven of these were associated with loss of hair; and five with feminisation.[6]

A Sertoli-cell tumour may also be associated with torsion of the spermatic cords – a rare condition. Mr H. Pearson and colleagues at the University of Bristol reviewed 13 cases seen over a 14-year period. In 11 dogs the testicle was inside the abdominal cavity, in one it was in the inguinal canal, and in one it was in the normal position in the scrotum. Of the 13 dogs, three died (one from uraemia due to retention of urine, one from shock before surgery could be begun, and a third following surgery).

The other 10 dogs recovered rapidly after removal of the affected testicle.

Symptoms of **torsion of the spermatic cord** (which consists of the vas deferens, spermatic artery, veins, and nerves, enclosed in a membrane) may include loss of appetite, distress – even yelping, abdominal pain, vomiting, and the passing of blood.

Inflammation of the testicle (**orchitis**) may be due to violence of some kind, e.g. a dog fight, blow with a stick, or an accident. There will be bruising, some local swelling, and the whole area will be very painful to the touch. (The pain is in part due to pressure on nerves of the inflamed testicle which has little capacity for swelling owing to its coverings.)

Infection may obviously occur following a bite and exacerbate the symptoms. Sometimes orchitis may be due solely to an infection, e.g. in a dog suffering from brucellosis. (See chapter 20.)

The penis of the dog is remarkable for the presence of a bone, the *Os penis*, within its substance, and also for the enlargement near its base which swells during mating, preventing withdrawal from the vagina and producing the 'tie' referred to in chapter 21.

Fracture of the *Os penis* is extremely rare and likely to be seen mainly in run-over accidents producing serious injuries elsewhere, though in one case a dog was caught up when negotiating a wire fence.

Case history. The dog showed no signs of haemorrhage, but did not pass urine, and the penis was bent downwards at its middle. Abnormal movement was possible when the part was handled, and it was very painful. A radiograph confirmed that the bone was fractured. This was reduced but the fractured ends failed to unite. Accordingly an operation was performed, and a titanium plate and screws used to fix them in the correct position. A catheter was left in place for three days after the operation, which was completely successful.[7] (In most cases no immobilisation is required, a catheter being left in for one week – Mr A. C. Stead, who operated in the above case.)

In the adult dog there is often a blob of yellowish mucus to be seen at the opening to the prepuce, but this is of no significance. It is only if there is a continuous discharge, or if the dog is constantly licking the part that inflammation of the penis or its sheath should be suspected. As a first-aid measure for this **balanitis**, as it is called, withdraw the penis (dog permitting) and look for signs of inflammation, discharge, or a grass seed – that most ubiquitous of foreign bodies – and if any of these are present, bathe the parts using pieces of cotton wool soaked in warm saline or diluted TCP in warm water. If in any doubt or difficulty, seek veterinary advice.

Bleeding from the end of the penis has already been referred to above – a possible association with a rare fracture of the bone – but a far more likely cause is a stone in the bladder or urethra; in this case other symptoms, such as unsuccessful straining to pass urine, will be noticed.

The penis may not be able to be extruded by the dog from his prepuce if the latter's opening is too small. This condition, called **phymosis**, can be put right by a veterinary surgeon, who will make an incision to enlarge the aperture.

Paraphymosis is a not uncommon condition in which the penis cannot be withdrawn back into the prepuce, which constricts it. Applications to the penis of water chilled in a refrigerator may, with a little manipulation, enable the penis to be returned whence it came. Vaseline, liquid paraffin or even cooking oil can, if necessary, be used as a lubricant. If such first-aid efforts fail, or are not tolerated by the dog, veterinary help should be obtained, owing to the risk of gangrene should the constriction be maintained.

While the testis produces not only spermatozoa but also sex hormones, the prostate gland and seminal vesicles are accessory sex glands which contribute a secretion which mixes with the sperms coming from the epididymis (where the sperms mature and are stored) on their way to the penis, and which protects and nourishes them during their journey in the female. The **prostate gland** partly surrounds the urethra at the neck of the bladder, and consequently any enlargement of the gland is likely to press upon the urethra and obstruct the flow of urine.

An acute inflammation of the prostate gland usually follows infection, and can sometimes be successfully treated with antibiotics, when most of the enlargement will disappear. One infection which should be mentioned here is brucellosis, which sometimes also gives rise to abscess formation.

In dogs five years old and upwards, enlargement of the prostate may be gradual, persistent, and troublesome. Veterinary advice is often sought because of wet patches (urine) found on the floor in the morning – through no fault of the dog. Treatment sometimes involves use of the synthetic female sex hormone stilboestrol. If this gives no more than temporary relief, castration will usually bring about a permanent reduction in size of the prostate, which atrophies, so relieving the symptoms.

The prostate is occasionally the site of tumour formation, including cancer. (See also the Appendix.)

REFERENCES

1 Joshua, Joan *Vet. Record* 101 (1977), 472
2 Poste, G. and King, N. *Vet. Record* 96 (1974), 574
3 Bicknell, S. R. *et al. Vet. Record* 99 (1976), 85
4 Smith, G. E. *Vet. Record* 63 (1968), 82
5 Browne, A. J. *Vet. Record* 94 (1974), 202
6 Steels, W. B. *et al. Vet. Record* 101 (1977), 142
7 Stead, A. C. *J. Small Anim. Pract.* 13 (1972), 19

23 The Care of Puppies

Bitches vary in their mothering ability. Some appear clumsy or neglectful at first, but improve later; others are very good from the start; a few remain indifferent mothers all their breeding lives.

Sometimes, usually with the first litter, there is an initial failure of the milk supply, a condition technically known as **agalactia**. This can often be corrected by a veterinarian administering a dose of the hormone oxytocin. If later the puppies are restless and not receiving adequate milk, the cause could be acute metritis in the bitch (see chapter 22). Mastitis, involving a painful inflammation of one or more of the mammary glands, may also result in the puppies being short of milk; the bitch being reluctant to nurse. Milk from the affected glands may be unsafe for them, too. Hot fomentations are helpful in reducing pain and aiding recovery, but antibiotic treatment by your veterinary surgeon is usually advisable.

The bitch provides her puppies not only with milk, but also with warmth, stimulation, and antibodies against infections. Her presence almost certainly has some other benefit which scientists have accepted but cannot yet fully explain.

The antibodies reach the puppies in the colostrum – milk secreted during the first two days or so after whelping. It is richer in protein and fat than her later, ordinary milk; it contains vitamins A and D, and antibodies against such infective agents as the bitch herself may have encountered, e.g. the virus of canine distemper. By this means the puppies are afforded a transient immunity against such an infection.

In her licking of the puppies, the bitch imparts local stimulation to nerve endings in the skin, which in turn has an effect upon the puppies' breathing. Similarly a bitch regularly licks her puppies in the appropriate places to stimulate them to defaecate and pass urine.

ORPHAN PUPPIES

The unexpected death of a bitch can leave her owner in the predicament of either having to find a foster-mother – no easy task at short notice – or to undertake artificial rearing of the orphan puppies. If members of a family can share the task, this will be less daunting but will still entail some loss of sleep, since the puppies cannot go all through the night without being fed. Puppies of the larger breeds can be fed at intervals of three or four hours; those of the smaller breeds may need their feeds more often.

Orphan puppies can be given a proprietary substitute (e.g. Lactol or

Esbilac) specifically intended for that purpose or, on the farm, one sold for rearing orphan lambs.

Bitch's milk is richer than cow's milk, containing about 7.6 per cent protein and about 11 per cent fat (as compared with the 3.5 per cent protein and 3.7 per cent fat of average cow's milk). The difference needs to be taken into account in rearing orphan puppies, for which the following may be prepared:

Fresh cow's milk		1 pint	1 teacup
Egg yolk		1 yolk	$\frac{1}{4}$ yolk
Cod-liver oil		2–3 drops	1 drop
Sterilised bone-flour	If available	1 teaspoon	$\frac{1}{4}$ teaspoon
Citric acid		$\frac{1}{2}$ teaspoon	pinch

Stir the egg yolk, bone flour and citric acid into the milk in that order. Add the cod-liver oil.

The local stimulation by the bitch can be simulated by a person's finger covered with tissue or the finger of a rubber glove.

However meticulous the care given to orphan puppies, they will not survive unless kept sufficiently warm. This is crucial. The recommendation for the first five days or so of life is a draught-free environment with a temperature of 75–85°F, gradually reduced to 70–75°F for the following three weeks. Obviously, a whole room does not have to be kept at this temperature – merely the puppies' rearing area or a covered whelping box.

TEMPERATURE

Should the body temperature of newborn puppies be taken, it will be found to be much lower than in the adult dog, only about 93–97°F on the first day after birth, and not above 98°F after a fortnight.

At their lower body temperature, newborn animals are susceptible to viral infections. For example, experiments with newborn mice have shown that an otherwise fatal infection with Coxsackie B1 virus can be modified to a symptomless infection by keeping the mice in an incubator so that their body temperature rises to that of mice eight or nine days old. Similarly if the body temperature of newborn puppies is artificially raised to that of adult dogs, there is diminished replication of canine herpes virus in their organs. The above is mentioned not to suggest that puppies' temperatures *should* be raised in this way, but merely to illustrate that temperature in the newborn really can be a critical factor.

FADING

Fading, or the fading syndrome, is a term for illness and death in newborn puppies, and **canine herpes virus** is one of the several causes of it.

Case history. In kennels housing about 40 adult dogs, 'fading' involved seven Greyhound pups. Three weeks before their birth, the bitch had been in contact with a Terrier whose litter had died within a week. The first Greyhound pup died on day 6 after birth, the second on day 8; the only symptoms were crying and shivering. On day 10 four more of the litter died, after showing a blood-stained discharge from the nose, arching of the back, and paddling movements with the limbs. The seventh pup died on day 14.

Veterinary pathologists Dr Daria Love and Dr C. R. R. Huxtable succeeded in isolating the canine herpes virus from the brain and several other organs of the dead puppies, and from the vagina of the bitch 18 days after she had whelped – a fact of some importance in understanding the nature of this infection and its method of spread.[1]

Other causes of 'fading' include the hypothermia already mentioned, canine viral hepatitis, *Bordetella* infection, and probably also a blood incompatibility; possibly *Clostridium parfringens* infection.

OTHER MATTERS

Docking and dew-claws. Before the puppies are one week old, their dew-claws may be removed and, if docking has to be done in accordance with Kennel Club rules for their breed, the tails dealt with at the same time. (A crossbred dog should never be docked.) The bitch should be removed, so that she does not become distressed while these tasks are being carried out. In Britain an anaesthetic is required by law for docking and dew-claw removal after the puppies' eyes open.

Early feeding. When the puppies are about three weeks old they may be encouraged to lap cow's milk. A week later they can be introduced to solid food; e.g. soft-boiled egg yolk, or minced meat. After five weeks, they can be given milk twice daily, with one meal of egg or meat. All changes should be made gradually, and quantities increased gradually; otherwise digestive upsets may occur. The meat should be butcher's meat, not knacker's meat. Drinking water should be on offer, and it should be ensured that each puppy receives its fair share of food.

Worms and Parasites. Parasitic roundworm larvae can pass across the placenta into the unborn puppy, and can also be transmitted in the bitch's milk. This applies both to hookworm larvae and to the worm *Toxocara canis.* In view of the danger to human health from the latter worm, and the fact that complete blockage of the puppy's intestine by it is not unknown in severe infestations, it is essential that all puppies are wormed. It is recommended that this be done when the puppies are between three and four weeks old; with the dose repeated at fortnightly intervals up to the age of 12 weeks. An anthelmintic (anti-worm drug) for use in such very young puppies should be obtained from, or prescribed by, your veterinary surgeon and used in accordance with his advice.

The sticky eggs of *Toxocara* adhere to the skin and hair of puppies (and of the nursing bitch), and to any old blanket or towel which may be used; and this is another reason why young children should not be allowed to handle pups or bitch at these times. If they do, they should certainly wash their hands thoroughly immediately afterwards.

Grass runs are usually provided adjacent to breeding kennels, but have the disadvantage that they become a fertile source of hookworm and *Toxocara* larvae. Concrete runs are preferable, despite their extra cost, since concrete does not readily support the parasites or their eggs and can be treated with a flame-gun or washed down with a very hot salt solution to destroy them. (Never use Lysol, carbolic acid or other phenol preparations, as poisoning can result from absorption of these compounds through the skin.)

External parasites must not be tolerated either. Some breeders greatly under-estimate the harmful effects of lice, which can cause severe anaemia in puppies. Fleas, too, must be removed from the puppy and its environment, not only because of the irritation caused, but on account of sensitisation to the flea's saliva which can lead to an allergy, and because fleas are carriers of larval tapeworms.

Puppy ailments which should be mentioned here include fits resulting from worm infestations or teething; puppy acne which is neither serious nor long-lasting; and diarrhoea which is serious if at all prolonged, owing to the dehydration which occurs.

At *five weeks* of age, the puppies' nails and temporary teeth may hurt the bitch, so that she may be reluctant to feed them; in fact, may refuse to do so. The nails can be trimmed in time to avert the first of these troubles.

By now the puppies should have been having, for the last week, the benefit of sunshine, and should be allowed to play where it can reach them, but not left out on a hot summer's day without access to shade or heat stroke could occur.

By *six weeks* of age the bitch may have little or no milk left, but may regurgitate some of her own food for the benefit of her pups. They should by now be receiving two milk feeds a day, with beaten egg yolk added to one of these feeds. Minced meat, boned fish, wholemeal bread baked in the oven, or biscuit can be given at one meal; and a knuckle bone to bite on. A drop of halibut-liver oil and the bone-flour can be continued; or a vitamin supplement if prescribed.

The bitch's food should be reduced at weaning. This should be completed by *seven weeks*; the pups now having four meals a day. The three months after weaning are a critical period, and feeding needs to be generous; the puppy requiring twice the adult amount per unit of body-weight.

Some puppies are taken from their dams when barely six weeks old and transferred to a pet shop or to a new owner. It is far better to leave the pups with the bitch, even if she has no milk for them, until they are eight weeks old, or nearly so. By then they will be stronger and better able to cope with a completely new environment and the stress of separation from their former one. Purchasers should be given details of the puppies' diet, so that there will not be a sudden change which could upset them.

When the puppies are *8 to 12 weeks* old some persistent temporary teeth may need veterinary attention. If not removed, they will force the permanent teeth out of their correct position, and their continued presence can be harmful. *Eight weeks* is also the time to fix an appointment with your veterinary surgeon for distemper inoculation (see chapter 7). The opportunity may be taken to examine the animal for any minor defects, such as inturning eyelashes, umbilical hernia, etc., and to pluck excessive ear hair from Poodles and Terriers with very hairy ears – a precaution against later ear troubles.

A vaccination certificate should be handed on to the puppy's new owner; it being made clear if and when a second inoculation is required. (It is essential that this is given at the correct interval, or the expected protection will not be conferred.)

REFERENCE
1 Love, D. N. and Huxtable, C. R. R. *Vet. Record* 99 (1976), 501

24 Middle and Old Age

Conditions of Old Age

Many middle-aged dogs tend to put on weight, and some become the victims of obesity. The latter condition is one to guard against, because the overfat dog is not only ungainly, but prone to various ailments less likely to affect the dog in good condition. Obesity imposes a strain on the heart and arteries, and may shorten the dog's life-span.

Adjust the diet of a dog which is becoming too fat. Reduce the total amount slightly, and also the carbohydrate and fat. If this does not check the tendency to over-weight, seek veterinary advice. Special diets can be recommended, including a canned dog food formulated for obesity. There may be some hormone imbalance affecting your dog, and this can sometimes be corrected with great success.

Elderly dogs, too, differ in their dietary needs from those of the young dog. Less fat, less carbohydrate, but adequate amounts of good-quality protein are indicated; with smaller meals three or four times a day.

Dogs with grey hairs are like old people. They can no longer do the things they once did. Old working sheepdogs should be retired from the hills to the lowlands, or worked only part-time. The elderly companion dog may well find very long walks, or rushing about, beyond him; but he still needs exercise. It is a good idea to take him out more often but for shorter distances. This, incidentally, will help prevent puddles on the floor indoors. Many old dogs suffer from chronic kidney disease, drink more, and need to pass urine more often.

The claws will need attention. If they are allowed to grow too long without being cut, the foot becomes raised in front, and the whole system of muscles and tendons is thrown out of gear.

Old dogs should not be given bones. They may succeed in gnawing a knuckle bone, but so often what then happens is that a hard mass of particles and spicules of bone cause a blockage in the rectum. The animal strains but can pass nothing, except sometimes a drop or two of blood. A dose of medicinal liquid paraffin may be tried, and repeated once; but if that fails it is best to obtain professional attention. An enema may be needed to remove the hard mass which is causing the blockage.

Old dogs' hearing and eyesight may begin to fail. **Deafness** may not at first be recognised by the owner for what it is, and the dog regarded as merely disobedient. **Impaired eyesight** may occur, since the natural elasticity of the lens of the eye decreases with age, and some old dogs develop cataracts. Nevertheless dogs usually adapt to such disabilities very well.

Decayed or loose teeth, or an accumulation of tartar around teeth and gum edges, can cause distress and difficulty in eating, as well as giving the breath a foul odour. Tartar removal, and the extraction of any loose or decayed teeth, can sometimes result in near-rejuvenation – to the surprise and delight of the owner – and undoubtedly in a happier dog.

Fainting fits may occur as a result of defects in the circulation. The owner should not become unduly worried about these – certainly not to the extent of trying to force brandy or whisky into the reluctant dog – but a short course of a suitable heart tonic may be advisable; so ask your veterinary surgeon. There may be disease of one of the heart's valves, and symptoms may resemble human asthma, with difficulty in breathing, and a cough.

It is usually possible to alleviate, over the short term, the severity of symptoms arising from defective heart action; but not to rectify the underlying cause. Owners should take comfort from the fact that many dogs with heart disease of one kind or another live to a ripe old age, and do not need to be kept permanently on drugs. A heart tonic as a standby for bad periods is all that is needed.

Cold east winds never blow through the pages of text-books, but in my opinion they can affect the health of a middle-aged or elderly dog, often leading to a dormant infection of the kidneys becoming an acute, active one. Confining exercise to more sheltered areas, out of the wind as far as possible, and buying or making a coat for the dog, may spare your dog a sharp attack of illness, and save you money on veterinary fees as well.

A few old dogs may go bald. Your veterinary surgeon, who may refer to the condition as '**senile alopecia**', may by judicious hormone treatment be able to offset any existing imbalance, so that hair grows again.

Especially in the giant breeds, a callosity may form on joints such as the elbow, hocks, and stifles. The term **hygroma** is sometimes used. The skin at these sites becomes thickened, sometimes greyish, and often wrinkled. In themselves such callosities are harmless if somewhat unsightly, but sooner or later the skin is likely to become damaged and this is followed by bacterial infection, leading to a chronic abscess or to a sinus needing surgical treatment. As pus is discharged, treatment will be needed both for the dog's sake and for reasons of hygiene in the home. So examine these callosities periodically.

I was asked recently whether I thought that letting old dogs sleep indoors, instead of continuing to sleep out in kennels, would be likely to prolong their lives. One can say that exposure to cold might well shorten the life of a dog in which old age had reduced the efficiency of heart and circulation, and hence the ability to cope with extremes of weather.

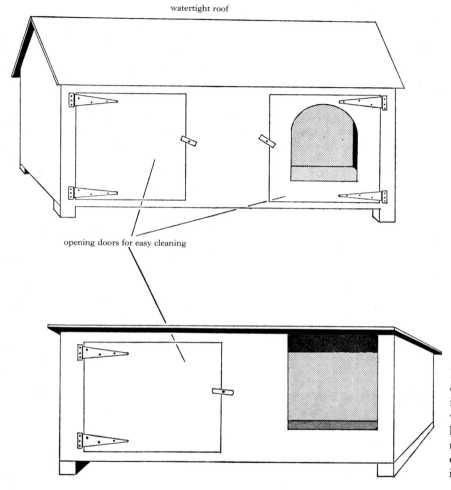

watertight roof

opening doors for easy cleaning

Kennels for use out of doors should be well insulated, but even if a well-constructed kennel is available, it may be better to allow old dogs to sleep indoors

Hypothermia is now a well recognised condition in old people living in rooms too cold for them to be able to maintain normal body temperature; and hypothermia does occur in the dog.

An old dog may not only have a latent kidney infection which can become active in extremes of cold, as mentioned above, but may also have arthritis, and on that account would be better indoors in warm and dry conditions. However, one must think of draughts. A dog could conceivably be worse off indoors than outside in a well-bedded kennel, if a change meant sleeping in a cold scullery with a draught blowing in under the back door. A raised dog bed will keep the animal off a tiled floor, or cold linoleum or concrete, and if there is a raised part on three sides protection from draughts should be achieved. (One has to get down to dog-lying level to find out whether there is a draught!)

Urinary **incontinence** has already been referred to, and in the old dog is seldom wilful but due to a sheer inability to avoid passing urine during the night. Putting down old newspapers may be helpful or the dog may be induced to use the type of tray containing absorbent material sold for feline purposes.

It is better not to let the dog sleep in a room where there is a solid-fuel stove as, if some fault of ventilation occurs, there may be a gradual concentration of carbon monoxide. Many dogs have been found dead in the morning from this cause.

Euthanasia

There comes a time when it may be kinder to end a dog's life than to allow a miserable existence to continue. For example, a dog so badly afflicted with arthritis that it can barely move without pain, or one with progressive loss of use of the hind limbs, is best not left to suffer. Cancer is another condition obviously calling for euthanasia; sometimes the deciding factor may be a combination of ailments, none of them severe, but which together add up to a life of discomfort, disability, and pain.

Another deciding factor may be the intolerance of one member of the family towards a dog which, in its old age, has become subject to chronic ear trouble (with an unpleasant odour), or is incontinent, or deaf and, owing to arthritis or rheumatism, unable to move quickly out of the way. Such a dog may be kicked or otherwise abused by an intolerant person, or necessary treatment may be neglected by the 'principal' owner, if I may use that term, who feels unable to afford the time and money necessary to cope with the dog. Euthanasia is then the best course.

In the canine context, euthanasia may sound a somewhat pretentious word to use, but it is a good one; it means to bring death quickly without pre-death fear or suffering.

25 Dog/Man Cross-Infection

Dog-Man Infections

Infections transmissible from lower animals to man are called zoonoses. By far the most important zoonosis, so far as the dog is concerned, is **rabies**. This is not only a horrifying illness in man, but once symptoms of it have appeared the chances of recovery are virtually nil. It should be noted that a lick as well as a bite can transmit the rabies virus to a person.

As explained in chapter 26, there are some countries in which cat-bites cause more people to have anti-rabies treatment than do dog-bites; and there are other countries in which the dog takes third place in this respect.

Some dog-bite wounds inflicted by a non-rabid dog may become infected with *Pasteurella septica* or other organisms. Medical men often advise a bitten person to have an anti-**tetanus** injection.

Tuberculosis is another important zoonosis, but the dog is seldom a source of infection to man nowadays, or so it would seem; but no statistics are available in the U.K. as the disease in dogs is not a notifiable one. It should be borne in mind if the symptoms discussed in chapter 20 appear.

Both forms of **leptospirosis** mentioned in chapter 7 are transmissible to man through infected urine, etc. Canicola fever and Weil's disease are the names given to the illnesses in man. A person is unlikely to become infected with either by a dog unless there is failure to wash the hands immediately after mopping up any urine from a dog ill or recently recovered from leptospirosis.

Dogs, like people, suffer from bacterial **food-poisoning** by *Salmonella* and *E. coli* organisms, and occasionally a dog may become a *Salmonella* carrier.

Case history. Two children and a puppy remained well in a household also comprising four adults who suffered from vomiting and diarrhoea. *Salmonella typhimurium* was isolated from all six people, and also from the puppy. The latter received veterinary treatment and was cleared of the infection. The puppy had been fed on raw knacker's meat, which had been kept among the human food, and might have contaminated either this or the kitchen utensils, so causing illness in the household. Alternatively, the puppy might itself have passed on the infection, though this was thought less likely in this particular outbreak.

Human **brucellosis** is almost invariably the result of drinking raw infected milk; of handling infected cattle or afterbirths (or in the case of veterinary surgeons, of accidentally pricking themselves with the needle of a hypodermic syringe containing live vaccine, or assisting at the calving of an infected cow). However, man can also be infected by a dog which is excreting these bacteria. The species may be *Brucella canis* in the U.S.A., for example, or *B. abortus* in Britain (see chapter 20). The disease in man can be a severe one, characterised by undulant fever, an influenza-like illness, sometimes muscular or joint pain, exhaustion, and headaches.

The worm *Toxocara canis* is the cause of the condition known as **visceral larva migrans**, or **toxocariasis**, in children. The effects of this infestation vary; there may be liver damage, or blindness, even death in very rare instances. This condition in children has, according to Dr Ronald Walker of California, a far greater incidence than the records of proven cases alone would suggest. This is because of the difficulties of diagnosis in the human host – especially the fact that the worm's eggs are not passed in human faeces, thus depriving the doctor of the easiest means of diagnosis. The larvae can be recovered and identified only by biopsy and this, states Dr Walker, is seldom achieved. The enzyme-linked immunoabsorbent assay promises better results than previous tests, he considers.

Dr Walker added: 'While common-sense should prevail over the more hysterical efforts of the anti-dog faction, we should be conscious that a problem does exist, and reflect on the fact that the high incidence of reported human cases in Louisiana results from the great interest shown locally by the medical profession in this disease.'

Children may become infested from grass or soil contaminated with *Toxocara* eggs in public parks and playgrounds, though the greatest danger is in the home where the sticky eggs adhere to the skin and hair of puppies (and of the nursing bitch) and to any bedding material used for them. Children are likely to swallow the eggs after getting them on their hands.

Hydatid disease is the formation of cysts produced in various parts of the human body (e.g. liver, lungs, rarely the brain) by immature forms of tapeworms. In the interests of public health it is extremely important to treat with a suitable anthelmintic any dog known to be passing tapeworm segments. This applies especially to sheepdogs, farm dogs generally, and those fed on raw carcase meat. Evacuated worms must be destroyed. (See chapter 6.)

Among skin diseases both **ringworm** and **sarcoptic mange** are transmissible from dog to man – in which mange is known as scabies. The dog flea will also parasitise man.

Man-Dog Infections

Diseases transmissible from man to lower animals are technically known as anthroponoses. They include **tuberculosis, mumps**, possibly a streptococcal infection from human cases of scarlet fever and tonsillitis; and infestation with the human flea. Psittacosis can be a two-way infection.

26 Rabies

An acute, infectious disease caused by a virus, rabies takes its name from the Latin word for madness. 'Hydrophobia' – the old name for rabies in man – is altogether inappropriate to apply to the disease in dogs, in which fear of water is not a symptom.

Since the rabies virus can produce disease in all warm-blooded animals, its victims vary from mammals to birds, from cat to camel, from tiny mouse to massive elephant. Not all animals are equally susceptible. Foxes, jackals and wolves are extremely susceptible; cattle, cats and rabbits are highly susceptible; dogs moderately so – according to a World Health Organisation classification.

Dogs transmit the infection from wild animals, by which they are bitten, to other dogs, to farm animals, to domestic pets such as rabbits, and to man; to a lesser extent, they transmit the infection back to wild animals. Stray dogs are always a serious problem from the rabies-control angle, and a source of infection to other dogs.

Below left: The bullet-shaped virus which causes rabies, as revealed by the electron microscope (× 400,000). *Below right*: A vampire bat (see page 197)

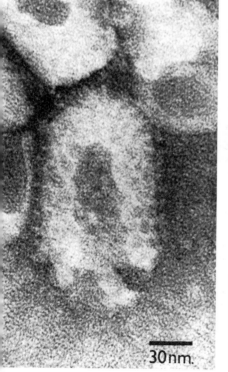

30nm.

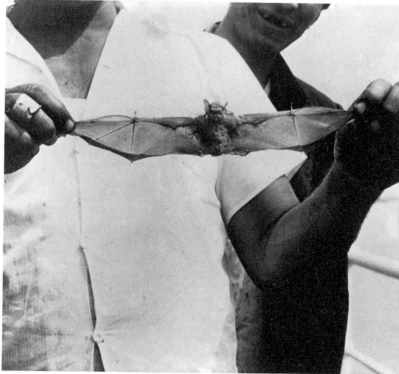

The furious stage of rabies

In many countries it is rabid dogs which remain the principal rabies hazard for man, requiring his preventive treatment; however, in a few European countries dog-bites necessitate this to a lesser extent than cat-bites, and in South Africa, for example, more people are bitten by rabid mongooses than by rabid dogs.

Although rabies virus may be transmitted violently by tooth and claw, it is important to think of rabies as an insidious disease. It may occur when least expected, and the symptoms may be suggestive of some entirely different canine illness. Indeed, occasionally symptoms may not be observed by the dog's owner at all. For example, in North America a mother, understandably enough, failed to connect in her mind two incidents that occurred on the same day – the finding of a slight wound on her baby's lip, and the disappearance from home of her puppy. The baby later died of rabies, which had not been even remotely suspected.

This running-away is an important feature of rabies, but not all dogs suffering from rabies do run away; it is just one characteristic of the 'furious' stage, one clue which may or may not be present.

SYMPTOMS

A slight fever and accompanying loss of appetite may pass unnoticed, but then a period of melancholy or anxiety may attract attention. However, all that the owner of a rabid dog may notice at first is a strange look about the animal's eyes, restlessness, and a tendency to hide in dark places.

One of the most important effects of rabies in the dog is that it induces a change of temperament; for example, noisy boisterous dogs often become

Dumb rabies, as illustrated in a nineteenth-century publication, 'drawn from life'

quiet and dull; while those which are normally of a quiet, gentle disposition may become sullen or bad-tempered. The unsuspecting owner is all the less likely to think of rabies if at times the dog is more affectionate than usual.

Vomiting may occur; occasionally muscular tremors may be seen. The site of the dog's bite wound may cause irritation or discomfort, and lead to the animal biting or scratching the part.

Rabies may affect the voice, so that the tone of the bark is altered.

Dilation of the pupils may occur, and later a vacant stare may be noticeable.

Appetite is capricious. The dog may appear ravenous, or decline both food and water, and eat pieces of wood, carpet, coal or metal. The latter symptom is associated with the 'furious' stage of the illness, during which the dog has the tendency to run away from home, to snap – sometimes at nothing, and to become excited, with saliva at the lips. The animal may by now appear obviously mentally deranged, yet have lucid intervals during which he recognises his owner. The dog will be liable to attack people, other dogs, cats, cattle, sheep, and horses, etc., during a journey which may take him twenty to thirty miles from home.

Sometimes a dog returns home after a day or two, by now looking bedraggled, thin, perhaps blood-stained and with saliva much in evidence. The anxious owner may be very solicitous and approach the dog which, especially if restrained in any way, may bite.

After a very few days, as a rule, this 'furious' stage merges into the 'dumb' or paralytic stage. Paralysis affects the lower jaw, which drops so that the mouth remains partly open, tongue protruding, and saliva dripping. The gait becomes staggering as the paralysis extends, and the animal tends to fall, at first able to regain his feet, but later unable to do so. Convulsions or 'fits' often precede death.

In some 75 per cent of cases the 'furious' stage is omitted, and the 'dumb' stage follows on from the earlier symptoms. The word 'dumb' is used because the paralysis prevents the dog barking; it may also make swallowing difficult. Excitement, the urge to run away, and aggressiveness are absent, and the animal as a rule remains passive. The dog's appearance is such as to inspire pity rather than fear.

Sometimes the dog makes sounds suggesting that it is choking, and the unwary owner may put his finger into the dog's mouth in an attempt to find what is causing the trouble, and to relieve it. This is an extremely hazardous proceeding, and one which has cost people their lives, since the saliva is likely to contain the virus and, if they have abrasions on their hands, the virus can infect them. The virus can also enter through un-abraded, i.e. intact, mucous membrane, so a lick from a rabid dog on the face, mouth or eyes can prove fatal to the licked person. Unfortunately, the virus is often present in a rabid dog's saliva before obvious symptoms are shown. This is why, in a rabies outbreak, it is so important to trace not only bitten people and animals, but also those that were in contact with a rabid animal and exposed to infective saliva.

Occasionally a dog is found dead, without any preliminary symptoms of rabies having been observed. Unless this occurs inside quarantine kennels, rabies is unlikely to be suspected; and disposal of the body may be fraught with some danger to the person handling it.

Differential Diagnosis. Diagnosis of rabies during life is often far from easy, since by no means all the symptoms mentioned above appear in every case. Sometimes the illness runs a course which is far from typical. Moreover, many of the symptoms of rabies are common to other diseases. For example, a tendency to snap when handled, salivation, a staggering gait, and convulsions are seen in cases of distemper when there is brain involvement. Vomiting occurs not only with rabies but also with canine viral hepatitis. A froth of saliva around the lips may be seen in fits due to epilepsy. A brain tumour can bring about a change of temperament, as well as the rabies virus. Convulsions may be a symptom of poisoning, or follow damage to the skull in a dog struck by a car. Salivation is profuse when a piece of bone is wedged across the roof of a dog's mouth. This is another condition for which rabies may be mistaken, and vice versa.

All this goes to show that a differential diagnosis is called for, and imposes a heavy responsibility upon the veterinary surgeon. He has to bear rabies in mind at all times, even in a country where the disease has not been present for many years, even in a dog which has already undergone six months' quarantine!

Such were the circumstances of the Camberley case in 1969, when the U.K. had been free of rabies (outside quarantine premises) for 47 years.

Case history. On a Tuesday morning an officer of the Royal Army Veterinary Corps, Major Morgan Jones, was consulted by another officer living close by, Major Helmsley, concerning his wife's dog, Fritz, which they had brought back from Germany, and which had been out of quarantine for 10 days.

Four days earlier Fritz had retreated underneath a bed and howled. Subsequently loss of appetite and refusal of water were noticed. On the Sunday and Monday Fritz made short rushes at his owners, never quite biting them. His bark was different from usual. On the Tuesday Fritz, when let out into the garden, bit through the milkman's shoe, rushed into the next-door garden and killed the neighbours' cat, and disappeared. Mrs Helmsley, with the possibility of rabies in mind, set off to look for Fritz and saw him jumping into a taxi full of school-children. Very pluckily, she managed to grab Fritz, now obviously mad, and – though bitten on the arm and leg – removed him from the taxi and took him to Major Morgan Jones, who locked him in his downstairs lavatory and telephoned the Ministry of Agriculture's divisional officer, notifying them of his suspicion that this was a case of rabies. 'The dog looked most odd with what I can only describe as an anxious expression on its face', he wrote later. There was no salivation, he noted, during the interval before Fritz was removed to quarantine premises.

Rabies was confirmed by laboratory means after Fritz's death. On the medical side, two bitten people and about 47 in-contact people received a course of anti-rabies vaccine inoculations.

The following year, 1970, a second case of rabies occurred, at Newmarket.

Case-history. A Terrier-cross bitch, Sessan, had been brought to England from Pakistan, where she was vaccinated 'three times', though dates and type of vaccine used were not known. Two days after coming out of quarantine kennels, Sessan's owner noticed that she was not well, though eating and drinking normally. The next day the animal vomited once. The following day food was refused, although a larger quantity of water than usual was drunk. During the night Sessan vomited three times. On the fifth day she was taken to a veterinary surgeon as 'a vomiting dog which would not eat'.

The bitch was obviously depressed, and salivating. No foreign body could be seen or palpated. A closer examination revealed that the lower jaw could not be closed. Normally this bitch barked a great deal, but had not done so since the third day of her present illness.

Differential diagnosis took account of four possibilities: distemper, gastro-enteritis, poisoning, or rabies. It was decided that the last possibility required further investigation, and the Ministry's divisional veterinary officer was informed accordingly.

Confined at home, the bitch was beginning to stagger when she walked, and swallowing had become difficult or impossible. Paralysis was complete on the sixth day, when removal to maximum-security kennels was effected. Sessan died on the eighth day.

These two case histories – one of 'furious' and the other of 'dumb' rabies – will probably give the reader a clearer idea of rabies than would a mere recital of possible symptoms.

Both cases were of special significance in two different ways, for subsequent investigation left little doubt that Fritz had been infected not in Germany but inside quarantine kennels, and this led to a tightening of regulations; while the incubation period of rabies had been 9 months in Sessan's case.

THE TIME-SCALE

Incubation period. In the dog the incubation period is commonly between 15 and 60 days, but periods as short as one week and reputedly as long as one year have been recorded.

Long incubation periods are of more than academic interest. They can give the owner an unpleasant surprise after thinking that all danger was past, and they can also breach the defence of even a 6-months' quarantine period. This length of time, adopted in Britain, is in the nature of a compromise, bearing in mind the average incubation periods on the one hand, and the expense of quarantine to the owner, as well as the stress to the dog, on the other hand.

Length of illness. The duration of rabies in the dog is usually under 10 days. In fact, it has frequently been stated that if a dog is still alive after 10 days, its illness cannot be rabies. This is a most dangerous assumption. Certainly, in parts of Africa and Asia, where rabies differs in many respects from the classical type seen in Europe and the U.S.A. (see the chapter on 'Tropical Diseases'), the illness is not restricted to a figure even double that. In Sri Lanka a person died of rabies before the dog which had bitten and infected this patient.

PREVENTIVE MEASURES

Quarantine and vaccination. All dogs entering British quarantine kennels are vaccinated against rabies, whether they have been vaccinated previously or not; no dogs are exempted from quarantine on the grounds of previous vaccination.

The reason for refusing to waive quarantine for a vaccinated dog becomes understandable on considering the Newmarket case. Here was a dog which had been 'vaccinated three times' yet became ill with rabies. What could have gone wrong? There are several possibilities. The vaccine used might have deteriorated through lengthy storage, or storage at too high a temperature; or it might not have been a reliable vaccine in the first place. Then again, it is important that the interval between doses is the correct one, and that one dose is not missed. Two cases of rabies in France were officially attributed to failure in this respect. In one, the two injections of vaccine were given at an interval of three days instead of the stipulated 15 to 21 days. In the second case, only one injection instead of the stipulated two which form the 'primo-vaccination' as opposed to the booster dose, was given.

If a dog already in the incubation stage of rabies is vaccinated, protection is not assured; the incubation period may be merely extended. Moreover, there are always a few individuals in which a vaccine – even an approved one from a highly reputable company – will not stimulate antibody production to an extent which will provide a useful degree of immunity. The fault can lie in the animal's own defence mechanism, and this applies to distemper vaccination, too.

One has also to bear in mind that the only 'proof' of vaccination is often a certificate – which obviously can be forged, issued by an unauthorised person in some far-off country, relate to a different dog, or merely be back-dated.

Despite these necessary qualifications and cautions, vaccination of dogs against rabies has proved one of the most successful methods of controlling the disease in many countries; thereby avoiding a great deal of human suffering. First-class vaccines are now available.

'Vaccination of dogs has proved one of the most successful methods of controlling the disease.' Here, dogs are brought to a public health office in Guatemala City for free injection

A PERSONAL EMERGENCY

Supposing that you suspected that your dog had rabies, what should you do? First, confine the dog, as Major Morgan Jones did with Fritz. Second, notify the police. If bitten, wash the wound immediately with soap and water or, if available, Cetrimide. Fourth, obtain medical advice without delay.

Importing and Exporting Dogs

Many dog-owners – including experienced travellers completely familiar with passports, visas, and vaccination certificates – overlook the fact that it is illegal to take dogs across many national frontiers unless local regulations have been fulfilled. Some nations exercise a total ban on dogs from countries where rabies exists, others require prior vaccination and production of a certificate, or the dog may have to stay in quarantine for a specified time.

Anyone intending to take a dog into the U.K. must obtain an import licence *in advance* from the Import Licence Section, M.A.F.F., Government Buildings, Toby Jug Site, Hook Rise South, Tolworth, Surrey, England. Arrangements for transport to approved quarantine kennels, for a 6-months' stay at the owner's expense, must also be confirmed in advance of the dog's arrival.

U.K. Control Measures. With the advance of fox-borne rabies towards the European mainland's coasts, and given the irresponsibility of animal smugglers, the disease could be re-introduced at any time. Once here, our State Veterinary Service would do its utmost to localise any outbreak and prevent its spread to wildlife – especially foxes which are very numerous not only in the depth of the countryside but in the suburbs, too.

Control measures within a designated infected area can include requiring all dogs to be muzzled and kept on a leash when out-of-doors; the impounding of all dogs wandering about on their own; a ban on movement of dogs out of the Infected Area; and compulsory vaccination.

27 In the Tropics

This chapter is intended for the dog-owner in the tropics and in sub-tropical regions. Some of the conditions described occur also in countries bordering the Mediterranean, or the hotter parts of the U.S.A. It is hoped, too, that information given may be of some value to owners of boarding kennels accommodating dogs which had previously (before their stay in quarantine kennels) come from hot countries.

HEAT EXHAUSTION

This may befall any dog in hot countries if unaccustomed to the climate, having been imported, or if subjected to exertion. For all practical purposes a non-sweating animal, the dog has to rely on panting as the chief means of losing excess heat, and this may prove inadequate. Symptoms of heat stress include a staggering gait, and inability to undertake physical effort. The dog may collapse, have convulsions, and die unless emergency measures are taken. These comprise moving the dog into the shade, and applying cold water to head, neck, and the whole of the upper part of the body. This can conveniently be carried out with a hose-pipe in the case of a large dog.

Case history 1. Six of 30 guard dogs at the Port of Aqaba, on the Red Sea, showed symptoms of heat exhaustion. Working only at night, these Army dogs were in kennels having extra thick walls and a double roof cooled by dampened matting. Despite these precautions, the six dogs were unable to tolerate the heat of a day on which the shade temperature rose to 118°F. All revived after being placed in an empty refrigerated meat van for an hour.[1]

CANINE TROPICAL PANCYTOPAENIA

This is a tick-transmitted disease caused by a rickettsia – a type of micro-organism which may be said to be intermediate between the smallest bacteria and the viruses. The rickettsia involved is known as *Ehrlichia canis*; hence the alternative name for the disease: canine ehrlichiosis. It occurs in many parts of Africa, the Middle East, South-East Asia, the Caribbean, and parts of the U.S.A.

Severe haemorrhagic gastro-enteritis often characterises this illness, and there may be bleeding from the nose also. There is a high fever. Vomiting may occur. Alsatians appear to be especially susceptible to c.t.p., and few survive the illness, which is associated with a marked reduction in the number of blood platelets. Confirmation of diagnosis requires laboratory methods. Treatment with an appropriate antibiotic (e.g. tetracycline hydrochloride) may prove successful in cases treated early enough.

CANINE RICKETTSIOSIS

This is another tick-borne rickettsial infection, transmitted by the common dog tick *Rhipicephalus sanguineus*, and occurs in countries bordering the Mediterranean, Africa and India. It is sometimes known as canine typhus.

Symptoms include fever (a temperature of up to 107°F or so), loss of appetite, thirst, swelling of the lymph nodes, a staring coat, and a brown discolouration of mouth and teeth. The breath has a unpleasant odour. A thick discharge from eyes and nose may be seen, and the eyes may become sunken. Nervous symptoms are present in some cases; e.g. hysteria, fits, or paralysis. An untreated dog may die within a week, or linger on, becoming emaciated, over several weeks. Treatment is as for c.t.p. above.

Canine rickettsiosis may be confused with canine babesiosis; the more so as both infections may occur concurrently.

CANINE BABESIOSIS

Also known as malignant jaundice, this is yet another tick-borne disease. A protozoan parasite – *Babesia canis*, or another species of *Babesia* – enters the dog's bloodstream when an infected tick feeds on the dog. Babesia destroys red blood cells, and anaemia results. This disease occurs in India, other parts of Asia, South Africa, etc., and is frequently fatal.

Symptoms include fever, marked weakness, and jaundice; yellow discolouration is seen on looking at the dog's gums or the lining of the eyelid. Blood may be passed in the urine. In less acute cases, symptoms are similar but milder.

Recovery will partly depend on whether the dog has come from a locality where the disease does not exist and consequently has no degree of immunity – imported dogs are less likely to recover. Treatment requires a specific drug for use against the protozoan parasite, such as Acapron or Phenamidine.

TRYPANOSOMIASIS

In several tropical regions, e.g. India, the Sudan and other parts of Africa, and Central and South America, blood parasites called trypanosomes infect dogs (though to a less extent, probably, than most other domestic animals and man). Two examples of trypanosomiasis are Chaga's disease of Central and South America, with symptoms which include fever, anaemia, emaciation, ascites, and often death from heart failure; and, in the other regions mentioned above, a disease called surra which also effects camels and horses, and in dogs resembles Chaga's disease except that oedematous swellings may affect several parts of the body. Treatment of these diseases is by injection of specific anti-trypanosome drugs.

CANINE LEISHMANIASIS

This disease is transmitted by sand flies and caused by minute single-celled parasites. It is identical with human kala-azar or dum-dum fever occurring in the Sudan, China and India. The parasites are found in cells of the spleen, liver, and bone marrow. Apart from fever, the only symptom may be wasting, with sometimes paralysis of the hindquarters. A skin form of leishmaniasis – 'oriental sore' of man – may affect the dog in the Middle East, North Africa, India, and South America. Drugs containing antimony are used in treatment.

Rabies

This disease is present in most tropical regions of the world. In Central and South America rabies is rarely seen in indigenous dogs in areas where the disease is commonly transmitted by vampire bats to cattle. This may be because local dogs have acquired some degree of immunity or are resistant to bat-transmitted virus. However, a very low incidence, or its virtual non-occurrence in indigenous dogs, is no guide as to what may befall the imported dog. In these areas, dogs may become infected through the grey mongoose (imported from India to kill snakes, but now constituting an important reservoir of the rabies virus). The mongoose and jackal are important sources of infection for dogs in South Africa and Asia. Other vectors are foxes and ground squirrels in Africa, wolves and bats in Asia.

In some parts of Africa and Asia a type of rabies different from the classical form has been recognised. In West Africa it is known as 'oulo fato'. Vomiting and paralysis are the main symptoms. A recurrent form is seen which may affect the dog for three seasons in succession, at the beginning of the rains. After a period of straying, there is hind-leg weakness. Recovery occurs after the first two attacks, but the third is fatal. A transient form, with mild paralysis or hind-leg weakness followed by recovery, is also known. Healthy carriers of infection have been noted in India, West Africa, and Ethiopia.

Good vaccines are available for the immunisation of dogs against rabies, and vaccination should be the rule in the tropics. (See also the separate chapter 'Rabies'.)

Botulism

This form of bacterial food-poisoning has already been described in chapter 20 'Less-Common Infections', but it is worth adding here that contamination of well-water by the carcass of an animal dead of botulism might contain sufficient toxin to produce botulism in the dog.

Anthrax

This disease is prevalent in the tropics. It has been described in chapter 20.

Parasitic Worms

Hookworm infestation is important in the tropics and sub-tropics. A voracious blood-sucker, causing anaemia, the adult worm is a dangerous parasite; its larvae, which can penetrate unbroken skin, damage the paws and cause skin irritation of the abdomen.

Serious damage to the feet of the dog may also be caused by the guinea-worm in parts of Asia and North America; lameness sometimes resulting from abscess formation. Contaminated water in ponds and ditches is the principal, if not the only source, of infestation with the worm (*Dracunculus*) for domestic animals.

Worms in heart and arteries. Mosquitoes and gnats transmit the minute larvae of the filarial worm *Dirofilaria immitis*, infestation with which is often called canine filariasis. The adult worm lives in the right ventricle of the heart as a rule, or in the pulmonary artery. If only one or two worms are present, no symptoms may be shown; otherwise coughing, rapid breathing, and a disinclination for exercise are shown, with collapse on exertion. Interference with the circulation may result in liver damage, and oedema.

The drug diethylcarbamazine is effective against the microfilariae (larval worms); less so against adult worms. It is advised that dogs taken to parts of the world where the disease occurs should be given daily doses of the drug, starting on the day of arrival. A proprietary preparation of the drug is called Nanocide, and available from the Wellcome Foundation (Veterinary Division)[2]

Spirocerca lupi is another worm common in hot countries. It infests the dog's oesophagus, stomach, and arteries, where it produces nodules or 'lumps'. These may develop a stalk and cause blockage; they may also become the site of a malignant growth. Symptoms include vomiting, sometimes difficulty in swallowing, or sudden fatal haemorrhage.

Case history. A $3\frac{1}{2}$-year-old Alsatian which, according to his owner, had been vigorous, alert and agile up to the previous midnight, was found dead at 6 a.m. Foul play was suspected and an autopsy requested. This revealed that the dog had died from internal haemorrhage, which in turn had been caused by damage to the carotid artery by six *Spirocerca lupi* worms. Dr T. T. Bannor found three worms in each of two nodules attached to the oesophagus.[3]

Worms in veins. Dogs are not immune from the type of worm, called flukes, which cause bilharzia in man. Also known as schistosomes, the male worm lives in a groove in the larger female worm. They are found in large veins; some species choose veins of the urinary bladder, others the nose.

The intermediate host is a water-snail, and larvae can penetrate the unbroken skin of an animal entering infected water. Symptoms vary according to the site chosen by the parasites, but include anaemia, diarrhoea, laboured breathing, and the presence of blood in the urine.

Drugs are available for treatment, including Antimosan. The disease occurs in parts of Africa and Asia.

Leeches. Another type of worm, leeches can kill dogs through loss of blood. The mouth and nose are common sites. Small haemorrhages lead to anaemia, and in severe infestations this proves fatal. Seventy leeches have been expelled from the nose of a dog after injection of chloroform water.

EXTERNAL PARASITES

These include the jigger-flea (*Tunga penetrans*). The female penetrates the skin and lives inside a cavity which it forms; severe pain and local inflammation – sometimes ulcers – is caused. The 'stick-tight' flea of chickens is also a troublesome pest of dogs in the tropics, and often attaches itself to the ears.

The larvae of several flies infest either wounds or the intact skin of the dog in the tropics. For example, larvae of the brownish-yellow Tumbu fly burrow into the skin, forming a subcutaneous swelling with a visible breathing hole. The dog's scrotum as well as other parts of the body may be affected. A drop of salad oil placed on the breathing hole may force the larva to emerge. The dog's sleeping quarters should be treated with a BHC or dichlorvos insecticide.

In tropical America larvae of the fly *Dermatobia hominis* cause similar swellings. The eggs of this fly are laid on the underside of a mosquito or gnat, which it captures for this purpose, and the larvae hatch out and enter where the mosquito has bitten.

For further information about ticks, and tick paralysis, see chapters 11 and 18 respectively.

DEHYDRATION

This occurs not only in cases of heat stress but also during the course of any illness in which diarrhoea is severe and prolonged. Dehydration is in itself a potential cause of death. The lost water and salts can be replaced by an intravenous injection of glucose saline.

In areas of the world where veterinarians are few and far between, it may be possible for the dog-owner to obtain UNICEF sachets of 'Oral Rehydration Salts'. These are sold for human use, and were introduced under the auspices of the World Health Organisation to treat dehydration in babies and young children. If such sachets are not obtainable locally, have the prescription made up:

Sodium chloride	3.5g
Potassium chloride	1.5g
Sodium bicarbonate	2.5g
Glucose	20.0g

Dissolve in 1 litre of water. *Do not boil.* To be given by mouth.

A TRAVELLER'S TALE

When a dog-owner living overseas decides to return home, he is faced with three possibilities: take the dog back with him; find a good home for him locally; or, if neither of these alternatives seems practicable, resort to euthanasia. Remember that, for dogs returning to Britain, an import licence must be obtained in advance for the dog, and quarantine arrangements made in advance too. See the address on page 194.

In the instance of which I am thinking, the first course was chosen and the dog – after what must have seemed a very long six months – was finally released from quarantine kennels to go to his new home. Although the animal appeared to settle down very well, he was noticeably thin.

At first this was put down to the result of pining in the quarantine kennels, and it was thought that being reunited with his owners, and a nourishing diet, would soon put weight back on him. Indeed, for a time there was some improvement but this was not maintained, and the dog's general health gradually worsened. Sometimes a cough attracted the attention of his fond owners, sometimes an apparent weakness of the hind legs.

The man took the dog for leisurely walks, and observed little wrong; but his wife, who was in the habit of throwing a ball for the dog to retrieve, noticed that this produced panting as though the exertion were too much for him. Once, in fact, the dog collapsed, rather like a person fainting. After that the ball was put away and not used again.

Veterinary advice was sought. 'Your dog is very anaemic,' his owners were told, 'and his heart is not very good.' They were advised to spare the dog all exertion, to include liver in his diet, and to use a prescribed tonic.

After three weeks the dog was again examined, and the veterinary surgeon expressed disappointment, but suggested that as the dog seemed a shade better they should persevere. The following week, however, their dog was chased by another, and was afterwards found to be in a very distressed condition. Reluctantly, they decided upon euthanasia.

An autopsy, requested by the wife who wanted to be reassured that 'they had done the right thing' revealed the presence within the heart of worms subsequently identified as *Dirofilaria immitis*.

I have included the above not in any way to discourage owners from bringing a dog back home, but merely to illustrate the fact that a tropical disease may first appear *after* the dog has left the tropics.

REFERENCES

1 Clabby, Brigadier J., O.B.E., M.R.C.V.S. *The History of the Royal Army Veterinary Corps 1919–1961* (J. A. Allen & Co.)

2 Munro, H. M. C. *Vet. Record* 103 (1977), 123

3 Bannor, T. T. *Vet. Record* 98 (1976), 302

28 Origins of the Dog

by R. N. Fiennes M.A., M.R.C.V.S.

There is little doubt that the dog was the first animal to be domesticated. Some authorities believe that the reindeer should take pride of place but this is unlikely, because primitive Northern tribes, such as the Lapps, are to this day unable to control their reindeer herds without the use of dogs. This being the case, the domestication of dogs is plainly an important turning point in human history; yet, it is one that has left very little in the way of concrete evidence to help us see how it happened. However, let us now examine what evidence still exists to see how and why this momentous event occurred.

In the view of most authorities, domestication was not a single event taking place at one point of time and place; rather, it seems that the parent canines were brought into domestication at approximately the same time in different places from whatever wild stock was available and had the necessary qualities. The evidence for this rests on two major foundations. First, in the American Continent, both North and South, there exist domestic dogs which are plainly derived from a great variety of parent stock. There are not only breeds evidently derived from the Northern wolves, either the grey wolves of northern Europe or the timber wolves of North America, but also from a variety of wild canines which are specifically different from *Canis lupus*. There exist domestic breeds evidently descended from the coyotes, (*Canis latrans*), from the so-called azara dogs (*Canis azarae*), and also from the strange little animal the bush dog *Icticyon (Speothos) venaticus*. One domestic dog, therefore, is derived from a member of the Canidae which is not even *Canis*.

The second point of evidence is derived from existing breeds of domestic dogs, which on examination can clearly be placed in at least four major categories, which may reasonably be supposed to have descended from four different parent stocks. The first of these categories, of which there can be no reasonable doubt whatever, constitutes the dingo group of dogs, which includes also the Middle and Far Eastern pariahs. This group comprises about 50 per cent of the world's canine population, and in many respects these animals are much closer to their parent stock than are most other breeds of dogs. The dingoes still live in a fully wild condition in the Australian continent; when the Aborigines need dogs for the home or for hunting, they acquire them by stealing the puppies; they do not breed them. The dingoes are very close in every respect of conformation and habit to the wolves which are their undoubted ancestors, the pale-footed Asian wolves (*Canis lupus pallipes*). They howl like wolves and only rarely bark; they come on heat and breed once a year only; and in their nesting and mating habits they resemble the wolves from which they have been derived.

A second quite distinctive group of dogs is that of the Greyhound, including the Greyhound proper, the Salukis, the Borzois, the Afghans, the Irish Wolfhounds, and the Scottish Deerhounds. There are a great many other local breeds and breeds, known to be crossed, but which retain greyhound characteristics. Apart from their characteristic conformation, these dogs have the unique property in the canine world, that they hunt by sight. Since their original distribution was evidently in hot dry desert country, it is reasonable to suppose that they have been derived from a desert wolf which had developed cursorial properties. The nearest candidate, existing today, appears to be the rather small desert wolf, designated by the late R. I. Pocock, F.R.S., as *Canis lupus arabs*.

A third group of dogs, which one believes to contain a motley assemblage, we have designated the Northern group; in this group the more primitive members show rather definitely their affinities with their parent-stock, namely the Northern grey wolf – the type species – *Canis lupus*. This group comprises the Huskies, Alsatians, Colbes, Spitz breeds, Terriers, and Maltese dogs. The Huskies are evidently very close to the parent wolves, and indeed every few generations are bred back by the Eskimos to the wild wolf stock. Intermediate between the Huskies and the more specialised breeds, are the Alsatians and Collies, the great sheepdogs of the world.

The fourth group of dogs may be termed the Mastiff group and appears to have been developed first in Tibet and along the great mountain ranges extending from there to Anatolia. This group appears to have been derived from mountain wolves, similar to the Tibetan wolf (*Canis lupus chanco*). It comprises as well as the mastiffs, the very large dogs of the world such as the Pyrenean mountain dogs, the St Bernards, Newfoundlands, also the great group of scent hunting sporting dogs with the true hounds, Retrievers, Spaniels, Setters and so on.

It is generally accepted today, that, although they have been derived from multiple ancestry, yet dogs – apart from those of the American continent – are derived from the many varieties of true wolves. This does not preclude the possibility that the jackal and other canine blood, even fox, has at some stage been introduced into domestic canine stock and that this could partly account for the great variety of form and character shown by different breeds. In the writings of Xenophon and Aristotle, it is definitely stated that some breeds of dogs are derived from dog/fox crosses. Furthermore, it would be most improbable that those great experimenters in domestication, the Ancient Egyptians, had not crossed their dogs with jackals, (which were after all sacred animals to them, the jackal-headed god Anubis being one of the major deities involved in the death ceremonies).

As regards the time when this happened, written or pictorial history opens in Chinese and pre-dynastic Egyptian times, with many breeds of dogs – some of them very similar to those of today – already well established. Prehistoric sites, such as those at Jericho and other places, dating from as early as 8000–7000 B.C. contained remains of dogs like herd dogs, and the neolithic sites of lake settlements found in Great Britain, Austria, Switzerland, Russia and elsewhere, contained the remains of very small toy dogs, some of whose skulls measured no more than 4 in. in length, probably related to the Maltese dogs and the Dutch Schipperkes.

It is evident that in semi-domesticated form, dingoes were taken by the original Aborigines to the Australian continent at a time not later than 15,000 B.C.: that is at the end of the last glacial epoch when the seas were low and it was relatively easy to reach this continent in the primitive craft then available.

The relationship of the Aborigines with the dingoes surely also gives us a clue as to how domestication first came about. Both dog and man appear to have become partially dependent on each other, living and hunting in the same vicinity. The dogs – perhaps we should call them wolves – became tolerant of man, and man brought puppies from time to time to his settlements and reared them.

The development of such a relationship can still be seen in the barren lands of northern Canada, where the Eskimos and the wild wolves inhabit the same terrain in a state of mutual tolerance, neither harming the other; indeed from time to time each renders assistance to the other. At the end of the last glacial epoch, we get a picture – still preserved in remote areas – of two major predators, wolves and man, living on herds of large game, hunting in rather different ways, but with enough to go round for all and thus without competition. Northern wolf puppies have on numerous occasions been reared in the company of man, of whom they have no fear and whose society they readily accept when adult, just as would a domesticated dog.

We may, therefore, suppose that domestication came about by a gradual process of adoption of a group of wild animals into human societies which had lived side by side with them amicably for a 100,000 years or more. Both man and wolf were social animals, requiring to be organised to hunt large animals which neither could successfully tackle single-handed. The established ways of life of the upper paleolithic era were rudely upset when the ice began to recede and the forests replaced tundra. Wolves, in these conditions, would have no difficulty in finding a livelihood; not so man, who was driven to live in settlements, thus abandoning his old nomadic ways of life. It was surely at this time that dogs began to be domesticated, in the sense that they were selectively bred for properties which could assist the human species in adapting itself to new ways of life. The mesolithic era, which succeeded the upper paleolithic, was largely transitional, lasting in the Mediterranean Near East only for a few hundred years, but longer in the north. It was succeeded by the neolithic, when man had overcome his problems; he had developed agriculture, domesticated wheat, barley and rice and also the progenitors of his farm animals. During this transitional period leading to the so-called neolithic revolution, dogs were evidently an important, if not an essential, ally of the human species. It is tragic that, since neolithic times, so large a proportion of these domesticated allies, the pariahs, have become neglected outcasts around Middle and Far Eastern cities.

For further reading: *The Natural History of the Dog*, by Richard and Alice Fiennes (Weidenfeld & Nicolson).

Glossary of words not listed in the Index

aetiology	cause, study of causes
anoestrus	not in oestrus
anorexia	loss of appetite
ascariasis	infestation with *Ascaris* worms
anuria	passing no urine
atypical	not typical
avitaminosis	a vitamin deficiency
bradycardia	slow heart action
clonic spasm	brief, spasmodic movement of a muscle
dorsal	uppermost; towards the back
dysphagia	difficulty in swallowing
dyspnoea	laboured breathing
endocarditis	inflammation of the heart's lining membrane
epistaxis	bleeding from the nose
fomites	infected objects; e.g. dog's collar, bedding, etc.
haematemesis	the vomiting of blood
hypertension	high blood pressure
hypotension	low blood pressure
lesion	any injury or tissue abnormality
melanoma	a tumour pigmented black

metastases	secondary growths, spreading cancer
myvasis	infestation of wounds with fly maggots
neoplasm	a tumour
parietal	relating to the wall of a cavity
pica	abnormal appetite
progestagen	a drug used in suppression of oestrus and acting like the hormone progesterone
pruritus	itchiness
pyrexia	fever
strangury	difficulty in passing urine
subclinical	an infection not giving rise to symptoms
syndrome	a group of symptoms
tachycardia	fast heart action
tachypnoea	rapid breathing
taeniacide	a tapeworm killing drug
titre	'high titres' means, in practice, that the blood serum contains high levels of antibody to a specific antigen, e.g. rabies virus
tonic spasm	a continuous spasm
urolithiasis	stone formation in the urinary system
ventral	undermost; towards the belly

Appendix

A Refractory Ear Condition

A bacterium called *Pseudomonas aerogunisosa* has in recent years been increasingly isolated from cases of inflammation of the canine ear which have failed to respond to normal treatment. Excessive wax, ulceration, and the later presence of yellow pus are seen. Fortunately at least one antibiotic, carbenicillin, has proved successful in overcoming this condition, but treatment is likely to take longer than when dealing with common ear infections.

Anaemia

This condition includes autoimmune anaemia, in which there is a defect or failure of the bodily defence mechanisms, with antibodies being formed against some of the dog's own cells. A deficiency of blood platelets may occur simultaneously with the shortage of red cells. The symptoms include pale gums, lethargy, weakness and collapse. Treatment may be successful, but is not always so.

Blood Transfusion

A single blood transfusion, without cross-matching or typing, is usually safe and may be the means of saving the life of a dog involved in an accident leading to severe haemorrhage, for example. In dogs there are nine known blood groups.

Canine Viral Hepatitis

Recent research has shown that two viruses are involved in this disease. A canine adenovirus (CAV-1) is associated with liver, kidney, eye, and respiratory disease; while CAV-2 is implicated only in respiratory disease. 'Blue-eye' (corneal oedema) may be caused by natural infection with CAV-1; or may follow use of vaccine containing live modified virus. Accordingly, vaccine manufacturers have mostly ensured that vaccine against canine viral hepatitis will not give rise to 'Blue-eye'.

Dogs for the Deaf

Over 200 'hearing dogs' are already at work in the USA, alerting deaf people to doorbells, alarm clocks, cooker times, etc. Now the idea has spread to the UK where Bruce Fogle – a veterinary surgeon – has been very active in raising funds for the new charity 'Hearing Dogs for the Deaf'. Stray and unwanted dogs will be selected for training, and supplied free only to very deaf people who are living alone. The Royal National Institution for the Deaf, London, is dealing with enquiries.

Electric Collars

The British Veterinary Association has commented on the radio-controlled dog collars used to punish the animal for misbehaviour. 'The shock inflicted can be considerable; it is always painful, and if excessive in voltage or duration can be actually injurious.' A transmitter fault could lead to inability to turn off the current, and other radio-controlled sources (for model aeroplanes, etc) might activate the collar. Incidentally, a Post Office radio transmitting licence is required.

Foreign Bodies

It might reasonably be thought that string would be the least dangerous of foreign bodies, but such is not the case. Gravy-soaked string may inadvertently be included in a dog's meal of chicken scraps or leftovers from a joint of beef. Occasionally string will form a loop around the base of the tongue, but more often it will pass into the stomach, causing local inflammation and sometimes obstruction. In the intestine swallowed string is apt to lead to an accordion-pleating appearance of the bowel wall, which may perforate. One dachshund had no less than 15 such perforations, each of which had to be sutured during the course of a life-saving abdominal operation.

Some wrapped loaves have a small, flat plastic fastener – a convenient means of resealing the package after some bread slices have been removed. This harmless-looking fastener should be kept out of the reach of dogs, as – like string – it has led to perforation of the intestine. Both these types of foreign body may be difficult to detect, since they are not opaque to X-rays.

Goitre

Lethargy is a notable symptom in the dog, in which the disease is not uncommon in the 3 to 5 year age group, especially in the bigger breeds. The thyroid gland becomes enlarged.

Haemophilia

This is an uncommon disease of male dogs of most breeds. It is caused by an inherited defect causing abnormally slow clotting of the blood; so that bleeding may occur and continue following only a minor injury. Bitches, though carriers of the gene for haemophilia, seldom show symptoms themselves. Fifty per cent of a carrier's male pups are likely to have haemophilia.

The signs are often vague and misleading, in that a temporary swelling on the forehead, for instance, or transient lameness, may be attributed solely to violence of some kind. Excessive bleeding sometimes occurs at teething, or if the toe-nails are trimmed too close to the quick. Haemophiliac dogs cannot, with safety, lead a rough-and-tumble life, and the owner must try to avoid knocks occurring. A bitch which is known to be a carrier should not, of course, be bred from.

Laboratory tests to *prove* that haemophilia is present are unfortunately very expensive and lengthy.

Heart Disease

Inflammation of the lining membrane of the heart is sometimes caused by bacteria, and technically known as **bacterial endocarditis**. This may result in outgrowths which interfere with the functioning of the mitral valve. One cause is the bacterium which causes erysipeloid in people and swine erysipelas: *Erysipelothrix rhusiopathiae*.

Case history. A 4-year-old Pointer had been unwell for four months, with lethargy, fever, and a shifting lameness. The dog was found to be weak, under-weight, with pale gums and enlarged lymph nodes. A sample of blood contained the above organisms.[1]

Congestive heart failure. Disease of the right side of the heart often gives rise to ascites, sometimes to swelling of one or more limbs due to oedema. Engorgement of the veins often occurs, with enlargement of the liver. The dog becomes easily tired and may lose weight. Ultimately congestive heart failure is likely to occur. This may also result from left-sided failure due to myocarditis or mitral valve incompetence.

Hormone-producing Tumours

Tumours affecting a gland may sometimes themselves produce hormones and cause disease. For example, a tumour involving the pancreas led to an excess of insulin in the blood and a consequent collapse, convulsions, and coma in a dog. Dr A. C. Palmer reported.[2]

Other instances have involved tumours on the ovaries. Dr I. A. P. McCandlish and colleagues described the production of sex hormones by such tumours. One resulted in a West Highland bitch, aged $11\frac{1}{2}$, being continually in oestrus for nine months. She was attractive to male dogs, but refused to stand for mating. Analysis of blood samples showed that levels of oestrogen and progesterone were similar to those occurring in normal pro-oestrus. Non-surgical treatment was tried but failed to do more than abolish her attraction for male dogs; so her ovaries and uterus were removed, after which she made an excellent recovery without any recurrence of the trouble.[3]

Insurance

Several companies cater for dog-owners and offer policies covering some or all of the following: third-party liability; death by accident, loss, or theft.

Even a usually non-aggressive dog may bite a teasing child, a postman, someone else's dog or cat; or may chase and injure sheep. Such incidents may of course result in the dog's owner being sued, and damages could be high. Anxiety on this account can be avoided by taking out an insurance policy which will cover sums up to £200,000 or more.

Veterinary fees (for treatment of injuries, illness, major surgery, minor ailments). Cover can be arranged for a yearly premium of between £8 and £30, with the dog-owner paying the first £5 or £10 of any claim, up to £200 or £300.

The June 1984 issue of *Which?* magazine made the point that insurance premiums are relatively cheap in comparison with veterinary fees. Their 'best buy' was the Holdfast policy – 'clear and straightforward, providing a good level of cover at a reasonable premium. For a few pounds more, Paws and Super Petplan provide good value.' Vetex was also commended. 'Apart from the annual premium, you pay only £10 for each course of treatment.'

Excluded from these policies are the cost of vaccination, and fees in connection with pregnancy, breeding, and neutering. The upper age limit for these policies is usually 9 or 10. A few companies will provide cover beyond that age, or even for life.

Fortunately few dogs require as much veterinary attention as the Viszla mentioned below. Even so, insurance is always worthwhile to cushion unexpected expense.

Case history. Some dogs do seem to be accident prone. Certainly a 3-year-old Viszla was. When six months old he fell out of a pickup truck, sustaining an injury to one femur which required surgical treatment. His next two visits to a veterinary hospital were on account of grass awns – one found lodged inside an eyelid, the other in his nose. Next he was hit by a car, which damaged his liver and spleen, and required more surgery. He was next seen by Dr Douglas L. Marks because the miniature electric light bulbs on a Christmas tree had canine appeal, and some were removed by the dog and swallowed. His seventh visit to hospital was made after he had been shaking his head and holding it to one side. His owner suspected another grass awn; but no, a grasshopper had got into his ear and died there. The dead insect measured one inch in length.[4]

Intersex

Recorded cases of intersex in the dog have usually involved one, or perhaps two, puppies out of a litter. When a 3-year-old Saluki's first litter of five proved to be all intersexes or hermaphrodites, an environmental rather than a genetic cause was suspected. Suspicion fell upon a proprietary vitamin supplement stated to contain testosterone and oestrogen, G. W. Hinsch stated in *Teratology*.[5] Two of the pups were classified as female hermaphrodites, because the internal anatomy of the urogenital system was that of a normal female, while the external genitalia were those of a male.

Case history. A 6-month-old cocker spaniel was noticed to have a very large clitoris when she came into oestrus. A fortnight later she behaved in a very aggressive manner at a dog show. When veterinary advice was sought it was found that she was a true hermaphrodite, with a combined ovary-testis on each side. The clitoris was found to contain a triangular bone – the equivalent of the normal *Os penis* of the canine male. The puppy's dam had been line-bred back to her grandsire, and the other puppy in the litter was also abnormal.[6]

Case history. Over 10-day periods a $2\frac{1}{2}$-year-old Dachshund had passed blood in his urine, and had also urinated during the night. These episodes had occurred when he was 9 months old, and again at 16, 22, and 29 months old. At these times, the owner reported, the dog was attractive to bitches. At all times he squatted to urinate.

Examination at the University of Glasgow's veterinary hospital showed that the *Os penis* was absent. No testicles were present in the scrotum. As the dog was suspected to be an intersex, a laparotomy was carried out, revealing a uterus and ovaries. There was also a vagina connecting with the pelvic urethra. After removal of part of the vagina and of uterus and ovaries, the Dachshund made an uneventful recovery and returned home.[7]

Itchy dog

Staphylococcal dermatitis may result in roughly circular, reddened areas of skin, which could be mistaken for ringworm. It is the fine skin, with relatively few hairs, on the abdomen and inside the thighs, which is mainly affected. As it is itchy, the dog is apt to lick or scratch the area.

Kennel Cough

In 1984 'kennel cough' appeared to be reaching epidemic proportions in many parts of Britain, and cases of associated pneumonia were reported.

Some cases followed dogs being taken to shows at which there were many coughing dogs, but no veterinary inspection. A vaccine is available for protection of dogs going to shows.

Lupus Erythematosus

This is an autoimmune disease; that is to say, a defect or failure of the bodily defence mechanisms in which antibodies become active against some of the dog's own cells. One form of the disease is characterized by symmetrical lesions on the nose, the rest of the face, and ears, where the skin tends to lose its pigment, become reddened, and scaly, with bald patches. These lesions are symmetrical. Exposure to sunlight exacerbates the condition.

A second form of lupus affects many organs and tissues, and symptoms may include arthritis, muscle pain, fever, enlarged lymph nodes, and sometimes nervous symptoms.

Nose Mites

A white mite, *Pneumonyssoides caninum*, is an uncommon inhabitant of the nose and nasal sinuses, and causes the dog to rub its nose on the ground or to shake its head. The parasite is present in Scandinavia, America, Australia, and South Africa.

Poisoning, Accidental

Dish-washing liquids should not be used for washing dogs, as some of these liquids contain ethanol which can cause poisoning. On farms, there is a similar danger from the misuse of sheep dips for washing dogs.

Case history. When food becomes unfit for human consumption some people give it to their dogs: a policy which has on occasion caused severe illness or even death. Here is an example: some cream cheese, stored in a refrigerator, was found to have a profuse growth of mould. After the household dog had eaten some of it, alarming symptoms developed. The animal became unsteady on its legs, had muscular tremors, and intermittent arching of the spine (as seen in strychnine poisoning). It was subsequently found that penitrem A, a mycotoxin, had caused these symptoms and originated without doubt from the mould, identified as *Penicillum crustosum*.[8]

Case history. A 6-month-old puppy ate some mistletoe berries. Fifteen hours later she had difficulty in controlling her hind legs and began nodding her head continuously. Her legs became paralysed some 10 hours later, when she reacted violently to touch, noise, or bright light. She died 50 hours after eating the berries.[9]

Prostate Gland

A ban on the use of stilboestrol in EEC countries came into force in 1982. As regards the symptoms, it should be added that sometimes the dog's owner may notice only malaise or hind leg stiffness.

Sarcocystis infection

A protozoan parasite which dog-owners seldom or never hear about is Sarcocystis. This has a two-host life-cycle, with cysts being formed in the muscles of cattle, sheep, and pigs (and occasionally people), according to the species involved. Dogs become infected through eating the raw flesh of animals having these cysts. The latter may cause no more than discomfort or local pain. A survey by T. V. Balmer and colleagues showed that 75 per cent of hounds in four north Wales packs were infected.

Whiskers

The thick, stiff hairs (*Vibrissae*), which project from the faces of dogs and other animals, are minor sense organs. They are reputed to help a dog to negotiate thorny hedges, for example; and without their whiskers sporting dogs are said to be more prone to facial and eye injuries. Whiskers should *not* be cut for Show purposes.

REFERENCES
1 Hoenig, M. & Gillette, D.
   JAVMA 176 (1980) 326
2 Palmer, A. C. *Vet. Record* 90
   (1972) 167
3 McCandlish, I. A. P. *Vet.
   Record* 105 (1979) 9
4 Marks, D. L. *Vet. Med/SAC*
   7 (1983) 519
5 Hinsch, G. W. *Teratology* 20
   (1979) 463
6 Sundberg, J. P. *Vet. Med/
   SAC* 74 (1979) 477
7 Weaver, A. D. *Vet. Record*
   105 (1979) 230
8 Young, M. *Carnation Res.
   Digest* 17 (1981) 14
9 Greatorex, J. C. *Vet. Record*
   78 (1966) 726
10 Balmer, T. V. *Vet. Record*
   110 (1982) 331

Index